THE MUTINIES IN RAJPOOTANA

BEING

A PERSONAL NARRATIVE

OF THE MUTINY AT NUSSEERABAD

WITH SUBSEQUENT RESIDENCE AT JODHPORE,
AND JOURNEY ACROSS THE DESERT INTO SIND,

TOGETHER WITH AN ACCOUNT OF

THE OUTBREAK AT NEEMUCH, AND MUTINY OF
THE JODHPORE LEGION AT ERINPOORA,
AND ATTACK ON MOUNT ABOO.

ILTUDUS THOMAS PRICHARD
LATE OF THE BENGAL ARMY

The Naval & Military Press Ltd

Published by
The Naval & Military Press Ltd

PREFACE.

I MUST solicit the indulgence of the public for any shortcomings in the following narrative, as it will not have the advantage of the author's supervision while going through the press. I may take this opportunity of stating that, if the public are sufficiently interested in Rajpootana matters to afford the necessary encouragement, I intend to bring out a second volume, containing an account of the military operations in Rajpootana and Central India when the army of retribution took the field.

CONTENTS.

CHAPTER I.

CHAPTER II.

CHAPTER III.

CHAPTER IV.

CHAPTER V.

CHAPTER VI.

CHAPTER VII.

CHAPTER VIII.

CHAPTER IX.

CHAPTER X.

CHAPTER XI.

CHAPTER XII.

CHAPTER XIII.

CHAPTER XIV.

CHAPTER XV.

CHAPTER XVI.

THE

MUTINIES IN RAJPOOTANA.

CHAPTER I.

INTRODUCTORY REMARKS—RAJPOOTANA.—AJMERE.

SOMEWHAT more than two years have elapsed since the exciting events occurred, which invested Indian subjects with so much interest that any journal or record, however hastily thrown together, of any part or period of the rebellion or the succeeding campaigns, was sure of a favourable reception from the public. In offering to the world after so long a lapse of time anything so commonplace as a narrative of adventures and experiences during the mutiny, some apology is needed. I have been induced chiefly by the following considerations to venture upon publishing the matter which will be found in the ensuing pages.

First. No narrative, that I am aware of, has as yet been written of the mutinies in Rajpootana; and as the history of the outbreak in almost every other part of India, and every station, has been laid before the public, it seems as if a link in the chain was wanting as long as there is no account extant of similar incidents as they occurred in so important a tract of country as Rajpootana.

Secondly. Although I can scarcely hope that my unpretending narrative will excite much interest in circles unconnected with India, the whole story of the mutiny and rebellion seems so wonderful that new details respecting it can hardly fail to be listened to or read with attention by any of those whose lot is cast in India, or who have themselves witnessed scenes similar to those which I shall attempt to describe, or by the friends and relatives of my fellow exiles who were exposed to the perils which in the eventful year of 1857 befell us all alike.

Thirdly. The real history of the mutiny remains yet to be written. Years must elapse before such a work can be undertaken with any hope of real success, or any prospect of dealing satisfactorily with the subject. Contemporary prejudices must be allowed to die out, and matters now involved in mystery be cleared up by diligent and patient inquiry; more evidence must be collected from every available source, and the whole carefully compared and arranged. To enable an historian to arrive at a correct view of the subject, nothing can be so useful as personal narratives that enter pretty closely into details, and convey to the reader as much as possible the very impression stamped on the mind of the writer by the events he is describing. The only way by which we can hope to solve the mystery of the mutiny and its origin, is by tracing every occurrence step by step, looking into every detail, and examining every part of the picture and every phase of character presented to us, and then making what deductions we can. In the hope that the following journal may not be without its uses in this respect, I have ventured upon offering it to the world.

By the side of the heart-stirring accounts of the campaign before Delhi, of the sufferings and deeds of the Lucknow garrison, of the miseries endured by the victims of Cawnpore and other places, given in such books as Hodson's *Twelve Years of a Soldier's Life*, Gubbins' *Mutinies in Oude*, Captain Hutchinson's *Narrative*, Captain Mowbray Thompson's *Story of Cawnpore*, Mrs. Copland's *Escape from Gwalior*, and numberless others, an account of a simple mutiny unattended by massacre or assassination to heighten the interest, may seem but tame and unattractive. The rebellion has been only too fruitful in themes of tragic nature. But it was not my lot to be present at Delhi or Lucknow, or with Sir Hugh Rose's victorious division in its triumphal march through Central India—a military operation, or rather a series of military operations, that I believe, all things considered, has scarcely a parallel in modern history, and whose importance has been strangely underrated by our countrymen both in India and England: it was not my lot to share in either the greatest dangers or glories of the war, but we had, like the rest, to go through the ordeal, and that in a position in many respects peculiar, isolated as we were in a remote corner of Rajpootana, and indebted for our safety, under Providence, to a strange concatenation of circumstances, over which we had certainly no control, and which ended in our eventual escape. Our adventures were not very startling, nor our sufferings very severe; we have no glorious victories to chronicle, no massacres to describe; we drifted into mutiny and we drifted out; many of our families found shelter at the court of one of the independent sovereigns of Rajpootana, and for a while were in safety, but the wave of rebellion rolled in and at last threatened us even there. Retreat was cut off on all sides save one, and on that we were separated from the nearest British territory, Sind, by a large tract of desert, almost uninhabited, with no roads, and where water and supplies were scarcely procurable. The commissioners of Sind sent an escort under the district officer to aid us; and our party, increased to six gentlemen, five ladies, and nine children, wended its weary way for 300 miles over a country almost as sterile as the African desert, and till that time less often visited by the European traveller, to Hyderabad in Sind. Such is the outline of the adventures and wanderings it is the purpose of the following pages to describe.

The accounts of the mutiny at Neemuch and Erinpoora, and the attack on Mount Aboo, have been furnished me by friends who were, like myself, eye-witnesses of the events they relate.

Had I remained in the army, it would have been necessary to suppress opinions that I have ventured to offer upon events, and in some cases on the characters of public men. But the deep distrust of the native soldiers with which the circumstances of the mutiny inspired me, and disapproval of the vexatious policy subsequently pursued by the government, induced me, as the only satisfactory course I could adopt, to resign my commission, when the danger was past, and to seek employment and support in another sphere than that in which I had been engaged during thirteen of the best years of my life.

It is indeed impossible for any one who has not experienced it, to realize the full effect upon the mind and feelings, of a mutiny of a regiment he was warmly attached to, accompanied as it was by treacherous and dastardly attempts at assassination. As the conduct of the Sepoys was strange and incomprehensible, so was their ingratitude and cowardice and deep villany utterly beyond the power of language to describe. That men with whom we had been associated for years, whose comforts and welfare we steadily and consistently attended to, and whose wants always met with due consideration from our hands, should have suddenly turned upon us, and attempted our lives, was so inexplicable, that had I not been present with the regiment, and witnessed and suffered from the outrage, I do not think any testimony, however unimpeachable, could have made me believe the story. When once the whole truth was realized, the revulsion of feeling was so strong that I determined never again to serve with native soldiers in any capacity whatever. Many of my fellow officers, who at the time were, I believe, impressed with the same feeling, have judged differently, and the new army is officered by men who have as much cause to complain of ingratitude and treachery as any of us. Each individual can judge best of his own course; but I must express my surprise at the infatuation of a government which, forgetting the experience of the past, is content to reorganize a large native force,* now more numerous than the old, and possessed of all its bad qualities, with none of its redeeming features.

The territory of Rajpootana consists of a large

---

* This was written before the late reduction was authorized.

tract of country between what are called the North-Western and Central Indian provinces on one side, and the desert bordering on Sind, the territories of Guzerat and of Holkar, on the other, and includes a number of independent states. At the courts of Jeypore, Jodhpore, Bhurtpore, Kotah, Oodeypore, and Malwa, a British officer always resides as political agent. The numerous other states, of which Alwur, Kerowlee, Tonk, Bikaneer, and Boondee are perhaps the most influential, are left to their own devices, and allowed to carry on their own affairs unassisted or uninterrupted by any British political officer at all. The Governor-General's agent, who usually resides a great part of the year at Mount Aboo, which is about 150 miles from Jodhpore, and just beyond the proper boundaries of Rajpootana, superintends the whole of the territory, and all the officers employed in any of the agencies are under his direct orders. The different states all send their Vakeels or representatives to the Governor-General's agent in whose immediate neighbourhood they reside, marching when he marches, halting when he halts, and repairing with him to the summer retreat in Mount Aboo. They assemble at stated times to discuss measures that may affect their sovereigns' interests which may be under the consideration of the British Government or its accredited agent. The plan is, in theory at all events, an excellent one, and I never heard any argument adduced against its practice. By it, the Governor-General's agent is placed in communication with the ruler of each petty state; he can make his wishes, or the orders of Government, known to them through the Vakeels, and by them be kept informed of everything of moment that occurs. The appointments given to British officers in this department are generally much coveted. They begin by being assistants to the agent, and eventually rise to be political agents themselves—the latter post, on account of its high salary, independent position, and influential character, being a prize deservedly valued.

Rajpootana, in some respects, is one of the most interesting parts of India. It was never thoroughly conquered by the Mahometans. They, indeed, overran it, captured its most famous strongholds, devastated its most fertile districts, and destroyed its richest cities. But the Hindoo inhabitants succeeded in recovering their independence, and though they yielded a nominal subjection to the emperor who reigned at Delhi, it was always unwillingly accorded, the tribute grudgingly paid, and very frequently withheld. The old Persian histories of the Emperors of Hindostan are full of stories recounting the prowess of the Rajpoots and the valour of the Mussulmans, and the pertinacity with which the war between the races was carried on, and the chivalrous valour of the leaders of the Rajpoots, who preferred death to defeat, and frequently divested the hardly earned victory of their foes of almost all its value, by consigning first their wives and families to death, and then sacrificing themselves by selling their lives as dearly as they could. In this part of India there are spots where the scenery, for grandeur and wildness and beauty, is not to be surpassed perhaps by any in the world; but for the most part it is a desolate region, flat and uncultivated. The traveller passes for miles and miles over an enormous plain where no vestige of a human habitation is in sight. There is verdure, for the country is by no means, as some may be inclined to fancy it, a sandy plain, and if inhabited and irrigated, would doubtless be most fertile. But where are the inhabitants? Judging from appearances you would suppose there were none. You ride through a village, and find it half in ruins; the houses that are standing, tenanted by a few male adults; two or three grown-up women and half-a-dozen children may stare at the stranger as he passes along the deserted streets; but there is an air of desolation and decay and poverty about the place that forces itself on the attention. The land in the immediate neighbourhood of the villages will perhaps be cultivated, and the road or cart track, most likely half a foot deep in sand or loose soil, will run for a little way between hedges formed of the earth heaped up on each side, and a few dry brambles fixed into the top; you soon emerge, however, into the jungle again, and ride on for miles and miles perhaps, before you see another human habitation, over ground covered with coarse grass and stunted shrubs; the deer are so unused to being disturbed in their lonely solitudes by the intrusion of man, that they come fearlessly almost up to your horse, or allow you to approach close to them. To lose one's way is, as I can speak from experience, a real evil, for you may have to ride many miles before you meet a human being from whom you can obtain directions or information as to your road.

In the mountainous parts of the country the scenery changes much, and becomes bold and grand. Grand it is anywhere, even in its most desolate wastes, for it is impossible to travel through these otherwise uninteresting regions without recalling to mind the wondrous traditions of old times, and the tales of patriotism and chivalry and devotion which the ancient history of Rajpootana is so full of. There is no need of fiction here, where facts are sufficiently imbued with the romantic to satisfy the imagination of the most wonder-loving reader that ever perused the pages of Scott, or waded through the voluminous works of G. P. R. James. Every hill almost that you see has an old ruined castle cresting its summit, to which some tradition is attached, and every now and then you pass the consecrated spot where the widow has in days gone by devoted herself to her deceased husband, and the rude sculpture of the man on horseback holding out his hand to the figure of a woman on foot, carved on the slab of stone, shows where the sacrifice of the suttee was made. Here you pass walled cities where in former days a resolute defence was made against the Moslem invader, till, reduced to extremity, the brave garrison first celebrated what they call there 'jauhar,' that is they made a huge pile of wood and combustible materials and kindled it, threw their wives and children, all they held dear to them on earth, and whose honour was dearer far to them than life, into the flames, and after watching them perish before their eyes, dashed open the gates of their city and courted death at the hands of their enemies. Here you pass the lonely hermitage by the clear mountain stream in a shady dell, the shade only too grateful where the burning summer sun at mid-day has tremendous power, whither the courtier or the soldier, wearied by the toils of ambition, deserted the world and retired to end his days in peaceful contemplation on the attributes of the Deity. Or you may see in other places monastic establishments, supported by the superstition of some raja who, after leading a life of crime, sought to obtain favour from heaven and satisfy his conscience by founding an institution for Jain or Buddhist priests, on the same system as our monasteries.

Everywhere you are reminded of the past, and see before you but too plainly the effects of ambition and avarice. What the Moslem conquerors left unfinished, the tyranny and selfishness of the rulers of the land completed.

In the centre of this wide tract is a little district marked by a red boundary line in the map, a sure sign that the hand of the Anglo-Saxon has been laid upon it. The principal city in it is Ajmere, which is beautifully situated on the shore of a lake in the centre of a fertile valley, surrounded by rugged and wild mountains of no very great elevation. The district is called by the same name, Ajmere, and is presided over by a Civil officer, holding the title of commissioner. The garrison of the district is quartered at Nusseerabad, which, being centrally situated, formed the principal military station for this part of Rajpootana. Nusseerabad is about sixteen miles from Ajmere, and stands on a bare rocky plain about eight miles from the outer foot of the hills that flank the E. and S.E. side of the valley which I have alluded to above. The road from Nusseerabad to Ajmere is a pretty one, leading through the hills and up the pass, from the summit of which you see spread before you the green fields of the valley, interspersed with clusters of trees, whose rich foliage forms a pleasant contrast to the colour of the inferior vegetation, while as you advance further on, passing the city and the romantic-looking old fort, you come upon the blue waters of the lake, sparkling under the rays of a bright sun, and a gloriously clear blue sky.

The summit of the highest peak about the city is crowned by a white temple, a place of Mahometan pilgrimage, a conspicuous object enough, and very sacred in the eyes of the devotees, who think, like many of another faith who ought to know better, that a compliance with certain outward forms or ordinances will compensate for non-compliance with others that involve the control of the passions and the exercise of real devotion.

In the eventful year of 1857 there were quartered at Nusseerabad a battery of Artillery (Native),—the same that fought with Sale at Jellalabad, and earned undying fame at that glorious siege,—the 1st Bombay Lancers, and the 30th N. I., which force was increased on the 1st May by the advent of the 15th Regiment, N.I.

CHAPTER II.

INTERCOURSE BETWEEN OFFICER AND SEPOY—MARCH TO NUSSEERABAD—NEWS OF THE OUTBREAK—GUMBHEER SING—INJUDICIOUS ORDERS—ATTEMPTS TO ALLAY EXCITEMENT—NUSSEERABAD—PRECAUTIONS—RELIEF OF AJMERE GARRISON.

WE landed in Calcutta in February, 1857, on my return from a furlough to England on medical certificate. My regiment, the 15th N. I., was then quartered at Meerut, destined so soon to become notorious as the source whence the tempest arose that desolated Hindostan. An officer who holds the office of interpreter and quartermaster to any native corps is necessarily forced into a more extended intercourse with natives, sepoys, native officers, and camp followers than most others. It is very generally supposed in England that European officers now-a-days seldom master the language of the men, and keep as much as possible aloof from them; and it has been frequently asserted that in consequence of their departure from the good old custom, as it is called, of former times, the mutiny, when it came, took us so completely by surprise. But the fact is, as it will be found when the different accounts of the outbreak are examined and compared, that we were by no means without warnings. Warnings we had, and plenty of them, but in some cases we disregarded them, and in others, and perhaps in most instances, we were utterly helpless from our peculiar position, and the only course open to us was to hope for the best; our strength was literally to sit still; in many cases escape there was none: and no officer could individually act so as to provide for his own safety without committing a gross breach of duty by showing distrust when he was called upon to exhibit confidence, and hurrying on a catastrophe which, to the very last moment, we believed might not be inevitable. I think all who have passed through the eventful period of 1857 will agree with me that the most distressing time of all was the interval, short in some cases, long in others, which elapsed before the troops actually declared their mutinous intentions. To trust them really was impossible, at the same time we could not actually distrust them. Yet it was apparent that an outbreak would occur, the consequences of which no one could foresee, the chances of escape varying according to position and attendant circumstances over which we had no control. Those of us who had families to protect, wives and children, whose fate might be so dreadful that the stoutest heart feared to contemplate it, and the bare possibility of which was enough to unman any one, experienced this anxiety to the utmost. But there we were, day after day, looking out eagerly for reports, discussing among ourselves anxiously the signs of the times and the feeling of our men, and the prospect of their remaining faithful, or the chance of escape, or the mode of action to be adopted if they mutinied. From the first thing at morning to the last thing at night we were kept with our mental energies strained to the very utmost, striving to maintain a careless unconcerned demeanour, and let the ordinary routine of life go on as usual, lest we should encourage disaffection by showing want of confidence. Knowing as we did what had occurred at other places, and afraid to impart the horrible information to our wives, or to breathe of it in our family circle, we were forced to smile when the heart was sick, and to assume a tone of confidence and freedom from anxiety, when we were expecting to hear almost every moment from the lines the sound of uproar that would herald in, we knew, a scene of outrage and massacre. We looked at our wives and little ones, and felt how powerless were we to save and protect those whom God had given us for protection, how at any moment they might become the prey of a lawless bloodthirsty rabble, drunk with lust and fury. Many have complained of the insolence and ill-behaviour of domestic servants before the revolt began, but I saw nothing or noticed nothing of it. I knew of course that not one was to be trusted in the hour of need, that is, I knew it in my heart of hearts, but it was difficult to realize it, and impossible to act upon it. No words can describe the distressing anxiety, the fearful mental struggle of those few days. Looking back upon them from this distance of time it seems as if months, ay, years must have passed; yet when I come to count them they were but about ten days, for the Meerut mutiny took place on the 10th May, and our own broke out on the 28th, and several days elapsed before any news from Meerut reached us in our remote nook in Rajpootana. Often did I envy from the bottom of my heart the position of most of my brother officers, who either had their wives in England, or were without any. Several stories have been told of officers shooting their own wives to save them from falling into the hands of the rebels. I do not believe there is any authenticated instance of such conduct, but I would here observe that though many tales of horror were exaggerated, the accounts of atrocities and indignities heaped upon the ladies at Delhi at all events, and many other places, were, alas, no fabrication. They were too true. This has been proved by investigations made upon the spot, though the detailed results of these enquiries will probably never be made public, and perhaps it is just as well they should not be. But at the time I speak of, let the reader recollect, we had had no contradiction of any of those dreadful rumours that were abroad, and a soldier may be as brave as a lion, and as brave as a British soldier almost always is, but he would have been more or less than human had he, in those days, looked into his wife's and children's faces and contemplated the fate that might befal them, as it had befallen others, as good, as innocent, and as much beloved in their own circle as they, without feeling his heart sick.

The assertion alluded to above, that officers used to keep aloof from their men, is quite incorrect. There were in every regiment some who made it their business to study the literature and language of the country; and all, more or less, were familiar with the latter, at all events as far as colloquial knowledge of it went. Of course there were exceptions, but as a general rule the behaviour of the European officers was calculated to win the regard and attachment of the Sepoys. It was customary to pay them the compliment of going to see their great festivals, nautches, &c. &c.; and though we took no further part in them, of course, than looking on, and affecting perhaps more interest than we really felt, and talking to the native officers, or to some man who acted as steward on the occasion, we were always conducted to the chairs placed for us with great ceremony, and our presence always appeared to give pleasure—the dancing, or wrestling, or singing, or 'tom-toming,' whichever it might be, went on with renewed zest, and it seemed to be a point of honour for each performer to redouble his or her exertions for the especial benefit of the white-faced spectators. And lest any exception should be taken to such a proceeding on the ground that heathen festivals having always more or less connexion with heathen worship, no Christian ought to sanction such ceremonies even by a visit, I would observe that the question, is it right or wrong, must be traced further back before it can be satisfactorily answered. If it be conceded that there was no anomaly and nothing wrong in an English gentleman and a Christian holding a commission in the late E. I. Company's army, a point I never heard disputed, it must be allowed that officers so situated were bound conscientiously to do their duty, the first step towards which would be to secure the affection and respect of those under their command. It was a regular custom for the sepoys to invite their officers to attend many of their festivals and ceremonies, and they would have been undoubtedly hurt by a refusal. For the latter to do more than this was not required; to do less would have been to lose the greatest chance of gaining influence with them. This should have been no inducement certainly, if the principle be wrong; but I do not think it was wrong, and indeed the officers of the Bengal Army have been generally charged with a fault the very opposite to this, viz., with neglecting to hold that intercourse with the Native officers and Sepoys which their peculiar position rendered necessary.

We reached Meerut in the middle of February. In March, the 15th N.I. was unexpectedly ordered to Nusseerabad, which station, in consequence of troops having been withdrawn for the Persian war, was without its full complement. Colonel Shuldham, commanding the regiment, joined us in camp one march beyond Delhi. Until his arrival, the command of the corps had devolved upon me, as next senior. The colonel was a strict disciplinarian, and in consequence very unpopular among the men, and strange reports were circulated about us while we were traversing the desert-like plains of Rajpootana, that his life had been successfully attempted by some malcontents in the regiment. However, we reached Nusseerabad without accident or adventure, and went quietly into quarters exactly ten days before the outbreak at Meerut occurred.

The first thing that aroused our suspicions that anything wrong had taken place, was the stoppage of the usual mail from the north-east. By degrees, rumours got abroad that a serious outbreak had occurred; how, I do not know, for no letters were received for several days. At last these uncertain rumours assumed a more definite form. There happened to be at the station a Mr. Courtenay, who kept an hotel at Meerut, and had left his family there while he went a tour through the provinces, in charge of an equestrian company, giving exhibitions at the different stations. This man received intelligence that the troops had broken out at Meerut, that his wife and family had been murdered, and his house burnt to the ground; all which was but too true: it was added, that the whole station was destroyed, and every European, man, woman, and child, at Meerut and Delhi massacred. This was all we heard for several days. At last more correct accounts reached us from neighbouring stations, whither they had been transmitted by indirect routes. All the roads were open to the south, the only one as yet closed being the direct one from the Punjaub and the north-west, Agra, and Delhi. We had cause for anxiety, situated as we were in a remote corner of Rajpootana, surrounded by independent states, who were *à priori* likely enough to take advantage of any opportunity that might offer to aggrandize themselves at the expense of the British Government. We had no European troops within 130 miles of us, Deesa, in the Bombay Presidency, being the nearest garrison where any English soldiers were quartered; and if the insurrection or mutiny—for we knew not then, with our imperfect information, what to call it, or what to think of it—had been of such a serious nature as to have made head at Meerut against a European force, consisting of the Carabineers, the 60th Rifles, and Artillery, there was not much reason for supposing that a Queen's regiment, the 83rd, and a troop of European Horse Artillery, 120 miles off, would be able to afford us much efficient aid. We were far from believing, however, that that aid would be required. As yet, we had no cause for suspecting that our men, who, be it observed, used to express the greatest indignation at the conduct of their fellow-countrymen at Meerut and Delhi, would prove disaffected. The officers of the artillery declared, that let the infantry do what they might, the artillery, the famous Jellalabad Battery, would never destroy its fair fame, and ruin the character this branch of the army had always held. In addition to these fancied sources of security, we had a more tangible one in the presence of a regiment of Bombay cavalry (Lancers), which could not be supposed to sympathize with the mutinous soldiers of another Presidency.

Still, in spite of these assurances, it was evident that considerable excitement prevailed. In the lines, in the bazaar, in the officers' houses, on the mall, all tongues were busy, all heads employed in ceaselessly discussing the events that were in progress—their origin, their probable result, their effects on other parts of India. The Sepoys were more than usually attentive to their duties, and more than usually in constant attendance upon their officers. But the non-commissioned and commissioned officers did not hesitate to tell us that disaffection was rife among certain classes in the regiment; they admitted there were ill-disposed men in the regiment ready and willing to create a disturbance, but they assured us that the well-disposed so far outnumbered them, that there was not the least chance of their committing themselves; and as long as they, the commissioned and non-commissioned officers, remained faithful to their salt, as they were, it was impossible for anything of moment to occur. 'But,' added *one* man, 'we are not so sure of the 30th; that regiment we know is mutinous, and planning mutiny.' The men of the 30th spoke in the same strain to their officers, and impressed upon their minds that though they were faithful, there was no doubt that the 15th, that had just come from Meerut, was deeply imbued with the spirit of revolt, and had they remained at that station, it was arranged that they were to have taken an active part in the insurrectionary movement there. The result of this, as evinced in the feelings and conversation of the officers, was sufficiently amusing; and although affairs were regularly assuming every day a more serious aspect, it was impossible not to be struck with the absurdity of our position. The officers of the 30th, as I have said, expressed their firm conviction, that though it was certain that the 15th would break out sooner or later, and possible that the artillery would join, their men, who were stanch, would be sufficient, headed by all the Europeans in the place, to capture the guns and protect life and property. The officers of the 15th said the same, and the artillery likewise, only that each reckoned on his own corps, or branch of the service, as alone faithful and trustworthy; it was indeed *quisque suos*, every officer maintaining not merely that his own men were the only faithful ones, but that the safety of the station, and of our own lines, depended on them. The cavalry officers were, on the other hand, confident that though the whole of the Bengal troops at the place were mutinous, and might break out any day or night, one charge of the invincible Lancers would at once put down any attempt at revolt. And this feeling was not confined to officers, but found expression even in the regiments themselves. I mention this to show the extent to which confidence was felt in the men by their officers; and there cannot be a better proof of the falsity of the charge, that the mutiny was owing mainly to the little intercourse and want of friendly feeling evinced by the European officers of the Bengal Native Army for their men. The very contrary was the case; they trusted them even to a fault. And so the time passed on, we daily, nay, almost hourly, enjoining on the native officers and non-commissioned officers the necessity of reporting the disaffected men in their companies (who were, as they allowed, fond of talking mutiny), while they, on their part, assured us they were only waiting for an opportunity, when they were in a position to adduce evidence in support of their charge, and that they would not fail.

Meantime, mysterious reports were circulated somehow, that served to feed the general, though utterly undefinable, spirit of disquietude that was abroad; the old story—old at least now, though it was new then—of bone-dust being mixed up with the atta sold in the bazaar, and of cartridges being composed of objectionable materials. These rumours fled about like will-o'-the-wisps—it was impossible to trace their origin or lay hold of them in any shape, or even to get them accurately detailed. A man would say he heard such and such a report; of course he disbelieved it; but when asked to give up the name of the person from whom he heard it, he would immediately reply, 'Oh, it was in every one's mouth, how could he fix upon any one in particular.'

There was a tank or artificial reservoir of water surrounded by trees a few hundred yards in front of the parade-ground, which was a favourite resort for the sepoys of the two infantry regiments, who used to repair to the spot for the purpose of cooking and eating their meals under the shade of the trees. As we believed that during the time they were assembled here a good deal of treason was talked, our men were desired to forego for the present the advantage of such a place for a cooking spot, as we had heard that it was a favourite resort for bad characters, and the name of the regiment might suffer. They promised willing compliance, and I believe acted up to their professions; for they expressed more and more, as time went on, their horror and dislike at the mutinous language of the 30th Sepoys, and the latter said exactly the same to their officers about the men of the other regiment.

In common with almost every other corps in the service, we had sent a selected party of men to the Musketry Instruction Depôt. It was at these depôts that it was generally believed the caste and religion of the Hindoo and Mussulman was to be systematically tampered with, by the new cartridges being forced upon the men. The attention of the Government had been given, when too late, to the matter that had caused and was causing so much mischief all over the country, and the depôts were broken up for the year, the men being ordered back to their respective regiments. Some days after the Meerut outbreak was known at Nusseerabad, and the disagreeable and dangerous state of excitement I have been attempting to describe had begun, we had notice of the approach of the small party that was returning from the depôt. It was an anxious time, for we thought we should be able to test pretty well the temper of the men by the reception they gave their comrades; and as many of those who had been selected to attend the depôts were men of the highest caste, and, as was generally supposed, of the greatest influence in the regiment, we expected that when they came and assured their comrades that they had seen and used these cartridges, and that their feelings and prejudices had not been offended thereby, a good deal of the groundless apprehension and excitement that prevailed might wear off. The head man of the party was a commissioned officer, a jemadar, or native ensign, and a fine fellow he was. When almost all are infamously bad, there is no great difficulty in excelling in virtue; and when the standard at last sunk so low in the Bengal Army that bad and good as applied to regiments of Sepoys came to define only degrees in villany and turpitude (a good regiment being one that mutinied without violence, and a bad one meaning a corps that killed, or tried to kill its officers), it is not giving a man much praise to say that he was a good soldier. But Gumbheer Sing was really, judged by a higher standard than that I have alluded to, a thoroughly good, trustworthy, faithful, and brave man. He had filled successively the posts of pay havildar (serjeant) to his company, havildar (serjeant) major to the regiment, and was now jemadar of the grenadier company under my command. When the mutiny actually occurred, this man's life was threatened before that of any of the European officers; he ran the gauntlet with us in company with three or four others, and that, too, at a great disadvantage, for we were on horseback and they on foot, though we had no idea at the moment that we were attended by a single man. They followed us in our wanderings, and returned subsequently with us to the deserted and ruined station, doing all they could to evince their sympathy and render what little service was in their power. About three months after, the brigadier, who acted, as he said, under the orders of the Commander-in-Chief, ordered these men to be disarmed on the parade-ground in public. The colonel tried hard to persuade Gumbheer Sing that it was a mistake, and would all be rectified—in vain—he sank from that hour, and died very shortly after completely broken-hearted. His family were in Oude, and he knew they would be sacrificed to the vengeance of the mutinous Sepoys; his honour was at stake, and he attempted to save it by sharing our fallen fortunes; but when the 'Sahibs' turned against him, it was too much for his proud spirit, and he got his wish, as he had frequently said to me; 'the regiment has disgraced itself; I only want one thing now, and that is to die.'

But to return. The report that these men gave was satisfactory in every way. They declared that the whole story of greased cartridges was a fabrication, that they had frequently seen and handled them, and that their caste (and they were some of the highest caste men in the regiment) had not suffered in the least from anything they had seen or done at the depôt. As far as we could tell, there was no ill-will whatever manifested towards any of these men in the corps, and taking this as a proof that disaffection had not yet spread very far, at any rate, we trusted we should get over the crisis safely.

But this crisis, though it was approaching quite fast enough of its own accord, was hurried on by every means the Government could adopt. The silly and injudicious treatment of the Barrackpore mutineers was pretty well known everywhere; but lest it should escape complete notoriety, the proceedings of the courts-martial were sent to every corps to be read out to the men; and, as if this was not enough, they were accompanied by about as absurd and injudicious remarks as could well have been added, the translation and proclamation of which devolved upon me as interpreter; and had I sacrificed my credit as a linguist, and made unintelligible translations of them, I perhaps might have staved off the mutiny for a day. So, lest the prevalent excitement should flag or die out (and our only chance was in allaying it), the men were repeatedly told how for the gravest crime in the catalogue of military offences, their fellow-soldiers in other parts of India had been let off with a nominal punishment, and how the Commander-in-Chief wished to assure them that their religion was not to be tampered with, an assurance which they would argue, with the suspicion inherent in the native mind, he would never have thought it necessary to give, had not there been some foundation for the supposition that Government intended to do the very thing he was declaring it never thought of doing. In their ideas, the object of all these orders was merely to throw dust in their eyes. Just at this time, too, the new platoon exercise was introduced, by which the men were made to tear with their fingers instead of, as of old, bite off the ends of the cartridges before loading. All our efforts were directed to allaying excitement, and, if possible inducing the men to forget for the time that there had been any discussion about cartridges at all. We set to work rebuilding the huts in the lines; the men were allowed a few days' leave to visit in small parties Pohkeer, a place of pilgrimage for the Hindoos, and of great sanctity, in the neighbourhood, and everything was done to draw off their attention from the topics of the day, and give them something else to think about; but all was of no avail as long as they were constantly reminded by hearing these orders read out to them, of what was going on elsewhere; and the introduction of a new system of platoon exercise, which appeared expressly adapted for the new cartridges, looked very bad beside our oft-repeated assurances that no innovations were intended.

Had they not derived from any other source the notion that there was an intention on the part of Government of tampering with their caste, the pertinacity with which the subject of the objectionable cartridges was forced upon their notice by the public orders alluded to, would of itself have been sufficient to excite distrust.

All this time, the men were especially attentive to their duties, most respectful and well-behaved; repairs were going on, as I have said, extensively in the lines; and I constantly had occasion to visit them on business, to see how matters were progressing and to settle disputes about this or that man's house, and I never had the slightest cause for the least suspicion that the bulk of the men were anything but well disposed towards their officers and the Government. They had not spoken out openly to us. Had they done so, and shown a disposition to aid in sifting the matter to the bottom, and to accept explanations, half our difficulties would have been removed; for we felt ourselves in a false position, and were unwilling to begin the subject by taking for granted that dissatisfaction existed; and by adopting open steps to counteract the impression that was evidently abroad, we should have at once admitted that there was a foundation (though slight) for the reports and ideas that they could not but know were very generally entertained. We tried, in fact, to ignore the whole thing as long as we could; we pretended to be unaware that there ever was a dispute between the sepoys and the Government; that the former had ever ventured on harbouring a thought of disaffection, and that the latter had ever had the slightest thought or intention of distrusting its soldiers.

When the party, however, returned from the depôt, we felt that we had a good excuse for speaking out, and under instructions from the commanding officer, we assembled the non-commissioned officers of our companies at our bungalows, and spoke to them. I had to address in this way the non-commissioned officers of three companies, the grenadiers Nos. 1 and 2. I alluded to the return of the depôt party, and the report they brought with them; told them that we had become aware that certain reports were abroad, to the effect that Government intended, by introducing new cartridges made of objectionable materials, to injure their caste, and I assured them that such was not the case; begged them to use every endeavour to counteract the impression that was abroad; and I guaranteed to them, on my word of honour, that if new cartridges were issued that were viewed with suspicion by the men, they should purchase the materials separately in the bazaar, or I would do so for them, and they should make them up for themselves. My short address to the non-commissioned officers had some effect, for I accidentally overheard their conversation (unknown to them) as they left the compound. 'It must be all right,' said one, 'for the Sahib says we may make up our own cartridges:' the rest murmured assent. This assurance of mine consoled them and quieted their fear, for they could not have had the smallest notion that I should overhear their conversation. I mention this because it proves that the men were labouring under the idea that their caste was in danger.

I can well believe that the public are pretty well tired of the cartridge question, but it had so much to do with the terrible tragedy of 1857, that no future historian of the rebellion can possibly ignore it.

It was a long time before we had an opportunity of examining any of these cartridges for ourselves; when we had, we were forced to acknowledge that upon inspection they presented a suspicious appearance. We felt ourselves placed in a very awkward predicament, to say the least, having on the faith of the instructions received from Government repeatedly assured the Sepoys, with all the force of authority backed by our own personal influence, that the cartridges, which we had never seen, were innocuous. That there could have been no real objection to them would appear from the fact that similar articles had been constantly used by flank companies of certain regiments with the Minié rifle; and those for the Enfield, which the Bengal Sepoys refused to touch, were taken by the Bombay army, or a portion of it, at all events, without a murmur. But it seems to have been a point of honour with our men, nay, more, of religious faith, to refuse these cartridges, and to resist their being forced on them even to death. The only possible way of accounting for it is, that they had been carefully instructed in the part they were to play. They had been persuaded by their priests or others that pollution would result from touching these things, and this they must have been brought to believe against their own convictions. I am speaking of the bulk of the men, the dupes, and not the active agents in the movement. And if this view of the case be correct, it goes far to prove, what is now almost universally denied, the existence of a premeditated plot and conspiracy, organized and worked out by some interested parties, as yet unknown.

Another strange feature in the case worthy of comment is, that at the same time that this report about the greased paper was circulated, another was equally prevalent, and had perhaps an equal amount of influence; and this was, that polluted flour had been prepared by Government for secretly destroying the caste of the men in the same way as the cartridges were to have done. For the latter there was undoubtedly foundation, greased cartridges having been introduced by a mistake—a mistake that was rectified as soon as discovered, that is, when it was too late—but for the other report there could possibly have been no foundation whatever.

The garrison of Nusseerabad was commanded by Brigadier M——, an old officer belonging to the Bombay Presidency. When I say that he had no love for Bengalees, as they call us, I only speak the truth, and most assuredly he had but little cause for liking us afterwards, for the accidental circumstance of Bengal troops being quartered at Nusseerabad was the cause of his being burnt out of house and home, and driven out of his station, like the rest of us. That Bengal officers should suffer by the mutiny of their men was natural enough, but that the Bombay officers should be involved in the common destruction was hard, and we cannot wonder at their wishing to be removed as far as possible from such uncomfortable neighbours as Bengal Native regiments undoubtedly were in those days. The Brigadier had met with an accident some time before these events occurred, and had broken his collar-bone, so that he had been a long time confined to his bed, or to his house, and was thus prevented from going about, and making personal investigations into matters that would have been all the better for inquiry; and was besides, in consequence of the accident, prevented from making the personal acquaintance of many of the officers of his brigade. He had, however, inquired from commandants of corps the temper of the men in their respective regiments. What answer he was likely to get, will be apparent from what I have said above; each officer of course assured him that his men were to be trusted; if this was the case, and he had no reason for disbelieving it, there was no cause for anxiety. That the Brigadier was deceived there is not much room for doubting, but the deception was not wilfully practised; officers were themselves deceived and deceived others. It was no proof of moral weakness in those days for us to be confident in the fidelity of our men; it was our duty; but if a similar catastrophe occur again, and similar confidence be shown, he will be a bold man who shall deny the charge of weakness almost amounting to insanity against an officer who allows himself to be duped.

The cantonment of Nusseerabad was drawn out in a contiguous line. On the right were the lines of the 1st Bombay Lancers, to their left those of the 15th regiment N.I., to the left of them again was a large space of ground devoted to the artillery, containing lines for native as well as barracks for European gunners, and to the left of this again were the lines of the 30th regiment N.I. The officers' bungalows were scattered about promiscuously in the rear of the Sepoys' lines, and in a vacant space of ground immediately behind the artillery barracks was the church, a thatched building, with as little pretence to grandeur or architectural taste as churches usually had that were erected at the same time that the Nusseerabad one was built—a time when it appears to have been desirable to ignore as much as possible, at all events, by any outward manifestation of support, the existence of such a religion as Christianity.

Soon after the news of the Meerut outbreak reached us, precautions were taken to prevent the occurrence of a similar catastrophe in our little cantonment; precautions I have said, but the means at hand for taking them were poor enough. However, a picket of cavalry under a European officer repaired every night to the artillery lines to look after the guns, and an artillery officer slept every night at the quarter guard; the cantonment roads were patrolled by cavalry, and every one who was found about after a certain hour, and could give no account of himself, was taken to the guard. At the same time, a troop of cavalry remained accoutred, horses and men, in their lines, ready to act at any moment they might be called upon. These precautions were excellent during the night, for it was only during the night that they were adopted. It will hardly be necessary for me to add, that in the daytime the mutiny broke out; the guns were captured without a struggle or even a dissentient voice.

On the 27th May the General Order reached us, issued in the emergency of the times (and the pangs that the centralizing red-tape Government of Bengal must have undergone before it gave birth to such an order may be imagined, but cannot, I am sure, be described), authorizing any local commandants to promote on the spot to the superior grade any Sepoy or non-commissioned officer or officers who performed eminently loyal service by giving up the name of any person or persons who attempted to corrupt them, or tried to induce them to join in any conspiracy against the Government. If this order had been issued six months before, it might have been of avail; now, like most of the measures taken by the Government, it was too late. It was to have been read out to the men upon parade shortly; in the meantime, we were at liberty to communicate it to them privately ourselves. There was a man in one of my companies (No. 1), whom I must briefly describe. His name was Bucktawur Sing, I had known him ever since I joined the regiment, and he had risen under my command from Sepoy to pay havildar. He was a powerfully made man, six feet four inches, at least, in height, and broad chested and muscular in proportion; indeed, he was almost a gian. The most remarkable thing about him was his voice; it was so powerful, that I believe he could make himself heard to as great a distance as an ordinary bugle. He appeared to have no power of controlling it. When posting sentries in camp, he used to roar or scream out the words of command almost as if, to use a common expression, he would wake the dead. If these lines happen to meet the eye of any of my quondam brother officers, they will recal to their recollection many a time when we have sat in the mess-tent and roared with laughter at Bucktawur Sing posting the sentries at the opposite extremity of the camp, and yelling at them as if they had stood at one end and he at another, instead of their being but two feet apart. I never heard that deafness was very common in the regiment, but I am sure it is a wonder any man ever went on sentry duty with Bucktawur Sing as his non-commissioned officer, and came off it with the tympana of his ears uninjured. This large mountain of bone and muscle came to me one morning some years ago with a very long face and down-cast countenance. He had fallen off dreadfully, his voice could no longer awake the distant echoes as it was wont, and Bucktawur Sing was but the shadow of his former self. He came into my room and said he wanted to speak to me. I saw by the sombre and melancholy expression of his countenance that something serious was the matter. I told him to speak on. He then informed me, that he was being charmed, and his life was wasting away under the influence of the evil incantations. He could not say who his enemy was, but he had one in the corps, and was quite convinced that he was the victim of magic, and his life would certainly be sacrificed. It is a common notion, I must here state, for the benefit of the uninitiated in these matters, among the Hindoos, that to get rid of an enemy, you have only to make a wax figure as much like him or her as possible, subject it to the usual incantations and dedicating ceremonies, then run a pin through it and plaçe it in the sun or before the fire, and as surely as it wastes away, so surely will the prototype sink into the grave by some indefinable, indescribable disease. I belief this unholy rite to have been pretty commonly practised in the lines; certainly it was universally believed in. I have often argued the point with the men, and they have, as they thought, clenched the argument and put dispute out of the question by adducing instances in which the incantation had been successfully practised against officers of the regiment. In these cases, the individuals alluded to had certainly died by premature death shortly after, or about the time that the incantations were said to have been practised, and this was sufficient in their ideas, and according to their mode of reasoning, to prove at once the efficacy of the charm. Unfortunately for this conclusion, there had been in all these cases of sudden and premature death other causes in operation which may have materially aided in bringing on the result anticipated by the enchanter; one of the victims of incantation had fallen from his horse and broken his neck, another had died of disease contracted in that unhealthy province, Sind; and in each case, there was some similar assignable cause of early death, but it was in vain to allege these commonplace circumstances as being in any way connected with the fate of the unhappy victims of malignity in the shape of magic.

I knew it was useless to attempt to persuade

Bucktawur Sing of the absurdity of this notion or to laugh him out of his fears; so I met him on his own ground, and observed, that if there was such efficacy as he supposed in this charming operation, it was quite certain that there must be an antidote. I advised him to apply to his spiritual adviser for a counter-charm; but he had anticipated me, and was provided with the talisman, in which, however, it seemed he did not place much faith. He took it off his arm and showed it to me; it consisted of a little scrap of dirty paper, on which a few words were inscribed in Arabic or Persian. I examined it gravely and attentively, and then returned it with a recommendation to him to wear and to put faith in it, and there was little doubt but that it would be a safe-guard against the evil he so much dreaded. He was greatly comforted by my assurances, and pleased with the interest taken in his fate, and went away with the amulet fastened on his arm, certainly a happier if not a wiser or better man than when he came.

From my fancied acquaintance with this man's character, I reckoned upon his being one of the most trustworthy non-commissioned officers in the Company, and though his personal influence among the men was not great, his position gave him considerable authority, and afforded opportunities for seeing what was going on in the lines, and being acquainted to a certain extent with the temper and feeling of the Sepoys. On the afternoon of the 27th, the day before the mutiny, this man came to me, and asked me if it was true that a European force was on its way to Nusseerabad. A requisition had been sent some time before to Deesa for a detachment of European soldiers and some guns to be sent to Nusseerabad; it was not generally known how large a force was on its way, and, as usual, the most exaggerated rumours were spread abroad. Indeed, the march of the Deesa detachment had been kept quiet by the authorities, as it was deemed unadvisable to give colour to any suspicions that the Sepoys were not trusted. But movements of this kind can never be effected in India without becoming publicly known, and, generally speaking, the attempts at secrecy only serve to give rise to exaggerated and improbable rumours; and in this instance, I have no doubt, acted most injuriously. It was given out, as it was so often in similar circumstances during the mutiny, that European troops were coming to enforce the use of the objectionable cartridges upon the Sepoys; in many places this report was so pertinaciously insisted on, and so cleverly worked, that regiments were induced by it to break into open acts of insubordination and defiance, and to commit themselves irretrievably to the insurgent cause. I asked Bucktawur Sing the object of his question, and he told me that the men were in a very excited state about it, and were displeased at the approach of a European detachment. Upon this I took high ground, and said the Government was not bound to ask leave of the Sepoys before it moved its troops; that it would send them wherever it was deemed expedient they should go; that there could be no possible cause for apprehension among the men if they were well disposed; and as for the silly rumours that were abroad, he, Bucktawur Sing, of course, knew how to treat them. I said a European force, the strength of which I did not know, was, I believed, on its way to Ajmere, and would pass through Nusseerabad; but I took the opportunity of making him acquainted with the new order we had just received, authorizing local commandants to promote on the spot any man who gave information leading to the conviction of any conspirator; and as he had often admitted to me that there were men in the lines who talked treason against the State, though, as he said, they were only talkers, I urged him to bring before me any man he caught behaving in this way, and guaranteed his promotion to a jemadarship. He appeared impressed with all I said, and promised to act upon it; but when I went still further to urge the necessity of action, remarking that this was a time when it would not do to shun responsibility, and that if in the execution of his duty he found it necessary, he would be justified in using force to bring a traitor to justice, and added, that the crisis might call for the sacrifice of life, his eye, generally so unexpressive, literally flashed fire. It was not very long before he acted on my injunction to the very letter, though not in the way that I had intended.

A few days before this, the light company of the 15th, under a European officer, had been sent to Ajmere to relieve a company of the 30th, in charge of the fort. The careless habits we had got into in this country were never better exemplified than they were in this case. Here was a fort, the walls of which were so old and rotten that it was generally believed a gun being fired from any one of the bastions would have brought them down, close to the large and thickly populated city of Ajmere, and commanded by the heights outside the town, containing an arsenal large enough to supply the troops in the whole of Rajpootana, capable of furnishing a siege train of great strength, guns, ammunition, besides an immense quantity of treasure, for the protection of which nothing more than a Company of Sepoys was allowed. When the excitement began, in consequence of the news from Meerut, the grenadier company of the 15th Native Infantry was sent, ostensibly to reinforce the light company in the fort, in reality to act as a check upon it. This may appear a curious arrangement to some of my readers, as if the protection of the fort was the object aimed at, it could scarcely be attained by doubling the strength of a traitorous garrison; but the grenadier company was generally supposed to be less tainted, or rather, I should say, more free from suspicion, than the rest, and in those days we were all deceived alike. When the grenadier company reached Ajmere, the light company at first refused to admit them, alleging that they were not trustworthy; but their objections were speedily overruled, and for a day or so the two companies garrisoned the fort. While there, one of the non-commissioned officers of the light company, a Mahometan, who was generally thought a good man and true, made a curious remark to his officer in connexion with the disturbance at Meerut. 'Ah, sir,' he said one day, 'this business has broken out prematurely, and you will get over your difficulties; but had preparations gone on three years longer, as was intended, you would have lost India.' A few days after, this man mutinied with the rest. This remark, if it is worth anything as evidence (and we cannot afford to throw aside the slightest thing that may help to unravel the mystery in which the origin and source of the revolt is involved), tends to show that the idea of an organized conspiracy throughout the country stands on better ground than is now generally believed.

Most fortunately, just before the outbreak occurred, the two companies of the 15th were relieved by a detachment from the Mhairwarra Battalion. This was a local corps raised chiefly for civil duties in the district, and quartered at Beeawr, a little place thirty-two miles south-west of Nusseerabad on the Deesa road. The Mhairs are a tribe of low caste men inhabiting that part of the country, and being a separate tribe and class altogether from the Sepoys of Oude in the North-west Provinces, it was supposed, as it indeed proved to be the case, that they would have little or no sympathy with them. The Mhairs remained stanch all the time, and did good service—that is, good service for native soldiers; and in taking charge of the Ajmere fort from the Sepoys of the 15th they saved Rajpootana. It was generally believed that if Ajmere had fallen, the Rajpootana states would have gone too, for the possession of the arsenal and all the military stores and treasure in the fort, besides the prestige which would accompany the acquisition of one of the most famous cities in India, a place of pilgrimage and great sanctity besides, would have given the insurgents' cause in that part of the country such an accession of influence and actual strength that it would have won over to its side one or more of the independent chiefs—the rest would have speedily followed suit, and British interest and power in Rajpootana would have ceased from that time to exist; while the destruction and capture of every European between Agra and the Nerbudda would have followed as a necessity. As long as we held Ajmere, there was a tangible proof of the existence, at any rate, of the British Government; for it could not, it would be argued, be in such a bad way as its enemies wished to make out, as long as it held possession of a city as important almost in that part of India as Delhi was in the North-west, or as Lahore in the Punjaub. Towards the latter end of May the garrison of the fort was surprised one morning by the approach of a strong detachment of the Mhairs under Lieutenant Carnell, who had made a forced march from Beeawr, so as to arrive before any notice of his movements could precede him: the two companies of the 15th returned to Nusseerabad, to share in the villany and subsequent fate of their comrades.

CHAPTER III.

THE OUTBREAK AND ESCAPE.

WE little deemed, on the morning of Thursday, the 28th May, 1857, as we got out of our beds, that it was the last time we should lie down in them. Things went on as usual, the ordinary duties of military life in quarters were gone through with their customary regularity, and the morning passed away as other mornings in the hot weather generally do. About noon I had a visit from the Moonshee, or translator and teacher of my regiment, a Mahometan, Meer Wakár Ally by name, who proved himself a thoroughly stanch servant of the State (for which, however, as was the case in too many instances, he never derived any benefit); and he told me that rumour with the thousand tongues was more busy than ever, that he had just passed a number of Sepoys who were returning from the bazaar in a very excited state, saying that the shopkeepers who sell grain (the staple commodity of food to a Hindoo, be it recollected) had told them that bone-dust had been mixed with the grain by the orders of Government, for the purpose of destroying their caste. Thinking that the Brigadier's notice should be drawn at once to this, I reported it to the Colonel of my regiment, requesting him to forward the report to the Brigadier, and get that officer to issue an order threatening with the severest punishment any man who could be proved to have given circulation to a report of the kind. The Colonel refused to concern himself about it, saying, which was very true, that the representation would be of no avail, that he would be called upon to prove the accuracy of the information, &c., and that no good practical results would follow. Upon this, I determined to push the matter myself, and, ordering my buggy, drove off at once to the Brigade Major, and urged upon him the advisability of bringing the matter to the notice of the Brigadier at once. It was useless going to the Brigadier myself, for he was too unwell to see any one. The Brigade Major promised compliance, and said he would speak about it 'the next day;' this was all I could get. The next day the station was a mass of smoking ruins; the spirit of revolt, of violence and outrage, had asserted itself; pillage and incendiarism were at work; the Europeans were driven into the jungle, homeless fugitives, and all authority save that of brute force was at an end.

In the afternoon, after lunch, we were startled by the report of a cannon. It was an unusual circumstance, and we knew something must be wrong. The report was followed, after a short interval, by a second: it was ominous. I hurried out to the gate of the compound that opened on a vacant space of ground, immediately in rear of the Sepoys' lines. The first thing I saw was a crowd of coolies (day labourers) who had been employed in repairing the huts, running as fast as they could from the direction of the lines. At the same time there arose the sound of many voices, a murmur, or buzz, as if a thousand men or more were all engaged in chattering, which was the case, for natives can do nothing without talking. Far from realizing that there was any danger to be apprehended, or that whatever occurred, our regiment, as a body, would behave badly, I returned to the house, and told my wife there was nothing to be alarmed about; but the excitement among the servants in the house and compound, and the noise outside increasing, I again went to the gate. I was there met by a man named Gopaul Sing (a clever, designing traitor, who I thought would attach himself to me under any circumstance, for he had reason to be grateful for many acts of kindness I had done him, and was much better informed on general topics than most men of his class, fond of attaching himself to European officers, conversing with them, picking up English words, and adopting as far as he could, without giving offence to his own comrades, European habits of thought and action)—this man came running up from the lines, apparently for the purpose of reassuring us, and persuading us nothing was the matter. The account he gave was, that a few Sepoys of the 30th had made a rush at the guns, taken them more in sport than in earnest, but they had been met by a party from our light company, who had driven them away;—between them, somehow, the guns had been fired off, but all was over, and there was no danger of any disturbance. I had scarcely time to reason upon the improbability of such a story, when I saw Captain Timbrell, the officer who commanded the artillery, galloping furiously up towards my house, which lay between the artillery and the cavalry lines. I called out, 'What's the matter?' He answered, 'Those rascals the 30th have taken my guns; I am off to turn out the cavalry.' This statement of course I never doubted; and as he had particularly specified the 30th, my confidence in our own men was only the more confirmed. I at once saw there would be a disturbance, but owing to the perfect faith I had in our own regiment, I trusted that matters would turn out favourably. It was best to take precautions; so while my charger was being saddled, I ordered the buggy to be got ready as well, and returning to the house, desired my wife to go across the road to Mrs. H——'s bungalow. This lady's husband belonged to the 1st Bombay Lancers, and as it was generally understood that the cavalry lines were the safest part of cantonments, we had arranged before, that if any disturbance occurred, my wife was to repair to Mrs. H——'s house, and follow her fortunes. Without taking anything, or making any preparations, she put her hat on, and followed by her ayah, ran across the compound towards Mr. H——'s house; the buggy and horse were taken there by the syce, as soon as ready. I had little time for thought, the hubbub outside was increasing momentarily, the servants were rushing frantically to the compound wall, upon which they climbed so as to look over. The whole station was alive, and the very air seemed full of excitement, horses neighing, men shouting, children crying, and that everlasting buzz from the lines, growing louder every instant. The effect was perfectly indescribable. It was totally unlike anything I ever experienced before. One's excitement is wound up pretty high on the occasion of a general action, but this was something totally different. In the one case, the genius of order is apparent everywhere, (at least, it is generally so; I have seen it otherwise); there may be a stunning, deafening noise of cannon and musketry; the clear sharp tone of the words of command rising distinct amid the confusion of sounds, the steady tramp of armed men, the clattering of horses' hoofs, the rumbling of light guns as the horses dash at full gallop across the field, the distant thunder of cavalry advancing to the front, or charging the foe—there may be all this, and a thousand different sights and sounds besides, all commingling by no means unharmoniously; but here there was nothing so satisfactory, all seemed confusion, hurry, anxiety, and wild excitement. The crisis had arrived, the worst passions that pollute the human heart were broken loose, and the consequences could not be foreseen. The conflict must bear the character more of civil strife than open war against an honourable foe. And with what instruments was it to be carried on? In the battle-field, men stand alone to face the danger; but here were our wives and families involved in the same risk with ourselves, requiring our protection and our care, and necessarily withdrawing our thoughts from the actual work before us, while their helpless state filled us with the deepest anxiety. Still I thought, the 30th only have mutinied; the bulk of our men are stanch; the cavalry are sure to be firm, and to fight well under their gallant officers; we shall have but to make a charge, the guns will be retaken, and the mutiny put down.

My wife had left, the house was empty, the servants had rushed to the compound gate and wall to look over, the dirzee (tailor), who was working in an inner room, composedly folded up the fabric he was engaged with, and asked for orders; I told him to make up his bundle, and to go for the present. I was alone, the last to leave the house, and after putting on my uniform and sword, reached the compound gate as my horse was being led out of the stables. The servants, who were looking over the top of the wall, and among them was the apathetic tailor, one and all attempted to dissuade me from going on to the parade-ground, saying I should be killed, as one officer had already been shot by his own men. I said, 'Never mind, it is in the hands of God,' and rode away. As I had to pass through the lines on my way to the parade-ground, the first Sepoys I saw were the rearguard, standing accoutred, and looking as if they did not know what to be at. I called out, 'The 30th have mutinied, we will show them what the 15th can do.' A large number of Sepoys were leaving their huts, and hurrying to the parade-ground; I called out to the same, and waved my hand. They must have thought me mad, their heads being full of murder and mutiny. I emerged on to the parade-ground close by the quarter guard, where there was a tree. Here I found the Colonel, and one or two officers on horseback, looking firm, but anxious. As yet, from the time the alarm had been given, my anxiety had been growing less, in consequence of the misapprehension I was under, that a few men of the 30th only had taken the guns, in which case our course would have been easy enough. The Sepoys were crowding to the bells of arms (small buildings of masonry, one to each company, used for keeping the arms and accoutrements in,) a few in uniform, many without, most half in and half out; that is, with their red coats, but no trousers—the dress which, I believe, is the best adapted for the native infantry soldier, as it is the one he likes best.

We were assembled in tolerable order, as for an usual parade. The Colonel took up his customary position; I ordered the column to form line at right angles to the lines, on the light company, which was done. All this time the mutineers who had possession of the guns kept firing at intervals; what at, I do not know. The whole thing seemed simple enough now; we had but to advance a short distance, charge, and the guns would be ours. In the fullest belief that this was the course we should pursue, I went and addressed the grenadier company, and called upon them to do their duty as brave and loyal soldiers. Meantime the cavalry I knew had been called out, and were to march down by the rear of the lines, between them and the officers' bungalows, where there was for the most part a clear space of ground; and as plenty of time would have elapsed for them to get to the position occupied by the mutineers—namely, the artillery lines, I momentarily expected to see their French-grey jackets and shining lances emerging from among the buildings on to the open parade-ground after charging through the ranks of the mutineers; I looked, but looked in vain, no cavalry came.

Soon after we had formed into line, the light company was brought out to the front and ordered to skirmish. The light company, obedient to command, opened out into extended order from the left. The immediate advance I had anticipated, however, did not occur; we waited—I could not make out the cause; perhaps it was to give the cavalry time to act first. By and bye the Colonel called out to the officer in command of the light company. 'Why don't you advance?' 'Because the men wont go, sir,' was the reply, though I did not hear it at the time. After some delay the bugle sounded for the light company to close on its left; it did so, and the grenadier company was ordered to the front and to extend. There was some hesitation here, but I believe they did extend; advance, however, they would not. I was still in ignorance of the cause; but I must plead guilty to such infatuation and over-confidence in the men, that since I had been on parade, the idea of their mutinying had never once crossed my mind.

The flank companies were then ordered to proceed to the lines and advance in column of sections between the row of bells of arms and the huts, so as to get close up to the guns under cover of the buildings—an excellent move, I thought, as now they will be able to act to advantage and co-operate with the cavalry. They went towards the spot indicated, but their movements were calculated to puzzle a spectator; for they stopped short just at the position from whence they could act effectively. I afterwards learned that when the two companies got to the place, they refused to advance, and some men of the grenadier company were overheard by Gumbheer Sing (the native officer, to whom I have alluded above) concerting a plan for shooting him, if he urged their advance further.

Meantime the Colonel had been to each company in succession and endeavoured to induce it to advance, but without success. They all refused to move to the attack on the guns; and at last my eyes became opened to the actual state of the case; the regiment was in mutiny.

By degrees reports came to be circulated, I do not know how, that the cavalry had refused to act too; it was said they had charged the guns, but had been driven back. This seemed incredible; at length the two companies were recalled from their position under cover of the lines, and we then learned that the cavalry had indeed failed to effect anything. The two companies, I must not forget to state, did not return before one man at least had rushed across the intervening space, in the face of his comrades and his officers, and joined the mutineers at the guns.

The cavalry had been formed in rear of the artillery lines, and ordered to charge by squadrons. They charged, but the men, as soon as they got within a few yards of the guns, went threes about, and allowed their officers to go on—if they pleased. Several did. Major Spottiswood fell mortally wounded, was carried back to his house, where he expired shortly after; Cornet Newbury was cut to pieces among the guns; Lieutenant Lock was badly wounded, and so was Captain Hardy.

Finding that nothing could be effected, the Colonel ordered our regiment back to its former position, that is in open column of companies opposite the lines. This formation was carried out, but the men were becoming more and more unmanageable every moment. They sat down in the ranks, asked for leave to go and get water to drink; it was very hot, as it always is in the latter end of May; a burning wind was blowing, and the sun's rays had been streaming upon our heads all the afternoon. With some difficulty we prevented the Sepoys from taking their arms with them to the reservoir, which as I have elsewhere said was in front of the parade-ground, for their object was to get away from the corps, and under pretence of going to the tank, to sidle up and join the mutineers. It was impossible to do anything; the men at last would obey no orders, and became insubordinate. I think it would have been better for the officers to have left them; but had we done so, we should not have experienced the depth to which their treachery, ingratitude, and villany could go, and consequently should not have properly appreciated the character of the Sepoy, which we (at least I can answer for myself) do now most fully.

I was spared a good deal of the anxiety I should otherwise have felt about my wife, by being informed that the ladies had all left the station for Ajmere an hour at least before, and as soon as I perceived that matters had arrived at that pitch that they could scarcely grow worse, I sent away my syce with orders to go up to the house, to get together as many things as he could, fasten them up in a bundle, and start them off to Ajmere after the fugitives.

The sun was beginning to get low in the heavens, when several fakeers appeared on the parade-ground. Where they came from I know not, but was told subsequently that about half-an-hour before the signal gun was fired, a band of about fifty of these fakeers was seen to enter the station, and make its way down the centre road towards the lines of the Sepoys. These men, whether they had been waiting in the lines or station, or whether they had that morning arrived, were not there without an object. They went down the ranks with a lotah (brass vessel) of water, at least I suppose it was water, and a quantity of what I presume was bhang (an intoxicating drug much used by the natives of India, which when taken in large quantities has a maddening rather than an intoxicating effect; it is very common for them to take large doses of it before fighting, as it gives them what we should call Dutch courage, makes them regardless of consequences, and capable of undergoing any amount of fatigue or exertion under its intensely stimulating and exciting effects), and gave each man a good quantity, with a little water to assist in its mastication. The effect was soon apparent: their eyes became fierce and bloodshot, and assumed the expression so familiar to those who have been long in India, and witnessed the change produced by this stimulant. No one who has seen natives under the influence of bhang, will be at a loss to account for the otherwise incredible stories of the frightful atrocities committed by the Sepoys during the late lamentable events. It has the power of transforming men into demons, giving them all the energy of madmen with all the recklessness of the drunkard. They began to talk or mutter incessantly, and evince the utmost disrespect for their officers by every means short of open and defiant insubordination. The Brigadier sent orders for the officers to leave, I believe in reply to a message from the Colonel informing him how matters stood, and soliciting instructions; and indeed it was time. The men I thought I could trust most were Gumbheer Sing, the jemadar of the grenadier company, and Bucktawur Sing, the pay-havildar of No. 1. company. I beckoned to the former, and asked him how many men, if any, he thought would be faithful to me and leave the rest. He was as unable to reply as I was myself. He said he was taken completely by surprise; had no idea that the men would act as they had; and mentioned one or two that he thought most likely to prove faithful, but plainly intimated that after the specimen of treachery we had had, he could trust no one. I then called to Bucktawur Sing, and put the same question to him; he said, 'he did not know, but would go and ask.' His answer was enough for me; I looked at Gumbheer Sing and smiled, it was evident he had no intention of proving stanch. About this time a musket-shot or two were fired at us by some man from among the mutineers at the guns, who came to the front and took deliberate aim; the ball passed harmlessly over our heads. The Colonel at last intimated his desire to leave, but wished if possible to save the colours of the regiment. Supposing the grenadier company to be more trustworthy than the rest, he desired the officer commanding it to ask for volunteers to take the colours, and leave with their officers. He went up to the front of the company and called out for volunteers, when the whole company to our surprise stepped forward. With an air of pride in his choice Pandies he marched them up in grand style to the neighbourhood of the quarter guard, and told the Colonel the whole grenadier company had volunteered; the whole regiment then moved forward, and each company called out, as well as we could understand in the confusion, that they would all volunteer to protect the colours. They were accordingly brought out, and given in charge to two non-commissioned officers, who took them and repaired with them to the rear of the grenadier company. The regiment had now become pretty well clübbed as it is called; the men were still in companies, and the companies were in column, but in consequence of the grenadiers having been brought up to the quarter guard, that company was in the centre, and No. I. in front. The officers and two serjeants were all mounted, the Colonel having taken the precaution to desire them all to mount some time before, so as to be in readiness if the men proceeded to extremities. The whole corps having volunteered to go away with the colours, a little time was spent in getting the men into something like order, and restoring silence. The sun had just set below the horizon when, with our faces towards the direction of the Ajmere road, the Colonel gave the word—Quick march. The centre companies, apparently from force of habit, made an onward movement, but the front company remained as if rooted to the ground. 'What is this?' said the Colonel; 'you said you were willing to go, and now you will not move.' The men only answered by muttering something about the cavalry cutting them up, a thing they had alluded to before in the same tone and spirit, and which goes to prove that they had no idea of being joined by the cavalry. There was a moment of hesitation. I was on horseback in front of the column a little in advance; the Adjutant, Lieutenant P——, was close by me; the Colonel was just behind, immediately in front of the men; the other officers were in different places all close to the men, and all more or less in their usual places near their companies. I was watching the column when I saw a movement in the centre, a Sepoy snatched one of the colours out of the grasp of the man who held it, and ran off towards the mutineers; the instant after, a native officer, named Tokey Ram, who held the other, followed, and several others followed him in single file, all running. I stood up in my stirrups and pointed at them, exclaiming in Hindostanee, 'Look at the treacherous villains;' but the words were scarcely out of my lips when another movement took place—every musket was raised and levelled at us, and crack, crack, went the reports; ping, ping, sang the balls as they flew round our ears, heads, and bodies; in short, we were under as heavy and as good a file firing as ever it had been my lot to witness either with blank or ball cartridge, on the parade-ground or on the field of battle. I turned to P——, and said 'Come along, we had better go now;' and we both set spurs to our horses, and galloped off as hard as we could. After riding a short distance while bullets were whistling by our ears, and knocking up the dust all round us in front and behind, so that it seemed a perfect miracle we were not riddled with as many holes in our bodies as a sieve, we reached the road that flanked the right of the cavalry lines. P—— called out, 'Left shoulder forward;' we turned our horses round, and being under cover, began to rein in our steeds. We reached the top of the road at the rear of the lines, where the cavalry were drawn up awaiting the issue of events; but P——'s horse could go no further, he had been struck in the abdomen, but had carried his master bravely out of danger, and there fell.*

* Lieutenant P—— was refused compensation for his charger by the military Auditor-general, on the grounds that the regiment having mutinied he had no longer occasion to keep a charger as Adjutant, and therefore it was not necessary to replace it. Sharp practice!

The Colonel, who came up almost immediately after, had had a still more narrow escape, for his horse had been shot in three places. Instead of galloping off when he first felt the spurs, the animal, being restive, turned round facing the column of mutineers (who would have been more delighted to inaugurate their entry into the service of the King of Delhi by murdering the Colonel, than by the assassination of any other officer in the regiment), and reared. This saved his life probably, for the animal received a ball in the neck that would otherwise have prostrated the Colonel himself; another hit him on his knee, and another on his nose, or else the same ball that penetrated his nose came out of the wound we found in the neck. The horse, however, strange to say, not only brought his rider out of danger, but recovered from his wounds, and is now as well as he ever was. The other officers and sergeants came in by ones and twos; all had had similar miraculous escapes. One had taken the direction of the lines, and was fired at by all the sentries at the end of each row of huts, till, just as he reached the last, he bethought himself of ordering the men to desist from shooting at him; he called out and made a sign not to fire, and they obeyed. Another rode between the bells of arms and the lines, and was fired at by three Sepoys from each building. What the men could have been doing there it is impossible to say; but there they were, with muskets loaded, and when this officer rode by for his life, took aim deliberately, and all missed. Another officer, as gallant and brave a man as ever breathed, who afterwards met his death in a melancholy way, having been murdered in the streets of Lucknow,

Lieutenant Thackwell, was in charge of a guard of about thirty men over the magazine. When the behaviour of the regiment upon parade rendered it apparent that we should be obliged to leave, an officer, Ensign C——, rode off to tell Thackwell to leave also, lest he should remain at his post, which he would be unwilling to desert without orders. C—— rode up, and not knowing exactly what to tell Thackwell, called out to him the Colonel wanted him, and he was to come away. Just then the firing began upon parade. Thackwell had no idea what it was all about; but the men of his guard had, for no sooner did they hear it, than they all levelled their muskets at this solitary British officer and fired; they missed. Thackwell by that time was mounted, but before riding off, levelled an old-fashioned six-barrelled revolver he had with him, (that was never known, I believe, to go off in its life). The coward at whom he levelled this innocent weapon of war actually threw down the musket with which he had the instant before, in common with thirty of his comrades, endeavoured to murder their victim, raised his hands in an attitude of prayer, and begged to be spared! Such was the stuff our brave Sepoy army was composed of, and such is the stuff our present native army is even now made of too. Thackwell, supposing the Colonel was on parade, and not realizing for the moment the awful lesson of treachery he had just seen, rode down to the parade ground. Here he found a strange scene; the European officers had left; the men were still firing in the direction he supposed they must have gone, but what were they firing at? They caught sight of him, and in an instant a hundred muskets were levelled at their prey; he rode straight out to the front for a hundred yards or so, then wheeled to the right, and rode off in the direction of the cavalry parade ground as fast as he could get his pony to carry him, fired at the whole time by each company in succession as he passed it in his flight, and reached us in safety after all, his scabbard having been struck and carried away by a ball. Truly we had reason to feel grateful to Providence, for never I believe in this world had men a more extraordinary escape.

There was rather less confusion certainly at what had now become the place of rendezvous, the rear of the Lancers' lines, for the cavalry were drawn up in columns, mounted, but doing nothing, the officers in knots and groups on horseback, and the Brigadier, with his arm in a sling, mounted on a camel. The first who greeted me was the husband of the lady to whose house my wife had gone for refuge, who told me she was all safe; it seemed the ladies had not gone to Ajmere as I was informed, but were still in the station. There was considerable indecision; no orders were given, and indeed no one knew what was best to be done. It was necessary to desert the station; the mutineers had it all their own way, and signalized their success by first setting fire to the church. The dry thatch was enveloped in flames almost immediately as the smoke rolled off in clouds; and the yelling and shouting of the insurgents was like that described by Scott, as if

> 'All the fiends from heaven that fell,
> Had raised the banner cry of hell.'

They proceeded from one act of violence to another, the spirit of outrage increasing every moment with the free indulgence now afforded it; and bungalow after bungalow burst into flames, while the yells and shouts of the mutineers grew louder and louder as their ranks were swelled by Sepoys and camp-followers and blackguards of every description, who literally revelled in wanton mischief, plunder, and incendiarism. It really looked as if the place had suddenly become peopled with demons, who had all broken loose to wreak their spite and vengeance upon everything that bore the impress of law, government, and order.

It was a disputed question whether we should proceed to Ajmere or to Beeawr. The former was sixteen miles distant, the latter thirty-two. At Ajmere there was a fort, but, as I have said, it was scarcely defensible; besides, what means had we of maintaining a siege if the mutineers marched against it, as there was every probability they would? for the plunder of so rich a city as Ajmere, and the possession of so valuable an arsenal as that in the fort, with an almost inexhaustible supply of arms, ammunition, military stores, and all the materials of war, were likely to tempt them in that direction. There were, it is true, many places on the Ajmere road which would have afforded an admirable position in a military point of view, and which might have been held by a small body of men against numbers, as long as they were not taken in the rear; but what security had we that we should not be attacked from the rear? who was to vouch for the fidelity of the Mhair battalion, part of which was quartered at Ajmere? and what security had we that the rabble of that thickly populated city would not rise and aid the insurgent cause? Besides, we had all the ladies and their families with us to be protected somehow; we were well into the hot weather, and though we might pass the night on the heights between Nusseerabad and Ajmere, how should we manage the following day for protection from the sun, for supplies, or water? On the other hand, Beeawr was double the distance; we were at the opposite end of the station, and should have to make a long detour to get into the road, and when we reached the place what advantage were we likely to gain? There was no fort, and the station was garrisoned only by another part of the Mhair battalion, a detachment of which was at Ajmere. Still we knew a European force was on the road between Deesa and Nusseerabad, and would necessarily pass through Beeawr, from which place they were supposed to be only a few days' journey distant. Leaving our destination to be settled by the senior officers, I set off in search of the ladies, feeling sure that they must be in a great state of alarm. Following the direction indicated by a bystander, I rode off towards the open country, which commenced a few hundred yards from the position we were occupying, as the cavalry lines stand at the extreme right of the whole station. When I emerged upon the plain, a strange sight met my eyes; it was covered, though not thickly, with almost all the non-combatant population belonging to us, vehicles of every description, men, women, and children, the latter innumerable, on foot, each carrying away a bundle or some article of household goods rescued from destruction. It was a hurried exodus indeed, and the whole crowd, for crowd it was, though scattered over a large space of ground, was making in a vague manner for the belt of jungle that ran along the foot of the hills.

My eye singled out of this motley group Mrs. H——'s bullock-cart and my own buggy, the latter empty, and on galloping up I found the two ladies with the children were in the former. I told Mrs. H—— of her husband's safety, for she heard he had been wounded, and was in great distress and anxiety, and making my wife get into the buggy with her ayah to lighten the bullock-cart, we proceeded on our way. Several officers had already joined their families, and driven off as I heard, in the direction of Ajmere; so thinking it was as well to follow that route, we struck into the road, and wended our way slowly towards the foot of the hills.

It may be as well to say a few words here about the adventures of the ladies previous to our joining them. Short as the distance was between our house and Mr. H——'s, the noise and uproar had increased sufficiently to excite considerable alarm in my wife's breast before she had crossed the intervening space. On entering, she found Captain H—— putting on his sword, preparing to go to parade, and Mrs. H——, pale and anxious, but composed; giving her little fair-haired boy his dinner, observing calmly that it was well to let him have a good meal; they did not know how long it might be before he got another. Her husband said a few words of encouragement to the ladies, and left them for sterner duties. Shortly after he returned, and desired them to leave the house (which, though in the cavalry lines, was next to those of the 15th Native Infantry, and therefore more exposed than others situated further to the right), and repair to that of Mr. D——, another officer of the same regiment, who lived in a large bungalow situated at the extreme right of the lines. And so Mrs. H——, with her two children, one about three, the other scarcely one year old, and my wife, accompanied by their two ayahs, got into a two-wheeled bullock-cart, a shagram, as the conveyance is called in Bombay, and rattled off to Mr. D——'s. There they found nearly all the ladies of the station assembled except Mrs. D—— herself, who had been spending the day with a friend at a distant part of the cantonment, and who had not yet returned. There was no small noise and confusion occasioned by the assemblage of so many of the fair sex, children, and female servants, under circumstances but too well calculated to excite the fears of the bravest and stoutest of hearts among them. After an interval passed in dreadful anxiety, the booming of the not very distant guns sounding ominously in their ears, without any certain information of what was going on further than that strife and bloodshed were almost at their very door, and that their husbands and brothers were more or less exposed to it, orders came, from what quarter is uncertain, for the whole party to proceed to the quarter or standard guard, where they were assured of the protection of the cavalry. A hurried move was accordingly made; they got into the vehicles—carts, carriages, buggies—and drove under the burning sun, which, however, was little felt in the excitement and alarm, to the standard guard. Mrs. D—— and Mrs. B—— joined them there with their children and ayahs. There was cause enough for sorrow and anxiety, but the elements of the comic were far from wanting to the scene. All the ladies set to talking, each describing the particular way the alarm was communicated, and each giving her opinion on passing events and their prospects. A lady, pointing to some prisoners in the quarter guard, whispered in a warning voice, 'Take care what you say; these men are prisoners, and will murder us all directly they can.' Another went off into hysterics, laughing and crying alternately. The children were difficult to manage, and the poor little things, far from appreciating the danger of their position, increased the confusion by roaring. They had only been in the quarter guard about half-an-hour when they were again told to move and take refuge in the lines; and now began a regular dispersion. The greater part set off for Ajmere, but my wife, with Mrs. H—— and her two children, went along with a native officer of the cavalry, who advised them to conceal themselves in his hut with his own family, and most gallantly escorted them there. In the hut they waited about three hours in a state of the utmost suspense, all the information they could get from the outer world being derived from reports whispered to them through the door, by informants outside, who went to see what was going on, and came and reported it. As may be supposed, the intelligence was vague and unsatisfactory to the last degree. The mutineers seemed to be getting the best of it; then they were told an officer had been wounded, but no name was given; that he had been carried home—was dead; another had fallen badly wounded—another, and so on. No particulars were added, and they were left to their worst anticipations and gloomiest forebodings. How their hearts must have sickened with anxiety and fear! Were the atrocities of Delhi and Meerut being enacted over again on the parade ground at so short a distance off? Were those they loved best on earth, whose protecting arms they might soon so sorely need, but whose assistance they might call for perhaps in vain, stretched lifeless or wounded on the ground, or had they already been hacked to pieces and mutilated by demons in the shape of Sepoys, as had been done but a few weeks before at other places? Were the few words of endearment, and the hasty adieu uttered at their hurried parting but a few short hours before, indeed the last words they were to exchange on earth? And their own fate, and that of the helpless little ones, deprived as they might be of all human protection, what was it to be? Three hours is a short time when spent happily, but under some circumstances may seem interminable. The action and behaviour of the other inmates of the hut served in a measure to distract their attention. There were three women and several children, the family of the native officer who had brought them there. At first they went on apparently undisturbed by the unusual circumstance of having lady visitors to watch them; squatted on the ground they smoked and talked alternately, their conversation chiefly consisting of evil prognostications. Every now and then one of the children who were playing about the hut, of any age from one to five, would go to its mother, and, kneeling down while she continued complacently smoking, imbibe a little of its natural food, and then run away and play again. The native ladies were, however, hospitable and kind in their way to the fugitives, and made them as comfortable as circumstances would allow, and, by way of showing attention, perpetually pressed them to drink water.

The long weary three hours at length passed; the reports, conveyed through the door to the frightened inmates of the hut, became worse and worse; at last the women appeared to give up all as lost, and began stripping off their ornaments, nose-rings and earrings, bracelets, &c., and preparing to bury them. By and by they told the ladies that the bazaars were being plundered, and the officers' bungalows burning, and all was lost; but they had scarcely time to speculate on the probabilities of the intelligence being true or false, before a volley of musketry almost close to where they were hiding rang out sharp and clear; the women threw open the door of the hut, and urged their guests to fly for their lives, 'for that all was over now.' In a state of mind that baffles all description they hurried out of the place, the bullets falling thick about them, and scrambled into the bullock-cart. The noise and confusion increased every instant; there was no time for thought or for inquiry; the only course was to hurry from the actual scene of danger; this they did, and reached the open ground to the right of the station in the direction of the Ajmere road in safety. By the time they got there the firing had pretty well ceased, so they halted; about twenty minutes after, as well as they could guess the time passed under such circumstances, during which their party was augmented by the arrival of several other ladies in a similar position to themselves, they were joined by some of the gentlemen, who rode up and relieved their worst fears by relating what had occurred.

CHAPTER IV.

THE NIGHT AFTER THE MUTINY—THE VICTORS—THE FUGITIVES—RETREAT TO BEEAWR.

THE mutineers had a glorious time of it all that night. They literally revelled in plunder, and gave free vent to their wildest and worst passions.

The cantonment was of course sacked. Two officers remained behind, one till 8 P.M., the other, much against his will, all that night and the following day. The first was Captain Fenwick of the 30th, who remained in the quarter-guard with his men from a sense of duty. The Sepoys of that regiment had offered no violence to their officers, as those of the 15th had done. They simply told them they had better go, and they went. They had been on parade with their men all the time that we had, but the distance was too great to allow us to see them, or for them to distinguish our movements. The 30th appear to have been more orderly altogether than the 15th, and a greater number of men from it remained eventually true to their officers, but they would not act against the mutineers, and met all the orders and persuasions of their officers with a sullen and obstinate refusal. Captain Fenwick, as I have said, remained in the quarter-guard. The place was full of men, all much excited. They were orderly, however, and respectful, and though constantly urging him to go away and leave them, proceeded to no open act of violence. The 15th perpetually sent emissaries to call upon the other regiment to join them; and finding they hesitated, about 8 o'clock in the evening they sent a threatening message to the effect that if they delayed any longer the guns should be brought down, and they would open fire with grape upon the recusants. The Sepoys in the quarter-guard now became more urgent that Captain Fenwick should leave them, and finding that if he did not do so willingly, they would proceed to use force, he consented. They sent an escort of four Sepoys and a non-commissioned officer, who saw him safe to the end of the cantonment, where they left him, an officer who had been brought up in the corps, and was universally respected—houseless and alone to wander forth into the jungle on foot as night was closing in. He had parted with his wife when the alarm was first given, he had no horse, it was an extremely hot night; behind him the station was in flames, and before him lay a large expanse of open country, a cheerless waste into which he might wander with the chance of stumbling on the rest of the party—a small chance enough, when it is recollected he could have had no idea which way we had gone.

Immediately after it was known that we had all abandoned the place, the work of destruction commenced in real earnest. There was an immense deal of confusion and disorder, as may readily be supposed: having got rid of their legitimate commanders, the men had no mind to subject themselves to any new authority till they had had a fling first, and tasted the sweets of liberty. So they set to work burning and plundering. The church was the first to go, and right merrily it blazed away as soon as fire was set to the dry thatch. The neighbouring bungalows went next, and mine being in close proximity to the lines, was among the earliest destroyed. The treasure chest was brought down, and put under a guard; very shortly after, I do not know exactly at what period, it was broken open, and pay, as it was called, distributed among all the Sepoys and registered camp-followers who chose to go and take it, and there were not many, we may be sure, who neglected so good an offer. But the whole night was spent by the bulk of the men in amassing plunder; books, clothes, ladies' dresses, furniture, ornaments, carriages, buggies, horses' harness, carts, bullocks, every conceivable thing was collected in the lines of the men in heaps. The scene was described by an eyewitness, the Munshi of my regiment,—who was forced by fear of his life to remain the whole night, and managed subsequently to escape and join us,—as being ludicrous in the extreme. All these useless articles of plunder they were bringing down to the parade, while a council of war was sitting, composed of the leading men among the mutineers, anxiously debating what course they should pursue. As soon as the 30th joined, they proceeded to elect a Brigadier, Commandants of Corps, Adjutants and other staff, and attempts were made to establish some kind of order, but without much success. After plundering the officers' houses, they next proceeded to loot the shops, and planted a gun at the head of the Sudder Bazaar, threatening to open fire if the inhabitants did not submit quietly to having their houses sacked and property taken away. They made terrible havoc with domestic ties; any good-looking woman they found was forthwith captured and carried off to the lines, to accompany her new lord and master on his victorious march through Hindostan. It was a reign of terror. But amid all this riot and disorder I never heard that any blood was wantonly shed; indeed in this respect the Nusseerabad mutiny forms an exception to the rest; two officers had been killed at the guns, and two wounded, and several of the Sepoys had fallen either killed or badly wounded by some of the cavalry officers who got among them, but there was no massacre, no butchery in cold blood, like that which disgraced so many scenes of the rebellion. No thanks to the Sepoys indeed for this, for the men of the 15th did their best to murder their officers wholesale, and would probably have shot, without the smallest scruple, any man, woman, or child that offered opposition; but no one did, they had it all their own way, and had no possible shadow of excuse for shedding blood.

Such a disorganized state were the mutineers in, all that night and the next day, that a very few resolute men could have retaken the place. Several times during the night an exemplification was afforded of the truth of what Shakespeare says, 'thus conscience does make cowards of us all.' There were in front of the parade ground, about 200 yards from the lines, some buildings connected with the conservancy of the station, surrounded by a low wall painted white; once or twice some nervous individual, or wag who wanted to amuse himself, cried out 'Look, there are the Gora log!' (the European detachment from Deesa was no doubt alluded to); when they all got up, left their plunder, and rushed for their arms in a state of the utmost bewilderment and anxiety; but the dreaded Gora log, on examination, proved to be nothing more than the white walls, and so their fears departed, and they were brave men again.

Meantime the fugitives, for we were little else, were wending their way by the uncertain light of a moon, not yet in its first quarter, across country, forming one of the most motley groups or processions I have ever seen. A body of Lancers went first, then came a line of bullock carts, shagrams of every possible size and form, buggies, &c., containing our wives and families, and lastly, another body of Lancers brought up the rear. We had started in the Ajmere direction, but before going very far an officer galloped up from the rear, and told us that the Brigadier had decided on going to Beeawr; we had therefore to make a detour, for Beeawr lay exactly in the opposite direction, and as we could not go through the cantonment, which by that time was in flames, we had to pass along the whole front of the station. We were very apprehensive of being followed, for the mutineers had a battery of horsed guns, and could easily have overtaken us and effected our destruction, hampered as we were with non-combatants; we therefore crossed the first or lowest range of hills, of very slight elevation, that flanked that portion of the Aravelli range of mountains which, as I have said, confronted Nusseerabad at about the distance of eight miles from the station. It was a long time before we could get into the Beeawr road, or any road at all, and we went scrambling and bumping among the rocks, bringing our buggy (in which my wife and the ayah were seated) over places that were certainly never designed by nature for wheeled conveyances of any kind. Many were the mishaps, many an upset took place, but we had no time to debate upon these little incidents; all we could do was to put the carriage upright again, tie it up with rope if it was broken, and push on. Very frequently we were obliged to stop the buggy at some place that looked more impassable than any other, and the ladies had to get out and walk over a large rock, or down the banks of a dry water-course, and up the other side. We might have laughed heartily at many of the ludicrous incidents that occurred in our flight at any other time; just then we were not much in a mood for laughing. The sky was red with the reflection of the flames that were destroying all our worldly property, and our future fate was most uncertain. Still, strange though it may seem to say so, we felt somehow happier and lighter of heart that night than we had done for a long time before. There are some things, the actual realization of which is undoubtedly much worse than the expectation of them, but suspense is very dreadful to bear long when it is raised to a high pitch. At last the worst, for the present at all events, was over; there was no more going to bed at night, to rise in the morning with the same thing on our minds, the same words upon our lips, 'Will our men be faithful, or will they mutiny? will they attempt to massacre our families? will they be content with the lives of their officers alone, or will they shed no blood at all?' No very pleasing alternative any way, yet it was what we had been revolving in our minds for so many long days and nights; and now it was all over, we were safe, and I thanked God that it was as often that night as I thought of what might have been. Our worldly property was all destroyed; but what mattered that, we had conveyances; a buggy for one, and a good horse for the other; all our friends and companions were in the same predicament as ourselves; many, indeed, for whom we felt deeply, who had young children to increase their anxiety, infinitely worse off. We were well, and most of us in good spirits, and very feelingly did we appreciate the force of t ose words, 'sufficient unto the day is the evil thereof.'

It was a weary night's march though, for Beeawr was distant thirty-two miles; by the detour we had made we must have increased the distance to forty. It was a most sultry night, a hot wind blowing, and the refraction from the sides of the mountains, not yet cooled after the day's sunning, increased the temperature. We had been out since three or four in the afternoon, and how thirsty we were! At last, about eight in the evening, we reached a well in a field near a village. How we all crowded round it! A kind Samaritan lent me a large tumbler, and another filled it with water; brackish it was, and muddy, but what of that! We took a deep draught to quench our present thirst, and lay in a stock of moisture to last till we got another chance of drinking—and it was doubtful when that would be; but we were not allowed a long halt, the trumpet sounded the advance, and the motley cavalcade moved on.

After a time the moon set, and the labour of finding the road, and getting over the innumerable obstacles that beset us, was increased tenfold. At length we passed through a village, the male inhabitants of which were all collected and armed; fortunately we had the Lancers with us, otherwise we might have fared badly at their hands. After this, each village we came to was in a similar state of preparation for hostilities either offensive or defensive; but they did not offer to molest us, contenting themselves with silently watching our column defile through their narrow streets, an operation that, owing to the length of the cavalcade, occupied a considerable time.

There was a great mixture of the comic with the tragic in all our movements; in fact, compared with what happened at most stations where the mutiny had been successful, and the rebels had carried all before them, and the European population had been driven into the jungle, our adventures were nothing but comic. They should be rather called melodramatic, for there was enough to make us anxious, and to temper our mirth. It was not every one that was as well off as we ourselves. Mrs. T—— was in the greatest agony of mind, for her husband had remained in Nusseerabad. He commanded the battery, and was in the artillery lines trying to control his men, when the mutiny had gained ground to such an extent that flight was out of the question, so he stayed there, his men concealing and protecting him all that night and the following day (Friday). It was not I believe till Saturday that he was able to get away, when he made for Ajmere, and wrote to his wife, who had of course joined our party, telling her he was safe. All this time she had been under the impression that her husband had been killed. We could not do very much to comfort her, for though nothing certain was known, it was generally believed that he had fallen. There were other ladies, too, in our party, whose husbands had not joined them, and they were suffering anxiety from the same cause; and there were husbands who had lost their wives, owing to their having missed the road in the dark, or gone to Ajmere, instead of following the main party of fugitives. A lady of our regiment had an English maid-servant, I do not know her surname, but she was always called Kate, and I never made further inquiries. Kate, it seems, was met wandering outside the station by Colonel P——, commanding the 1st Bombay Lancers, who was driving in a buggy, and, having a vacant seat, kindly took up the girl, but owing to bad roads or difficult driving, he upset his companion three times, when she declared she preferred walking to running the risk of a fourth turn-over. Colonel P—— subsequently mounted his horse, and rode with the regiment, but during the night, while the column was making one of its numerous halts, uncertain which way to proceed, and trying to find the road, I heard a noise close behind me, and looking round saw Colonel P——'s horse trotting towards us; he appeared to have no power of controlling the animal, though it was moving at a very ordinary pace, and as he approached, he uttered an exclamation, and suddenly fell heavily on the ground. He was raised up by two of our faithful Pandies who accompanied us, and with difficulty put inside a carriage; the next time I inquired about him, I was told his dead body was being brought along in a country cart obtained for the purpose. We had no time for coroner's inquests. The Colonel's death is supposed to have resulted from apoplexy. It was intensely hot, and he had been exposed to the sun all the afternoon; this, and the excitement, and the natural predisposition to attacks of the kind, was supposed to account satisfactorily for that officer's melancholy death, making the third casualty that had occurred in the 1st Lancers on that disastrous day. About one or two o'clock in the morning we reached a place called Leree, where there was a small dâk bungalow, that is, a little thatched house with two rooms for travellers to rest in. A bivouac was ordered here, and not before it was needed. The ladies and children got a little sleep inside, and the officers lay down on the ground and on the steps and verandahs of the house. This place was eighteen miles by the direct road from Nusseerabad; we had about sixteen more to go before we reached Beeawr. The Brigadier and some of the senior officers held a council of war. The former was for halting here altogether, and sending a reconnoitring party into cantonments to find out what the mutineers were about, and what chance of success an attempt at re-occupying the place would meet with, but he was overruled by the others, and it was finally decided to push on to Beeawr, as originally intended. Here we fell in with the officers of the 30th, of whose fate we were until that time in ignorance. As their lines were situated on the left of the cantonment immediately fronting the Beeawr and Deesa road, they had, when forced to leave, at once set out in the direction, and consequently reached Leree long before the rest, who were forced to make a detour. As there was very little, in fact, nothing, to be got at this place in the way of food or refreshment, after making a short halt, I determined to leave the column and make the best of my way on to Beeawr, so as to arrive there as early as possible; and accordingly, being joined by a few officers and their wives who were of the same opinion as to the advisability of pushing on before the heat of the succeeding day was upon us, we set out again, and reached Beeawr without further adventure about ten o'clock the following morning.

Among the ladies who accompanied us were Mrs. Fenwick and Mrs. T——, who were driving in the same buggy; they were both in the deepest anxiety about their husbands, neither of them having joined us, and there was cause for apprehending the worst. But about daylight, Mrs. Fenwick was overjoyed at seeing her husband ride up; he had left the burning cantonment as I have described above, and walked as far as Leree, where he managed to get a horse; her feelings may be better imagined, but our sympathies were deeply excited for her companion, who was now the only lady of our party uncertain of the fate of her husband. We feared the worst for him, and felt that it was the kindest course to let the stream of grief flow on in silence, unchecked by the suggestion of hopes which we could not offer with the conviction that they were well founded.

CHAPTER V.

RECEPTION AT BEEAWR—RETURN TO NUSSEERABAD—A SACKED CANTONMENT—DOMESTIC SERVANTS—PROPERTY RECOVERED —DETACHMENTS ARRIVE.

WEARIED, dispirited, hungry, and thirsty, begrimed with dust and dirt, we rode into the compound of the Commissioner of Ajmere on the morning of the 29th. Accustomed as most of us were to campaigning and roughing it, the want of rest and food would not have excited more than—an Englishman's right—a good grumble or two, but the poor ladies and children were in far worse plight than we, as the temporary hardships we had undergone pressed tenfold upon them. Knowing that Colonel D——, the Commissioner of the district, was at Beeawr, and knowing also that he must have been informed of what had occurred long before we arrived, we fully expected to find every preparation made for giving us as kind and cordial a reception as strangers and fellow-countrymen—more especially when in distress—are always sure to meet with from English officers in India. But, alas! we were doomed to disappointment. We waited in the compound, in which, though it was full of native servants and hangers-on, not a man came forward to hold our horses; no one appeared to welcome us, or to express a word of sympathy. The most charitable supposition is, that it had been previously settled that Colonel

D—— should receive the bachelors of the party, while other arrangements, of which we knew nothing, were made for the ladies and their families. The Commissioner of Ajmere was a venerable-looking old man, and in very bad health, and, as he died shortly after, I shall so far attend to the old proverb, 'De mortuis nil nisi bonum,' as to say no more than I have already said regarding our reception at Beeawr. As soon as I found there was no prospect of our getting the least relief at the Commissioner's house, I returned to the disconsolate party in the compound—having been selfish enough to procure for myself a glass of water, which I had to beg from one of the Colonel's sable attendants—and related my experience. There was no help for it. The first thing was to get under cover, as the sun's rays were fiercely hot. There was an empty bungalow hard by, and to this we hastened; here was shelter to be had, at any rate; we fastened up our horses in the deserted stables, took what measures we could to procure some grass for them, and then returned to console our hungry families with bare words of sympathy and comfort. We sent the first thing to the baker's for some bread, for some of us were half starved; to our dismay the baker returned answer that he would not let us have any bread till we sent the money for it. This was a sad blow to our hopes, for of course we had not a farthing among us. So far had the respect for British character sunk in a few short hours, that an answer was returned to an application which no native in India would have dreamt of giving twenty-four hours before. Misfortune makes strange bedfellows, they say, but it also teaches many lessons that may be useful in after life. We were fairly at our wit's end to devise means for providing the commonest necessaries of life; never before, during my wanderings over pretty well half the continent of India, had I known what it was to want for a moment a cordial reception and kind hospitality wherever there was a British officer to be found. What had happened? The Sepoys, whom we liked and trusted, had nearly murdered us. Had human nature become suddenly diseased?—were our countrymen affected by the same spirit that led the natives to attempt our lives? This was, indeed, the hardest blow of all.

But a 'Deus ex machinâ' came to our relief in the very moment of our utmost need, and this was the husband of one of the ladies of our party, who had discovered that there was a good Samaritan at Beeawr after all, and that we had only to make our way to his house to get food and shelter and rest. Overjoyed, we lost no time in acting on the good intelligence, and made our way on foot through some deserted gardens and dried-up compounds, and over ruined walls and broken-down hedges, to the house of Dr. Small, medical officer to the local battalion, and in medical charge of the place. Here we found Dr. Small's little bungalow literally crammed. He and his wife, who were kindness personified, put themselves and child as much out of the way as possible, to make room for the needy and numerous visitors; as many as nine separate families found refuge under his roof, and a curious scene it was. The breakfast-table, not large enough to admit all at once, was crowded, and the food quickly dispatched.

Many of us were too fatigued to take more than a mouthful, but a cup of tea or a glass of beer were relished as they were seldom relished before. After breakfast we lay down, as we could and where we could, carrying on all the time a fierce discussion on the events that had led to our present flight. We all related each his individual experience, compared notes, and speculated on the cause of the mutiny, &c. —topics that have now fairly grown threadbare under oft-reiterated discussions. How Dr. Small could have managed to receive us all as he did, and how we all managed to squeeze into his house, is a wonder. The Commissioner, however, whose house had ample accommodation for all of us, did not escape the ravages of the locusts, in the shape of hungry visitors, for all the bachelors of the party, and the officers of the 1st Lancers, which regiment reached Beeawr a few hours after us, put up within the walls of his spacious domicile, and a wholesale consumption of beer and cheroots and provender of all kinds succeeded. It was Friday morning when we reached Beeawr. By Sunday evening, as the reader may suppose, we began to get very tired of our sojourn there. A small house full of ladies and children in the hot weather, and in such a state of utter destitution as we were, or should have been, had it not been for the kind exertions of our host and hostess, was not the place for gentlemen to stay at longer than was necessary; so as soon as we heard that the mutineers had left Nusseerabad, I determined to accompany Capt. B——, the commissariat officer and bazaar master, back to the ruined station, and see what amount of damage had been done, and what chance there was of recovering any of our lost property. The Lancers returned to Nusseerabad before us, so the road might be supposed tolerably safe, though there were said to be a number of Sepoys loitering about the country. I must not forget to mention that a party of the 30th N. I., under a native officer, said to be about 120 strong, had left the rebels, and followed us to Beeawr. They were ordered to halt outside the station, and to give up their arms. An officer, Captain Fenwick, was sent to meet them, and receive their submission; and accordingly he repaired to the spot. It was a very hot day, and the walk made him feel very thirsty, but there was difficulty in getting water from the well, as natives, either Hindoo or Mussulman, will not allow a European to drink out of their vessels. But the native officer of the party, a Hindoo, came forward, and offered his, remarking, 'Take mine, Sahib, and drink, there is no such thing as caste now.' I merely mention this to show how universal was the feeling that the authorities were bent upon the destruction of caste, and that all who sided with the British must do so at the sacrifice of their religious prejudices.

The same evening that we returned to Nusseerabad, this party of Sepoys was unexpectedly ordered to march thither also under two of their own officers They had received no warning to prepare, and the sudden intelligence of the move excited their suspicions, already actively at work. A short time was given them to complete a few arrangements, such as packing up their bundles, &c., but when they fell in before starting it was found that a large number, about half, had made use of the interval to desert.

A curious scene met our eye as we entered the ruined station on Monday morning about sunrise. The first thing I noticed was the white appearance of the roads we were riding on; it looked as if it had been snowing, and the snow had left innumerable patches all over the place. We soon found that this white appearance of the ground resulted from an immense quantity of paper strewed about, chiefly private letters, taken evidently out of writing-desks and cabinets, where they had been no doubt placed with the idea of keeping them from the eye of strangers. Here was a revelation of secrets and family matters. I observed that nearly all I picked up were overland letters, and began at first collecting them with a view of returning them to the owner, who had evidently made a point of preserving them for some object, but I soon found that the attempt would end in my overburdening myself, for I could have collected a donkey-load in half-an-hour, and by evening should have required a camel to carry the product of my day's gleaning.

The houses were mostly blackened ruins; the compounds, like the roads, strewed with papers, notes, letters, private and official, fragments of books; the ditches round most of the compounds, too, were quite full of papers, and what chiefly attracted my attention, was the immense quantity of music lying about, Trashy stuff, I dare say, as old music generally is, but, had I chosen to collect it, I could have laid in a stock that would have put most regimental bandmasters in ecstasies. In one compound I observed a singular result from the wholesale plunder that had been going on. The house was apparently one of the last that had been gutted, for there were more remnants of property here than in any other estate: when I say more remnants, I must not be understood to imply that there were any remnants at all at other places except paper; the sacking of the station had been most complete, indeed it had undergone three sackings, first by the Sepoys, then by the villagers, and lastly by the bazaar people,—or very likely the latter had the second chance; but it was wonderful how every single shred of everything in the shape of property had been carried away, except in the house I speak of, which had been inhabited by one of the married officers of my own regiment. There was a little crockery actually unbroken in the compound, and a plate-chest, alas! empty; still the chest was there, and that was something wonderful. The usual havoc had been committed among the papers and books here as elsewhere, and the whole ground was strewed with fragments of literature; but it seems the scene of devastation and plunder had been disturbed by a westerly wind, and the consequence was, the paper had been blown away. Immediately behind the house was a field covered with stubble about six inches in height. The effect of the wind among the papers had been to blow them away into this field, where they all lodged, one piece against each bit of stubble, standing upright over the whole ground in such a position that you could read the contents of most as you walked up and down between the furrows. A most excellent plan for peripatetic philosophers to exercise both mind and body at the same time. We rode through the bazaar. On entering it I was greeted by two or three of my servants, who came running up, pretending great delight at my return; said they had been hiding in the bazaar in imminent fear of their lives ever since the outbreak. This account of themselves I professed to be satisfied with, as I was in great want of servants, for very few indeed remained with us. Their conduct was, to say the least, open to inquiry, for had they been so solicitous about our safety and so anxious to return to their avocations, there was nothing in the world to have prevented their going to Beeawr. My companion, Captain B——, had been sent in by the Brigadier with orders to reassure the inhabitants of the bazaar, both by his presence at his post and by his conduct and language, as it was a great object to allay the general panic, and get the people to return to their ordinary business as soon as possible. The bazaar bore evident traces of having been subjected to rough usage, still there was nothing to be seen of the ruin and desolation we had heard so much about. A house here and there had been set on fire, and the doors, and doorposts, and roof burnt, but as a general rule they were intact, and at least half, I should think, were shut up and locked, showing that the owner had left the place for the present. The large shopkeepers, of whom there were two, the principal native residents at Nusseerabad, did not appear to have suffered anything at all. One of these, a Parsee shopkeeper, complained indeed that the Sepoys had gone into his shop and smashed everything, but we reached Nusseerabad about thirty-six or forty hours after the rebels had gone, and certainly in the interim he could have had no means of replenishing his shop, and I saw no signs of such violent outrage. He told the wildest stories; that one Sepoy had broken open his treasure-chest and taken away 19,000 rupees—rather a large sum in cash for him to have by him, especially in troublous times, when natives had been for long expecting an outbreak. The other shopkeeper, who had a very large establishment and extensive godowns well-stocked with furniture, &c., kept his doors locked up. Externally his house had suffered nothing, and when I first went inside, which was some days after my return, I found things pretty much in the state they were before the outbreak. One of our officers, Dr. de R——, who had lately come from England, had brought with him a good deal of nice furniture, in the shape of ornamented cabinets, &c. Immediately on his return to Nusseerabad, he went straight to this man's shop, and insisted on its being opened; with considerable difficulty he effected an entrance, where, not much to his surprise apparently, for he seems to have suspected something of the kind, he found all his furniture safely lodged in the shop, and exposed, to all appearance for sale, along with the rest of the stock in hand. Of course he claimed his property, but the wily native, who was not to be caught napping, came forward, and smilingly assured him that he had removed the property to his shop for safety, and was only too glad to return it. I afterwards went to our mess-house. It had for some reason or other escaped being bu nt, but had been pretty well gutted. There were two or three pieces of a table here saved by one of the Sepoys of the regiment, who, under very suspicious circumstances indeed, was found in the lines on our return. We had had a good supply of beer, and wine, and stores in our godown when the outbreak occurred. Where were they all gone to? The Sepoys certainly could not have carried away bottles of beer and wine, and oilman's stores. Had they been smashed, and the contents spilled out of wanton mischief on the floor, still we should have found the fragments in the one case, and the empty bottles in the other. But no, everything had been carried away, bottles, boxes, and all. There was not, and is not to this day, a shadow of doubt in my mind that the whole of these stores, and a very large proportion of the private property that was lost, fell into the hands of the native tradesmen in the bazaar (who, if they had not been in league with the rebels, or at any rate had means of influencing them, would never have escaped ruin at their hands), and were retailed subsequently when troops returned to the place. Under this impression it may be imagined how anxious I was for the return of the Brigadier to the cantonment, as I never doubted for a moment that the first thing he would do would be to authorize a thorough search for property in the bazaar. Will it be believed, it was not allowed!

Captain B—— had been sent in, as I have observed, with a view of reassuring the inhabitants of the bazaar. I was much amused at the way he did so. We stopped every now and then as we rode through, and were of course immediately surrounded by a crowd of natives, who complained loudly and bitterly of the terrible losses they had met with, and the barbarous manner they had been treated. 'Never mind,' replied Captain B——, in a soothing tone and manner, 'it will be all right now; there are so many pultans (native regiments) on their way, and so many European soldiers; the first instalment will be here immediately.' Now, considering the experience these men had just had of native regiments, it seemed but a poor source of consolation to them to know that though the dreaded Sepoys had just gone off to Delhi laden with plunder, there were plenty more coming. The prospect of a garrison of European soldiers might have been deemed a tower of strength at any other time, but just then the value of soldiers and everything else European had fallen considerably in the market; the public feeling was anything but one of confidence in us, and it was a question whether, to the excited imagination of these people, the advent of the Gora log (English soldiers) was not looked upon as a worse calamity than even the occupation of the place by Sepoys.

After reassuring the minds of the inhabitants in this effectual manner, and sitting for a short time at the Parsee's shop, the owner of which gave us what refreshment he could, and promised to have some curry made for us and sent up to Captain B——'s office, which had escaped demolition, that officer rode off to look at his ruins, and I went to look at mine. Numberless are the associations connected in our minds with the magic word Home; but it is very rarely that in India, more especially to those in the army, and in the roving, unsettled life we lead in it, a temporary sojourn at a military station can invest our places of residence with even the imaginary attributes of home. Still our bungalows are the only homes we have, and one cannot walk over the yet warm ashes of the house he has lived in even for a month, without feeling more or less the force of the calamity that drove him and his, houseless (even if he considered himself homeless before), into the world.

The ruins of my late bungalow did indeed present a sad scene of desolation. I sank up to my ankle in ashes, which, as I have said, were still warm; everything was destroyed—it was a total ruin. I found a number of our visiting cards strewed about the compound, but, strange to say, no papers scarcely; the demon of destruction had revelled here even with greater violence than at other places, and even books and papers had been totally destroyed. I had had a nice library, at least for India, and a number of pictures; engravings, books, papers, all were burnt to ashes. On the mantelpiece in the drawing-room there had stood a stereoscope, and a pile of stereoscopic pictures on subjects of family interest. The glasses were still there, partly melted, but of course no traces of the images represented on them. A coloured daguerreotype of some members of my family, done upon a brass plate, still remained; it had been subjected pretty well to the action of fire, but the figures and colour were still discernible. In the compound I found stems of moderator lamps fused and half melted; on the wall, as if placed there in derision, a broken tortoise-shell tea-caddy, an old family relic; and in the servants' huts and outhouses several empty broken boxes, chiefly those which had contained ladies' wearing apparel, dresses, &c.; and this was all I found. I looked about, and moralized a little, and then, mounting my horse, rode down to the lines and regimental bazaar.

Here all was much as it was elsewhere—ruin and desolation; the lines had been burnt, a portion of the huts escaping, and the bazaar also, but, before leaving, the mutineers had wantonly destroyed a small Hindoo temple that stood in a central position in the bazaar, and was always regarded by the men of that religion with the usual veneration and respect paid to places of the kind. Here was another enigma in the unaccountable conduct of the Hindoos. What could have induced them to violate the sanctity of one of their own objects of worship? It was not to be supposed that the Mussulmans, the smallest party numerically in the corps, would have ventured on such an act, even had they wished to sow the seeds of dissension in the rebel army; and why should the Hindoos commit an act of religious suicide?

The regimental bunneahs, or shopkeepers, from whom the Sepoys purchased grain, were still hanging about the deserted and ruined shops. I had found out that their debts in the regiment and accounts with the men had, by dint of the most inexorable dunning and the greatest exertion on their part, been settled before the day on which the outbreak occurred, which was pretty strong circumstantial evidence that they were all aware beforehand when the mutiny was to commence. The regimental hospital was empty. What had become of the sick? There was one case certainly in which removal must have been attended with serious consequences. About a fortnight before the outbreak, a murder had been committed in the Sudder bazaar, attended with unusual results. In a fit of jealousy a man armed himself with a sword, and rushed suddenly upon a party, consisting of his wife, a lover, and the wife's mother; the wife and the lover were both killed, and the mother-in-law was supposed to be, for the murderer left her on the ground with an immense gash in her head, her arm cut clean off, and several other wounds about her body;

in this state she was found next morning, and, strange to say, was yet alive. The injured husband who had thus revenged himself was captured with difficulty, for he took refuge in a godown or store shed, filled with sacks of potatoes, the property of the commissariat contractor, and, ensconced behind these bulwarks, bade defiance to the myrmidons of the law when they came to arrest him. He was taken at last by a small party who went after him armed with muskets, against which the potatoes would have offered a vain resistance. The woman, with but a feeble spark of life remaining in her, as may well be supposed, was taken to our regimental hospital, where I saw her once or twice during my rounds. It was found necessary to re-amputate the arm, though it had been cut clean off, and, as the wound in the head alone had been sufficient to have killed half a dozen mortals with the ordinary amount of vitality in them, it was quite contrary to all the experience of our medicos that she survived. However, she did survive, and though weak when I saw her some days after the outrage had been committed, was in no bad case. When I revisited the hospital after my return, the old woman was gone; the murderer had been, of course, released from prison, and joined the rebels. I hope he offered his poor old mother-in-law an arm, at any rate, as they trudged along the road to Delhi.

The mutineers were closely pursued by two officers, Lieutenant Walters and Heathcote, the former a civil officer, and the latter Deputy Assistant-Quarter-Master-General of the Rajpootana Field Force, as the Nusseerabad garrison was called; these officers were accompanied by a body of men called Raj troops, which signifies armed retainers of the neighbouring independent chiefs; some belonging to the Jodhpore and some to the Jeypore states. The men would not fight, and they were too much afraid of the Sepoys and the guns to attack them, had they wished, but they made no secret of the fact that their sympathies were with the rebels; they believed that we had tried to tamper with the religion of our men, and evidently thought they were right to act as they did. Still they went along with these two British officers cheerily enough, and, keeping just behind the rebel column, followed it nearly up to Delhi. It is a strange thing that though they were on the look-out for stragglers, they found none. The rebels made good long marches, the roads were in many places very heavy, the men were encumbered with immense quantities of plunder, and must have been badly off for carriage, yet the pursuers could pick up no stragglers. They parted with a quantity of the plundered property in the villages as they went along, from which a portion of it was subsequently recovered; but that they should have managed to carry along their sick and women and children and baggage in their hasty march, ill-equipped as they were, is not one of the least curious parts of their strange history.

The behaviour of our domestic servants during this crisis was, as a general rule, most infamous. Whatever grievances the Sepoys may have had, or fancied they had, the other class, at any rate, could not plead even this excuse. They were not called upon to use obnoxious cartridges, nor was it ever whispered that any attempt was to be made against their caste and prejudices, unless, indeed, the absurd story of the bone dust atta, which would affect them as much as the Sepoys, may be considered in this light. Without any exception almost, the officers' servants aided in plundering their masters and mistresses, by whom, as a general rule, they had always been well and liberally treated, and accompanied the mutineers to Delhi. One of the grossest cases of treachery and ingratitude in this class was that of a servant Colonel Shuldham had had in his service sixteen years; and the Colonel was most particular in his treatment of natives, and towards this man especially he had always behaved with the utmost kindness and good-nature. The man was a sirdar, or head of the Colonel's establishment, and a great man evidently in his own estimation and that of his compeers. Instead of repaying sixteen years of kindness and liberality by following his master and sharing his fortunes, he took his fill of plunder and joined the rebels. In our own case we had pretty much the same experience. The inferior servants in the household, as I afterwards learnt, made up bundles of clothes, and any articles they liked to select out of the house, and went off with them. My wife's ayah had accompanied her in the buggy, so she could not very well desert, and was subsequently joined by her husband, who presented himself at Beeawr a day or two after we got there, with a spare regimental sword, a pair of pistols, and a pair of boots; the last two no mean addition to my then slender stock of goods and chattels. Having recently arrived from England, we had no old servant with us, but one or two that we had entertained at Nusseerabad; these men rejoined me on my return, and

I was therefore much better off than many others who could get no servants at all for a long time, though I was perfectly conscious all the while that my faithful domestics had helped themselves very liberally to our moveable property.

They had the grace to return a few articles which were then most invaluable to us, but what spirit of disorder or incongruity could have influenced them in their selection it is impossible to conceive. They professed to have gathered up what they could, and preserved it by burying the bundles in the earth; but one would have supposed from an inspection of the property thus returned to us, that the rebels must have first of all collected every article of apparel, every book, every material object inside the house, put them altogether in a heap, with as much disorder as possible, and then let a man blindfold put his hand upon it, and draw out a certain number of things. There were a few little books among them. We had, among other relics, several old prayer-books, which after being half worn out by age, as is usually the case, had been replaced in general use by others, but the old ones we had kept, though of course they would not be allowed to retain their place in the book-shelf. These, to the number of six, were preserved. I also found two little volumes of Jeremy Taylor's works, and strange to say, two copies of the same book, *Disce Vivere,* which I had by me, one of these being, I recollected, on the drawing-room table; the other, which was a superfluous one altogether, was, I know, on the shelf; yet these two books were brought back. The rest of my library, a valuable one, particularly in oriental works, was totally destroyed. I discovered in raking up the rubbish, which, rubbish as it was, I was glad enough to get, a few ladies' dresses, a few articles of apparel, apparently the oldest and most worn in our wardrobes; a lace cambric handkerchief was wrapped round the bit of a very old bridle, and lots of new ribbon were intermingled with old shoes. Out of my wife's stock of jewellery, one brooch and one bracelet were brought back.

In a few days after my return to Nusseerabad, the reinforcement so kindly promised to the inhabitants of the bazaar arrived; a detachment of the Jodhpore legion, a wing of the 12th Bombay N.I., a detachment of the 2nd Bombay Cavalry, 3 guns Bombay Horse Artillery (European), and about 200 men of H.M's. 83rd. The officers I had left at Beeawr accompanied this part of the detachment, as also did the Brigadier and his staff. The ladies remained at Beeawr. We (*i.e.*, the officers of my regiment) took up our abode in our mess-house, each occupying a corner of one of the rooms; purchased at exorbitant prices in the bazaar a few plates and cooking pots, got a servant or two to attend us, and made ourselves as comfortable as circumstances would allow.

CHAPTER VI.

AFFAIRS AT NUSSEERABAD—PROPERTY BROUGHT IN—WANDERING PANDIES—HOW THE MUTINY WAS MANAGED.

I CANNOT say that matters were in a very satisfactory state at Nusseerabad. We set to work to gather up the fragments, as it were, of our regimental institutions, and settle as far as we could, while things were fresh in our memory, band and mess accounts, &c.; we had to draw out returns and rolls for transmission to head-quarters, committees sat to investigate losses, and altogether, the horse being gone, we did our best to shut securely the stable door. The detachment of the 83rd and the guns having re-established British authority in the district, orders were issued to all who had stolen property to give it up, and a party of cavalry under a British officer went out every day to visit the neighbouring villages and scour the country, taking carts with them to bring back anything they found. The property the cavalry brought in was deposited in the standard guard, and another building attached to the regiment. The greater part of the miscellaneous collection of worldly goods thus restored consisted, as may readily be supposed, of nothing but empty boxes; the contents having been abstracted, the boxes were returned. The more valuable property was placed in the school-room, and after it had been allowed to accumulate for some days, people were summoned by a public notice to go and claim their own; it was necessary to have it taken away to make room for more.

Words would fail to enumerate the miscellaneous genera of articles heaped together; the only thing I ever heard of, to which it might be compared, is the fabled castle in the moon, where all lost articles are deposited. The reader must imagine a heap of the most heterogeneous things it is possible to concentrate together, all of course more or less damaged; ladies' silk and lace dresses had been dragged in the dirt; books and pictures had been kicked about; plate and cutlery exposed to the damp air; but it is useless attempting to describe the mass of confused and jumbled property.

This was nothing, however, to what was to be seen at the Kotwalla in the Sudder bazaar. This place had been appointed for the reception of everything brought in by police, discovered in the bazaar or cantonments, in short, for whatever came to light on byeways or byeroads, and that was not recovered by the cavalry, whose expeditions to the surrounding villages ceased after each had been visited. The inhabitants of one had turned out and pelted the troopers and the officers with them on one occasion, of which fresh outrage against British authority the usual notice was taken, that is, it was passed over in silence. Cartloads of odds and ends were being brought in all day long, and thrown upon the ground; each succeeding cart emptied its load upon the former deposit, and so on, till at last there grew into existence two heaps, which, if collected into one, would have equalled in bulk and size a small house. A great part of this, however, was clothing, Sepoys' great coats, uniforms, &c.; but there was an immense quantity of books and music, besides a room full of ladies' dresses in a neighbouring house. People were in this case, too, invited to select their property and carry it away, and the reader will understand what the probability was of one's being able to find and recognise anything amid such a mass; the chance was ten thousand to one that the article he was in search of was not on the surface at the time he was looking for it, and of course to penetrate into the under strata of such a formation was more than the most enthusiastic geologist would have ventured on. And it was a curious thing, and not unworthy of remark, that although every one seemed to find something that he recognised as belonging to some one else, I scarcely ever heard of any one recognising his own property. Certainly I rescued nothing of mine, though I used to repair daily to the Kotwalla as a matter of business. There were a number of Sepoys, will it be believed, straggling about the cantonment. They were men we found there on our return who had joined the mutineers in their plunder of the place, but not feeling inclined to make so long a journey as that to Delhi, had deserted their comrades when they started, and returned to the empty lines, giving themselves up, or reporting themselves, as they called it, to the first British officer they came across, and of course making out that they had been usefully engaged in some way or other. These men were permitted to reside in cantonments, and used to go swaggering about the place claiming property, as they called it, armed with huge bludgeons, and ready for any mischief. In their behaviour to English officers they were most rude and insolent, regardless of orders, with no duty to do, as they drew no pay. They used to throng the Kotwalla in such numbers, pulling about the things there on the pretence of looking for property, that it became an absolute nuisance. At last the Brigadier ordered a subaltern officer to go on duty at the Kotwalla daily to preserve order. On one occasion, when an officer, who has been mentioned before, Lieutenant Thackwell, was engaged in the duty, a crowd of Sepoys came round the place, as was their wont, interfering with the object for which the property was being brought there, insubordinate and insolent as usual. Thackwell ordered them back two or three times: most of them retired sulkily, but one of the number was determined to have his own way, and refused to move; on which Thackwell put his hand to his shoulder and pushed him off. The man had with him an iron-bound club, manufactured expressly for breaking heads in village rows; he raised it in the most approved Indo-Tipperary fashion, and in one second more it would have descended on Thackwell's skull and fractured it. He was, however, a powerful man—more powerful than his opponent, who was one of those enormous six feet two men which we used to be so fond of seeing in our ranks—and clenching his fist, he sent it with the whole force of his muscular arm right in the Pandy's face. He turned a sommersault backwards, and fell senseless.

The matter was reported, but no notice taken of it, the Sepoy's attack having been supposed to be cancelled by the officer's unconstitutional way of defending himself.

Before proceeding further with the narrative, it

will be necessary to say a few words in explanation of what has gone before. We had been so taken by surprise that we scarcely knew how the catastrophe which had involved us all in a common misfortune had occurred, and it was not till some days afterwards that the real story of the mutiny was arrived at. Even now there is considerable difference of opinion among officers of different regiments as to the share taken by their respective corps in the general outbreak; but I believe the following is as true a statement as can be obtained of the manner in which the mutiny began at Nusseerabad. I had been told it was the Sepoys of the 30th who had taken the guns, and this had not been contradicted. I did not observe that many of our own men were absent from parade; and though conscious that a few of them had gone over to the mutineers, as I saw them go myself, yet I was still under the impression that the leader of the mutiny, and the bulk of the men who had captured the guns, were from the 30th. The contrary, however, was the case. The artillery was posted between the two regiments, and was consequently flanked by the light company of the 15th on the right, and the grenadier company of the 30th on the left. The mutiny began by a few men of the light company of the former regiment, a smaller number still of the grenadier company of the latter rushing upon the guns when the horses were away at watering, and only the ordinary artillery sentries on the look-out. I believe at first the number of mutineers that held possession of the guns was not more than twenty-seven; the bulk of the 15th did not openly join them till after sunset—that is, three or four hours after—and the bulk of the 30th did not join them till night. How was it, then, the mutiny occurred at all? It was just this: there were a certain number of active leading spirits in both regiments and in the battery determined upon mutiny, and determined also upon getting the majority of their comrades to join them. How these men were influenced, or who they were that stimulated them to rebellion, or what connexion they had, if any, with other parties at a distance, bent on attempting the overthrow of the British Government, or whether or not they were acting in concert with, or in obedience to, instructions from the royal families of Oude or Delhi, this is not the place to inquire. There is no doubt, I think, that the mutiny at Nusseerabad, and at other stations also, took place immediately in consequence of instructions or communications from certain strangers, who came into the lines under the disguise of fakeers. Who they were it is impossible now to say—whether Sepoys of one of the regiments so foolishly disbanded at Barrackpore—as if it were our object to send emissaries into every corner of the country, and sow the seeds of rebellion and disaffection broadcast over the land—or messengers from Delhi or Lucknow. They did not cease tampering with the native troops even after our men had marched for Delhi, for I have seen them coming from the lines of the Bombay troops.

In every case of mutiny there were a few designing traitors in the corps bent on crime; they knew that the whole army was composed of very inflammable materials; if a spark once ignited the train, the conflagration was sure to spread. The way for mutiny was well prepared beforehand, perhaps had been preparing for years; very likely, as Hidayah Ally says, ever since the Affghan war: the leaven was at work, and good care was taken that its action should not cease. At last, about the month of May, the men were wrought up to the highest pitch of excitement by prophecies, and traditions, and warnings, and threats, and every means that craft could suggest to work upon superstition and ignorance. They were taught to believe that something tremendous was about to happen; that our empire must be overthrown; that an attempt was to be made to corrupt their minds, and put down the practice of their religion, and to destroy the distinction of caste. All this the bulk of the men, I believe, really laid to heart. The ignorant and superstitious, probably the most honest, were thus made sure of: they would join the mutiny directly the portentous sign they were on the look-out for commenced, either in the heavens or on the earth. The utterly unprincipled—a very tolerably large class—whoc ared little either about God or man, as long as they kept out of mischief and made money, would join whichever side carried the day. The remaining class, who were really well affected towards the British Government, were so weak in number that they might be easily overpowered when the crisis came.

This view of things will account for much of the otherwise incomprehensible conduct of different regiments, and many of the phenomena of the mutiny which at first might appear so extraordinary as to be utterly inexplicable by any of the principles or instincts which usually influence human nature. I believe, that if we had had a small party—say, a company only—of Europeans at Nusseerabad we should have prevented the outbreak altogether; at least, we should have prevented its success. If we had been able to recapture the guns, we should have been joined by the cavalry, who would then probably have really exerted themselves, and a large body from both infantry regiments, especially the 30th—for the well-disposed would have thrown all the weight of their influence into the scale with us. At Nusseerabad, however we were utterly helpless; and considering all things, it is not much to be wondered at that, when the mutiny broke out, the bulk of the men thought everything was gone against us, and determined to go themselves too. The handful of daring spirits who first rushed on the guns knew of course that the artillerymen would offer only a nominal opposition; the rest of the men wavered and waited; for three or four hours or more were we on parade doing nothing but looking at one another. The cavalry failed to take the guns; the wives and families of the officers had fled, or were hiding themselves; the men were given large doses of 'bhang,' and became intoxicated and reckless. An attempt was made to secure the colours, and the whole thing was over: they had now but to get rid of their officers and join the King of Delhi.

A good deal was said at the time, and subsequently, about the behaviour of the Bombay Cavalry, and no small amount of ill-will has been engendered by the opinions which have been offered on the subject. I am sorry to say anything that may give offence to any man, especially to any of the gallant and hospitable officers of the 1st Bombay Lancers; but the truth must be spoken, and it is better for all parties that it should be told. Why did not the cavalry take the guns from the mere handful of men who had possession of them? To say they could not is a far worse compliment to the corps than to assert that it was disaffected. That attempts had been made to tamper with them there can be no doubt. I believe half the troopers were Oude men, from the same province, and connected by common interest (and in many cases by actual and close relationship) with the Sepoys of the 15th and 30th Bengal N.I. But there were several things that fortunately prevented their attempts at seducing the cavalry from their allegiance from being successful. The chief was, the system that prevailed in the Bombay army, which undoubtedly was infinitely better adapted for native soldiers than that which prevailed in Bengal, the latter being founded on the principle the adoption of which exhibited the greatest possible ignorance of human nature. I will not enter upon the subject now further than to repeat what has so often been said before, lest any of my readers should happen to be ignorant of it—that in the Bengal army commanding officers were nothing but serjeant-majors, the other European officers were nonentities as far as actual authority went; the adjutant-general commanded the whole army, and the commanding officer could neither reward or punish. In Bombay, on the contrary, commanding officers of corps had all the power which men in their position must be entrusted with if they are to have that influence over their men which is absolutely necessary in dealing with any troops, either native or European. Besides this, it is the custom in the Bombay native regiments for the men to keep their families with them in the lines; this the Bengal Sepoys seldom did; and it is obvious that although such a practice might interfere occasionally with the efficiency of a regiment, rendering it more difficult to march when means of transport have to be procured for the women and children, as well as the men, it renders the chances of a general mutiny much less. The wives and families of the Sepoys then become a kind of hostage for their good behaviour. This motive was not calculated, however, to operate so effectually in keeping the Bombay native army true to its officers as the mixture of races and castes that were to be found always in its ranks.

That the Bombay Lancers, led as they were by as gallant a set of officers as ever drew their swords, could not have captured the guns is scarcely credible. It is evident that the men had not been seduced from their allegiance, because they behaved well afterwards, protected us when we left the station, and not only that, but left their own families in the lines when the whole of the rest of the station was in possession of the mutineers; and indeed remained faithful to the British Government under circumstances subsequently that must have been very trying to the confidence of Asiatics; indeed, their fidelity, never doubted by their own officers—but suspected, as was natural, perhaps, by those who had experienced practically too much of the treachery of Asiatics to trust them under any circumstances while recent events were so fresh in their recollections—underwent the severest ordeal it could well be subjected to. But making all allowance for their position, and for their attachment to their officers and to the Government, I do not think it likely that they were unaware of the intentions of the mutineers, and am inclined to believe that some sort of understanding existed between the two parties, to the effect that, on the one hand, the cavalry would not act against their brethren, if, on the other, the lives and honour of their families were respected. It is hardly possible to believe that otherwise they would have abandoned the station with us that night as they did, leaving their unprotected households to the mercy of the rebels. A party, it is true, remained behind under a native officer, but not strong enough to make any resistance had the mutineers really meant mischief. We certainly owe our lives to the conduct of the 1st Lancers on this occasion; for, had it not been for the protection they afforded us, we should probably have fallen by the hands of the Sepoys, and those who escaped would have shared a similar fate at the first village they reached.

That the cavalry had not fair play must be allowed. Instead of being taken up on the open plain, where they could have formed up leisurely, and out of range of the guns, and then have charged with every advantage that position could afford, they were hurried along over ground where cavalry could scarcely act at all, formed up hastily in a cramped space, though under cover, on ground surrounded by buildings, and then called on to charge a battery, manned, it is true, by a handful of mutineers; but there were enough of them to work the guns, and, for all they knew, supported by the strength of the whole of the two infantry regiments.

As a mere matter of speculation it is useless to repeat it, but as a warning to the Government the words may not be thrown away—One company of European infantry, or half a troop of European dragoons, would have saved Nusseerabad.*

---

* Since the above was written, I have accidentally fallen in with an officer of the Bombay army, Major ——, who gave me information strongly corroborative of the views I have here expressed. Major —— told me that in course of conversation with a jemadar of the 1st Bombay Lancers, the man admitted to him that there was an understanding between the Lancers and the mutineers of the 15th and 30th Native Infantry regiments. It had been previously agreed upon that the Lancers would not act against the mutineers, on the condition that the latter refrained from molesting the families of the Lancers, who would, as they foresaw, be left in a measure unprotected in the lines when the desertion of the station by the European officers, &c., took place; an event that was perceived would inevitably take place when the outbreak had commenced. It was also agreed upon that the mutineers were not to touch the quarter-guard of the cavalry, where a considerable amount of cash belonging to the native officers and men of the Lancers was kept.

CHAPTER VII.

OUTBREAK AT NEEMUCH—FLIGHT OF THE EUROPEAN RESIDENTS—PROGRESS OF THE MUTINEERS.

WE had no sooner recovered in a measure from the shock which our own share in the general mutiny had given us, than we began to be very anxious about our neighbours. Neemuch was the nearest station to us where there was any considerable body of Bengal native troops quartered, and we daily, hourly expected to hear that, in the common phraseology of the day, Neemuch 'had gone.' For some time the intelligence we received was cheering: at last we heard of excitement prevailing among the Sepoys there. The report said they had been quieted by the judicious measures adopted by the Brigadier; then ensued an ominous silence; and at last came the rumour of a mutiny, accompanied, as was always the case at first, with dismal stories of an European population massacred.

I am indebted for the following particulars of the Neemuch mutiny to Colonel Abbott, 72nd Native Infantry, who commanded the station. This place is about 120 miles from Nusseerabad and from Mhow; it is a very favourite garrison for troops, having the reputation of being one of the healthiest stations in the Presidency. The cantonment is built on an elevated ridge running north-west and south-east; in length about two miles and a half;

the soil is well adapted for horticulture, and most of the bungalows had gardens attached to them. A kind of fort or fortified square had been erected for the protection of the European inhabitants or garrison if reduced to extremities, and was generally used, I believe, as a magazine. The troops stationed there in May, 1857, were:—

Fourth Troop First Brigade Horse Artillery (Native), left wing 1st Light Cavalry, 72nd Regiment N.I., 7th Regiment Gwalior Contingent. Some excitement on the receipt of the intelligence of the mutiny at Meerut and the seizure of the city of Delhi showed itself, and on the subject of the greased cartridges; but as there existed at Neemuch none of these objectionable articles, the matter was apparently set at rest. It is supposed that the first treasonable designs arose from an assembly of the Mohammedan portion of the force on the occasion of a dinner given in celebration of the Eed by an influential moonshee attached to the Meywar agency, who resided in a bungalow near the cavalry lines. This moonshee had a most extensive correspondence (as was discovered from the numerous letters we recovered after the outbreak), and at this dinner subjects were doubtless discussed in a manner which true loyalty to the State would have forbidden.* One

* It is only fair to this man's character to state that he was subsequently sent to Ajmere, charges of treason having been brought against him, and by order of the Governor-General's agent subjected to trial before a commission consisting of the late Captain Hardcastle and Lieutenants Impey and Walter, the two former adjutants to the agent, the latter adjutant to the Commissioner of Ajmere, by whom he was fully and honourably

responsible person, native doctor Buksh Khan, of the 72nd Regiment N.I., absented himself from the feast, and gave out to his friends that the reason he did so was, that he could not join in the sentiments which were expressed by the host. This moonshee, shortly after his dinner, removed the whole of his family from the station to Jowrah, which did not fail to cause some panic in the Sudder bazaar. The mutinous spirit showed itself first at about 11 A.M., 28th May, 1857, when, on a rumour that the Sudder bazaar was being plundered, the 72nd Regiment and 7th Gwalior Contingent rushed to their arms. Order was restored by the officers, who instantly repaired to the lines, but the excitement was not allayed, and several other panics got up by designing men disquieted the force; and, to put a stop to this, the commanding officer assembled the native officers, of the whole force, and remonstrated with them. They appeared convinced that the conduct of the men was unwarrantable, and took an oath of loyalty to Government and to their officers. However, things did not appear straight, and the commanding officer, accompanied by his staff, visited the lines of the artillery and cavalry on the afternoon of the 2nd June. The news of the Nusseerabad mutiny of the

---

acquitted. The man at the time was, and is now, in receipt of a pension from the British Government, granted by Lord Hardinge for services rendered in the political and intelligence department during the Affghan war; he was very highly spoken of by the officers under whom he was employed, and has testimonials of ability and fidelity. Brigadier-General Lawrence, Governor-General's Agent in Rajpootana, gave him an excellent character; but he has, I believe, never been reinstated in the position he held at Neemuch.

28th May had undoubtedly produced some impression. The men of both arms (with one exception in the cavalry) were most orderly and respectful, and hopes were entertained that the crisis had passed; but as the force could not be *certainly* relied upon, it was deemed necessary for the interest of Government to call upon the Raja of Kotah and the Rana of Oodeypore to march some troops towards Neemuch for the protection of the gaol, &c., in case of an outbreak. These requisitions were promptly attended to by Captain L. Showers, officiating Governor-General's Agent in Marwar, and by the ever-to-be-lamented Major Burton, political agent at Kotah; and it had been agreed to by the active and zealous superintendent of Neemuch, Captain B. P. Lloyd, that in case troops should mutiny, the European community could not do better than fall back on the village of Dharroo, twelve miles south of the station, on the road to Oodeypore, from which direction the Rana's troops were advancing.

On the night of the 3rd June, about half-past 9 P.M., four or five troopers of the cavalry galloped down the front of the 72nd N.I. calling out, 'Get ready'—'Get ready.' The men rushed to the bells of arms, demanding their weapons, which they represented were for self-defence. All the officers of the regiments were in the lines. The native officers came to the commanding officer, and begged him to permit the men to take their arms. The order was given, when all having got their arms, they retired to their huts, and everything was quiet. At about 11 P.M. two guns from the direction of the artillery, fired in quick succession—evidently an appointed signal—

roused all to action. The men of the 72nd Regiment came out of their huts, and were formed into companies in rear of their respective bells of arms, and the cavalry were seen galloping with torches lighted in their hands in the direction of the gaol. They released the prisoners, the officers' houses began to blaze, and the dull sounds of the artillery guns moving were distinctly heard. The tumult increased: the commanding officer of the 72nd Regiment was endeavouring to restore order on the right; the companies of the left wing attempted to join the mutinous artillery by the front, across the parade, but on being ordered back, they returned; afterwards, however, they went off by the rear. Order was now at an end; a company of the 72nd, led by an old mutineer, Subadar Nuthoo Pattuck, joined the artillery; the cavalry galloped about the road firing off their pistols at everything and nothing, and the only thing that remained to be done, was for the European officers and families to abandon the station. As the cavalry had possession of the centre of the cantonment commanding the road leading from the 72nd lines in the direction of Dharroo, their only plan was to try and reach Jacond, which place was distant ten miles, in a northerly direction, and on the route of the advancing troops of the Kotah Raja. The officers were assembled in the regimental quarter-guard, and the artillery becoming aware of this, brought a gun to bear on it. The native officers assured them their lives would be sacrificed if they remained any longer; so, after making an unsuccessful attempt to get the colours, they determined to leave the station. This was about one o'clock in the morning. Of the fate of the civil officers, of the artillery, cavalry, and Gwalior Contingent officers and their families, they were in total ignorance; but there was no time for inquiry, and no means of making any; so, guided by the flames of the burning houses and the pale light of the moon, they set out on their way to Jawud. Leaving the high road, and striking across country, the party wandered all the remainder of the night, and at dawn found themselves still five miles from Jawud, which place, however, they reached at about 7 A.M., and were most kindly and hospitably received by Mr. Charles Burton, Assistant-Superintendent of Neemuch, who, with his inestimable mother, Mrs. Burton, and her daughter, afforded the ladies of the party every comfort in their power. They proved themselves the kindest friends in need and deed. Major Burton, who had left the Kotah troops at Deekeen, arrived at 11 A.M., and by his cool demeanour restored some spirit into the minds of all. However, their perils were not over, for about 1 P.M. a man rushed in with a letter in the Mahratta character, purporting to be written from a man in the Neemuch brigade, which stated that a force of all arms was about to start for Jawud. After some consultation it was deemed right to fall further back to the camp of the Kotah troops at Deekeen, distant twenty-five miles, and the harassed party, at 2.30 P.M., in the hot sun of June, without shelter, had again to move. They reached their destination at about 9 P.M., and most of the party passed a dismal night. It was intended to have marched the next morning, 5th June, to Jawud; but as the Kotah troops, which consisted chiefly of vagabonds dismissed for their crimes from the

Company's army, showed a decided disinclination to move in the direction of the mutineers, a halt was the only alternative. During the day, Mr. Charles Burton, who had been forced to leave Jawud (where he had with the greatest self-devotion remained at his post on the departure of the Neemuch party), owing to an *émeute* among the police, came in. On the morning of the 6th the camp moved to Moorwun twelve miles, and on the 7th to Jawud.

I must pause here to describe the adventures of the officers of the 7th Regiment Gwalior Contingent, which I have been enabled to do by the kindness of Captain Macdonald, commanding the regiment, who has placed his journal at my disposal. For some time previous to the outbreak, this officer had remained in the fortified square with the right wing of his regiment, for the purpose of watching the behaviour of the men, and feeling naturally anxious, in the state in which affairs then were, regarding the treasure, &c., entrusted to the safe keeping of the corps.

When the eventful night of the 3rd June arrived, he had about 200 men accoutred, with their muskets loaded, upon the walls, and intended to pass the night himself on one of the bastions, so as to be on the spot in case of need. A little before midnight some of the men awoke him, and told him that a couple of signal guns had been fired by the artillery. Being ready, dressed he was instantly on the walls. Everything seemed perfectly quiet, but the tranquillity was only temporary, for a few minutes afterwards he plainly saw that attempts were being made to set fire to the officers' houses in cantonments; this was quickly effected, those bungalows being the first to burst out into flames at which night guards were posted.

The gate of the fort was that night in charge of the 3rd company of the regiment, under command of a subadar named Hurrie Sing; this man is described as being by no means a leading character in the corps, and on this occasion he kept constantly by Captain Macdonald's side, apparently exerting himself to carry out that officer's orders. It is curious how often it was the case that leading parts were taken in the several regiments by men or native officers of whose character their European superiors had had no great idea. Either talent was latent, and only showed itself when opportunity called it into action, or we were very often lamentably mistaken in the characters of those with whom we had to do. This was especially the case in my own regiment. The first man to snatch the colour out of the hand of the havildar, and carry it in triumph, albeit hastily, over to the rebels, was a subadar who I thought would be the last man in the regiment to take a leading part in anything. I had observed him, when matters were drawing to a crisis, leave the ranks, and repair to his hut in the lines, from which he shortly afterwards emerged in a bran new uniform, coat and trousers, looking more spruce and officer-like than he had ever done before, even on the occasion of the 'annual inspection.' He kept his best clothes ready to inaugurate his entry into the service of the Great Mogul by wearing them. When Delhi was sacked, a number of papers were picked up, and some of these fell into the hands of Captain Shebbeare, for some time attached to the Guides, who showed them to me. They were General

Orders, issued daily by the rebel commander-in-chief, written in Persian characters, and stamped with a seal. They were curious relics. The daily disposition of troops, of regiments, brigades, &c., the relief of guards, picket, and so on, were detailed in them, just as they were, I fancy, in the camp outside the walls by Generals Barnard and Wilson. The 15th and 30th Regiments were constantly mentioned, as also of course many others; but what astonished me was to find the rapid promotion a friend of mine named Bhagerutty Misr had gained. He was a Brigadier-General, with frequently as many as four or five regiments of all arms under his command. He was attached to the light company of the 15th, and held the rank of subadar when the mutiny occurred, but from what I knew of his character I never should have divined that he was destined to fill so high a post as that he had attained in the service of the King of Delhi. In person he was very like a large crow, with sharp features, hooked nose, very thin limbs, and protruding chest. He had, however, a good expression in his face, and a not unpleasant smile. How we were deceived! The man was a Brahmin, and little indeed could we see into his heart. The Colonel placed every confidence in him—at least he thought him more trustworthy than the rest—and the evening before the mutiny was walking up and down his verandah with him talking to him confidentially. He rewarded the Colonel's confidence by annexing his charger, and probably also his uniform, and it is not impossible that he may have owed his subsequent rapid advance to efficiency of equipment, for natives are influenced a good deal by externals.

When there was no longer any room for doubt that the expected crisis had arrived, Captain Macdonald ordered a messenger to be sent to his second in command, Lieutenant Rose, who was in the lines with the left wing of the regiment, directing him to bring his men down to the fortified square. He heard the order repeated by subadar Hurrie Sing from the gate, but nevertheless it struck him while standing on the wall that no messenger left the fort. On inquiry he was assured by the subadar that his order had been attended to. Lieutenant Rose, however, subsequently informed him that no message had been received.

It had been previously arranged that, in the event of any crisis like that at hand occurring, Lieutenant Rose was to parade the left wing with a view of joining Captain Macdonald: he accordingly did so, and while getting the men under arms was deliberately fired at by a Sepoy of the 4th company, fortunately without effect.

When affairs were in this state Captain Macdonald heard his second in command calling out to him from some little distance on the left flank of the fortified square. He said the men would not come with him, and begged Captain Macdonald to go in and see if his influence could be of any avail. On receiving this officer's orders the wing, after a little hesitation, marched down and entered the fort. An additional company was now told off to each face of the square, the gate was shut, and the drawbridge raised.

Being under the impression that the gate would be the first part attacked, Captain Macdonald directed Ensign Davenport, 21st Bombay N. I., who was doing duty with the 7th Regiment Gwalior Contingent, to join the party at the gate: at the same time another strong party on the walls was told off to support the defence of the gate, if needed. Captain Macdonald then went round and visited all the posts, endeavouring to induce the men to remain faithful, and promising a pecuniary reward to them if the treasure, &c., was preserved. He was met everywhere by assurances of loyalty and good behaviour, the only doubt expressed of their making an effectual defence being in the event of guns being brought to bear upon the place. He then pointed out to them that nothing but heavy ordnance could be of the slightest avail against the fortifications, and this the mutineers were totally unprovided with, the guns of the troops being nothing more than six-pounders. The mortar would be useless in the hands of any but an experienced European officer. The colours of the regiment were unfurled and placed on the bastion, and the men called on to protect them from dishonour. Nothing was left undone that could add to the security of the place, or induce the men to act properly, and every confidence was felt that their efforts would be attended with success.

Time wore on; at half-past two, men were observed leaving the walls in small parties and in silence. On inquiring the cause, Captain Macdonald was told by subadar Hurrie Sing that they were going for their bedding; he ordered them back, and they returned, but about half-an-hour afterwards a similar and more combined movement was made, and at the same moment Lieutenant and Adjutant Gordon and Ensign Davenport came up and told their commandant that the gate had been thrown open by the subadar's orders, and that they had been forced to quit the post at the point of the bayonet. Nothing but consideration for the lives of the small body of Europeans now entirely at the mercy of the mutineers prevented these officers from using their fire-arms. Captain Macdonald hastened to the gate; it was indeed wide open. For a short time he succeeded in keeping the men in, but the check was only temporary, and they went out in a body.

The officers followed, leaving the now almost empty fort, and on coming up to the regiment seized the colours, Captain Macdonald snatching one from the hands of the havildar who carried it, and the Adjutant the other. They then endeavoured to recall the men, and induce them to rally round the colours, but at that moment two guns were fired by the artillery—no doubt intended for a signal—and cavalry were heard advancing. Nothing could be done, the men would listen to no orders, no entreaties; to have remained longer with them would have been uselessly risking life, so the European officers allowed the regiment to leave them. As they turned to depart, they were accompanied for some distance by about twelve men, who threw their arms round their necks, and made every demonstration of strong feeling. They, however, dropped off one by one like inconstant lovers, and eventually four men alone were left, who accompanied their officers about three miles, when two of them disappeared. The remaining two stayed with the officers till the 5th, and went as far as six-and-thirty miles with them; they were hungry and footsore, but they left to rejoin their comrades. It was subsequently discovered that immediately on rejoining the main body of the mutineers they were seized, accused of having aided the escape of the European officers, and cruelly put to death.

Foremost among the mutineers was jemadar Lalla Tewang, a man who had been transferred from the 2nd Regiment (Grenadier) Bengal N. I. He was on duty over the treasure, and was observed after the mutiny had openly broken out to place guards over the tumbrils, and was heard calling out to his men to allow no one (especially referring to Captain Macdonald) to approach them. This native officer subsequently took possession of all Captain Macdonald's private property, donned that officer's epaulettes, mounted his charger and rode off, carrying with him a quantity of plunder on horseback. Ten days previously he had received his commission from the hands of the officer he thus plundered, and some time before had been indebted to him for exposing a conspiracy that had been formed against him in the regiment, and saving him from dismissal from the service. Another act of Pandy gratitude.

The mutiny of the 7th Regiment Gwalior Contingent thus described, was remarkable for the following features :—

No great excitement was to be observed among the men, nor was a word of disrespect uttered by them. The mutiny proceeded step by step as if everything had been arranged beforehand. The outbreak commenced in the cantonments before midnight, and though all the Europeans—except the few who remained, as detailed above, to the very last—had left the fort by one o'clock, the hours were struck regularly up to three. At that time the place was in the hands of the mutineers, and signal fires were lighted in the four bastions. In every case the men upon whom the officers placed the most confidence were those who were considered the least trustworthy. As in our case at Nusseerabad, the regiment made a clean sweep of their lines, taking every one belonging to the corps with them; even old widow pensioners, and men who had passed the committee, and were on the point of being invalided, and all the sick; many of the latter died shortly after. Within eleven hours of the mutiny, the whole force had left the station, carrying away with them their families, spare clothing, camp equipage, all the ammunition they could find of both service and practice, as well as the spare arms and accoutrements of men absent on furlough; so it is difficult to believe but that arrangements must have been made previously for transporting so large a quantity of baggage, for we may be sure each man had amassed a tolerable amount of plunder. At Nusseerabad the same thing occurred to a great extent, except that vast quantities of clothing and several tents were left behind. The camels attached to the commissariat department, and kept available for service (as the Nusseerabad brigade was a field force, and always had its marching establishment ready), were driven off loose into the jungle by the man in charge directly it became known that the Sepoys had broken out, so that they were hard pushed for transport, and were forced to put loads upon the officers' chargers and ponies, and fill the buggies and carriages with their ill-gotten property.

Before concluding this chapter I would draw attention to the gallantry displayed by Captain Macdonald and the brave band of officers who stood firmly by him during the crisis. Their names deserve to be recorded, more especially as no recognition of their services has ever been made by Government. Besides Captain Macdonald and the officers of his regiment, Lieutenant Rose, who was killed at Gwalior, and Lieutenant Gordon, there were present Ensign Davenport, Drs. Murray and Gane, Sergeant-Major Nesbitt (since dead), and Quartermaster-Sergeant Lane.

CHAPTER VIII.

NEEMUCH MUTINY CONTINUED — PROCEEDINGS OF THE OFFICERS.

THE following extract of an official report of the Neemuch outbreak may throw further light on the subject:—

'*From* CAPTAIN B. P. LLOYD, *Superintendent of Neemuch, to* COLONEL G. ST. P. LAWRENCE, *Commissioner at Neemuch, and Agent for the Governor-General in the Rajpootana States.*

'SIR,—I have the honour to submit a report upon the events preceding and subsequent to the late mutiny of the troops stationed at Neemuch, as per margin,* which has already been demi-officially notified to you.

'My daily demi-official communication will have acquainted you with the state of feeling which pervaded the troops after the occurrences at Meerut and Delhi became known, but, until the outbreak of the troops stationed at Nusseerabad, the best hopes were entertained that those here would be restrained from following in the tide of rebellion.

'Every effort was made to preserve the confidence of the men, and to make that of the officers in them

* 4th Troop 1st Brigade H.A., (Native); Two troops 1st Light Cavalry (Native); 72nd Regiment N.I.; 7th Regiment Gwalior Contingent.

apparent. Colonel Abbott slept every night in a tent in the lines of his regiment without a guard or sentry, and latterly all officers did the same, even with their families. One wing of the 7th Regiment Gwalior Contingent held the fortified square and treasury, and the other wing was encamped close to, but outside the walls. Captain Macdonald, commanding the corps, resided entirely in the fort, for the purpose of better observing and controlling his regiment. Although it is not for me to comment on the actions of commanding officers, I cannot refrain from expressing my admiration of the firm and conciliating conduct of all officers in command of corps and detachments throughout the trying period, and especially of the tact and calm judgment exercised by Colonel P. Abbott, 72nd Regiment N.I., commanding the station, by whose management the outbreak was without doubt delayed many days.

'On the morning of the 2nd, Colonel Abbott informed me, in his own regimental lines, that, from the occurrences of the previous night, and from information he had received, he was of opinion that the outbreak could not be delayed more than a few hours. I left him to secure a few of my most valuable records, and endeavour to secure a line of retreat for fugitives by the Oodeypore road, by means of a detachment of police sowars. Meanwhile Colonel Abbott undertook to assemble all the native officers of the force, and endeavour to bring them to a sense of their duty, and to remove the distrust in each other which there was reason to believe was one cause of the prevailing excitement. After some discussion all took oaths, on the Koran and Ganges water, that they now trusted each other, and would remain true to their salt. The commanding officer was requested to swear* to his confidence in their faithful intentions, and did so, when the meeting broke up, all apparently being satisfied and loyally inclined. All continued quiet up to the evening of the 3rd, when some excitement again appeared, arising it was said from a rumour of the approach of troops to the station.

'It is necessary to mention here that for many preceding days the utmost panic had prevailed in the Sudder bazaar, and great numbers of persons had removed with their property. The wildest reports were constantly set afloat by designing persons to increase

---

* That this proceeding of Colonel Abbott's must have had great weight is evident from the fact that it was told me by a native at Nusseerabad, who had heard the story in the bazaar some considerable time before the news of the outbreak reached us. The report further said the minds of the Sepoys were entirely calmed down, and their confidence fully restored, as Colonel Abbott Sahib had sworn to them on the Bible that the rumours in circulation about a strong European force being at hand to coerce them, and force them to lose caste by using the cartridges, were all a fabrication. Subsequently I heard from the same source that the confidence of the men remained unshaken till the evening of that same day, the 3rd (the mutiny took place in the night), when a peon or chuprassee attached to the Sudder bazaar, appeared in the bazaar with a forged document, bearing the signature of the political officer, directing supplies to be got ready next morning for the European troops who were expected to arrive at Neemuch. This he showed to every one, and the people were convinced by it that a European force was at hand, and that they had been deceived. A few hours afterwards the outbreak occurred. The active agents in this business were clever men, and understood their work well.

J. T. P.

the distrust, and the commonest occurrences were distorted into phantoms of evil intended against the troops.

'The move of the Kotah force under Major Burton for the protection of Jawud had been determined upon in consultation with Colonel Abbott, commanding the station. The troops at Neemuch had been told of the intended move some days before, and, assured that no part of the force was intended to approach Neemuch, the Kotah troops were ordered to Jawud with a view to preserving the peace of the district, and protecting the town from marauders. I believe there is no reason whatever to suppose that this movement precipitated the crisis, while subsequent events have proved it to have been a most fortunate and happy one for the interests of Government.

'On the night of the 3rd symptoms of violence were shown by the artillery, and Lieutenant Walker could only restrain them for about two hours, when some of them rushed to the guns, and, loading them, fired two off, evidently as a preconcerted signal. Upon this the cavalry rushed to join them, and shortly afterwards the 7th N.I. broke from their lines also. The wing of the 72nd Regiment Gwalior Contingent, encamped outside the fort, had been marched in by Captain Macdonald on the report of the signal guns, and every preparation for defence made, but, after holding firm for some time, the gates were ordered by a subadar, Hurrie Sing, to be opened, and the officers were told to save themselves, and eventually escorted to a place of comparative safety. Captain Macdonald and his officers remained in the fort till the very last, and only left it on the gates being forcibly opened, and their lives in the greatest danger, with no hope of being of the least use.

'I was roused on the report of the two signal guns, and quickly on horseback. I proceeded to arouse my assistant, Lieutenant Ritchie, and Assistant-Surgeon Cotes, who resided in the next bungalow. While there, Lieutenant Barnes, Artillery, galloped up, begging us to aid in bringing away Mrs. Walker and child, whose carriage had been fired at four or five times by mounted troopers. We immediately hastened to assist, and succeeded in getting out of the station on the Oodeypore road. By this time fires were appearing in every direction. Having seen the party safe to the village of Daroo, Lieutenant Ritchie and I returned towards cantonments in hopes of assisting fugitives. We met the officers of the 1st Cavalry, but no others, and, after hovering about the burning station till daylight, we returned to Daroo.

'It had been the intention of Captain Showers, officiating political agent of Meywar, to return to Neemuch on the morning of the 4th. His dâk was laid and a tent was pitched for him at Baru, twelve miles from cantonments. Thither, therefore, I determined to proceed, in hopes of concerting measures with him for following the mutineers and preserving the peace of the country. He, however, did not come (having, as it subsequently appeared, altered his plans), and about noon I received a note from the Thakoor of Daroo warning me that a party of the 1st Light Cavalry were searching the country for me.

'The party assembled at Baru consisted of Lieutenant and Mrs. Walker, Lieutenant Barnes, sergeant

Supple, Artillery; Captain Macdonald, Lieutenant Gordon, Lieutenant Rose, 7th Regiment Gwalior Contingent; Lieutenant Davenport, attached to do.; Captain Sir J. Hill, Lieutenant Ellice, Lieutenant Stapleton, 1st Light Cavalry; Captain Lloyd, Superintendent; Lieutenant Ritchie, Assistant-Superintendent.

'I therefore determined on moving to Chota Sadree, a walled town of Meywar, which would afford protection, and, at the same time, be nearer to Neemuch. The whole party arrived there late in the afternoon much exhausted with the heat, but refreshments were obtained from some of the residents of cantonments who had removed there a few days before the outbreak. Dr. Cotes, Civil Assistant-Surgeon, had also arrived at Sadree direct, early in the day.

'The Hakim (Governor) was alarmed at so many Europeans entering his town, and earnestly recommended that an adjournment to Burra Sadree, ten miles further on the Oodeypore road, should be made, and this plan was adopted by all the party except Lieut. Ritchie and myself, who remained to watch events at Neemuch.

'I found to my great disappointment that the force of Meywar troops which I had been led to expect was collected at Chota Sadree, had not arrived, and it was not till the morning of the 6th that I could get an escort to enable me to move towards Neemuch. My police sowars had been stationed at various points on the road the night of the mutiny, to assist fugitives, and had not rejoined me. Early on the morning of the 6th, with seventeen Sadree sowars, and accompanied by Lieutenant Ritchie, Adjutant Superintendent, and Lieutenant Stapleton, 1st Light Cavalry,

I started for cantonments, which I had learned the evening before had been evacuated by the mutineers, and soon had the melancholy satisfaction of re-occupying the deserted and ruined station.

'On the 7th the Kotah troops under Major Burton reached Jawud, and greatly restored confidence. A detachment of 100 Boondee horse came into Neemuch on the evening of the same day, and, at my urgent request, Major Burton, with the rest of the troops, marched into Neemuch on the night of the 8th, leaving 100 foot and ten horsemen for the protection of Jawud.

'Colonel Abbott and officers and ladies occupy the fortified square, which has been put into the best state of defence possible, by mounting the Kotah guns, two brass 3-pounders, on the bastions, planting an 8-inch mortar in the centre, and a 24-pounder gun, which is too heavy for use on the ramparts, has been placed so as to bear on the gateway. The drawbridge is in working order, with ropes attached, ready for instant use.

'The station of Neemuch is almost all destroyed. Some twelve or fourteen houses escaped fire, but all have been plundered, and the wanton destruction of property is almost incredible. The Sudder bazaar has been plundered, and a great part of it burnt. The gaol prisoners were released by the mutineers, but some have been already recaptured.* I have already reported the plunder of the treasury. The

* There were several instances during the mutiny of prisoners that had been released from gaol by the mutineers returning and giving themselves up.

amount carried off was 126,900 rupees, besides the contents of the military chest, amounting to about 50,000 rupees, I understand.

'I have the honour to be, Sir,
'Your most obedient servant,
(Signed) B. P. LLOYD,
Superintendent, Neemuch.

'*Dated, Neemuch, June* 16, 1857.'

Let us return to Colonel Abbott's journal.

When the fugitives reached the once pretty station of Neemuch, how sad was the spectacle that met their eyes. For three miles before they reached the cantonment, the road was white with fragments of papers and letters that were clinging to the roots of bushes, where they had been blown by the high wind. It was found that the mutineers of all arms had assembled on the parade ground on the morning of the 4th of June, in front of the fortified square, after plundering the bazaar and treasury; they then went to the parade ground of the 72nd N.I., where two months' pay was issued, and subadar Gurres Ram nominated to the command of the regiment, subadar Suderree Sing, 1st Light Cavalry, having been appointed Brigadier, and jemadar Dost Mohammed, Major of Brigade. Small parties were then detached in all directions to collect carriages. About 1 p.m. a panic arose in consequence of a report that European troops were marching on the station; they all packed up their plunder hastily (vast quantities being abandoned, owing to want of transport), and marched out of the place with the band playing. The first halt they made was at Nimbhera, a town belonging to the Nawab of Tonk, sixteen miles from Neemuch on the road to Delhi. Here they were entertained by the native authorities of the town. The next morning they continued their march, after shooting some troopers of the 1st Light Cavalry, and some Sepoys of the 7th Regiment Gwalior Contingent, who had rejoined the column after seeing their officers to a place of safety.

It was found that all the officers, civil, artillery, cavalry, and infantry, with their families, had reached Daroo in safety, and that the wife and children of a non-commissioned officer had been brutally murdered by either the cavalry or the blackguards of the Sudder bazaar. On the 9th the cavalry of the Mehidpore Contingent, which had been sent by the officiating agent for the Governor-General from Central India to the assistance of the Neemuch party, mutinied fourteen miles from Neemuch, after murdering the two officers attached to the corps, Lieutenants Hunt and Brodie, whose mangled bodies were found in the road, and interred by the native civil authorities. Fears being entertained that the rebels would advance upon Neemuch, the utmost exertions were made to provision the fortified square, which was effected by the zealous and unremitting exertions of the Bazaar Master, Lieutenant Williams, 21st Bombay N.I., who, with Captain Laurie of the same regiment, the station staff-officer, deserve all praise. The measures taken for the defence of the fort have already been detailed in Captain Lloyd's letter. The rebels, however, deterred either by their fears or the masterly arrangements of Major Burton and Captain Lloyd, returned to Mehidpore, marching upwards of eighty miles in two days, where they attempted to seduce from their allegiance the artillery and infantry of the

Mehidpore Contingent, but without success; they then left, marching through the country levying contributions from the defenceless villagers, and eventually joined the Neemuch brigade somewhere beyond Deolee, by which they were at first rather coldly received, as they brought no treasure.

The brigade of rebels thus augmented, gave us considerable uneasiness at Nusseerabad, for with our very weak force we had three different places to protect, Nusseerabad, Ajmere, and Beeawr. Most of the ladies were at the latter place, a few at Ajmere, and none at Nusseerabad. Had they attacked us, it would have been necessary to leave the cantonment and fall back on Ajmere; for with the small available and trustworthy force at his command, Brigadier-General Lawrence, who had by that time assumed control of all matters, military as well as civil, would have been hardly justified in going into action. The movements of the mutineers, too, seemed uncertain; they hovered about the neighbourhood, taking first one road, then another, then returning, marching and countermarching, so that we could not tell what their plans were. They carried on their movements, too, with the utmost precision, and showed that they had not forgotten the lessons that had been taught them in the service of the Government. They made a great point of gaining accurate intelligence, and had scouts mounted on fleet riding camels scouring the country and always accompanying the brigade at some little distance on each flank. Their camp regulations were conducted in the most approved military style, and they made a point of always halting on Sunday!

At last they made up their minds, after sacking

Deolee, to proceed to Agra and Delhi; the former place they reached on the 5th July, and were attacked by a force under Brigadier Polwhell, with what result is well known: from thence they marched *via* Muttra to Delhi, where they were merged with the great rebel army collected round the throne of the last of the Moguls. The designation of the Neemuch brigade was, however, retained till the memorable action of Nyjufghur was fought in August, when the column under Nicholson totally defeated the enemy, and the Neemuch brigade as a separate force was never heard of afterwards. On the capture of the city, the remnant fled with the rest of the rebels to Lucknow, and after that place, too, had fallen, they went into Rohilcund and joined Khan Bahadar Khan, since which all trace of them has been lost.

Meantime what befel the officers and ladies? Their adventures may as well be recounted here (though in doing so I am somewhat anticipating my narrative in point of time), as they joined the Nusseerabad party, and shared in their troubles and wanderings. The fates led me in another direction altogether, and before continuing my own narrative, it will be better to detail in a few words the proceedings of our friends at Nusseerabad, to which I shall not again have occasion to do more than allude.

On the 6th July, the officers of the mutinied infantry corps at Neemuch were ordered to proceed with their families to Nusseerabad, and even promised an escort of 50 cavalry and 100 infantry of the Rana of Oodeypore's troops. When the time for starting came, however, the number dwindled down to 10 cavalry and 25 infantry, which must have been rather a matter of congratulation than otherwise, I should think, as in those days one's chances of security were in inverse ratio to the strength of the native escorts furnished. After a most toilsome and distressing march, exposed to the full force of the rains in the height of the wet season, and furnished with tents inferior to those the Government deems necessary for its Sepoys, the party reached Nusseerabad on the 17th July. Every kindness was here shown them, and they were enabled to put up in some of the bungalows that had escaped destruction; but lest they should be disposed to make themselves too comfortable, they were warned that their stay would probably be short, as the Lieutenant-Governor of the North-west Provinces had sent an order for all the officers of mutinied corps in Rajpootana to proceed as soon as possible to Agra; the Neemuch party were to join the officers of our brigade. They were all kept on the *qui vive* by being told they would certainly start in a day or two, and consequently were prevented from taking any steps in making any arrangements to supply themselves with wearing apparel and other necessaries beyond what was absolutely required for actual use, of which the mutiny had deprived them. So they stayed till the 28th of August in the most uncomfortable and unsettled state that can be imagined. Nusseerabad is not a lively place at any time, but what must it have been then? Four-fifths of its houses were in ruins, and the other fifth tenanted mostly by officers whose men had just mutinied, destroying all they ever had in the world, and who were living really in the greatest destitution and want, with nothing to do but to talk over and over again of what had passed, and speculate on the uncertain future, while they suffered from a ceaseless longing to do something in the way of revenging themselves on the ruthless enemy. They had no means of amusement and no employment; no books; were forced to live without any of the appliances for comfort they had always been accustomed to, and which are in the hot weather in India not luxuries but necessaries; crammed several families in one house, with few or no servants and little or no money; and the only occurrence in the way of change, an occasional panic excited by the report that the Bombay regiments had broken out. Compared to many other places in India at that time, of course, Nusseerabad was a happy abode, but I think even the fort at Agra, full as it was, must have been a pleasanter place of residence, for it was nearer the seat of active operations, and if there was but little to do, there must have been a good deal to see and hear.

They might have started many times between the 17th July and the end of August with comparative safety, but it was not till the 28th of that month, when Brigadier M—— had just heard of the mutiny of the Jodhpore legion, that the peremptory order for a move was given. The whole country was under water, and they had a long detour to make before they could reach the first encamping ground. They did reach it at last, but only to receive an order to return immediately, because the few camels they had with them to carry the miserable remnant of their worldly goods and chattels and tents were wanted; so back they went. The camels were required for a force that was about to start in pursuit of the mutineers of the Jodhpore legion, of whom more anon; but the officers and ladies were told that they would have to start again immediately, for camels would be procured in a short time; so they waited in suspense till the 7th September, when they were again ordered off. This time, to add to their difficulties, resulting from the state of the country and roads, the rebels were in dangerous proximity to their route; the Gwalior Contingent were supposed to be either on their way, or thinking of going to Agra, and the Jodhpore legion were infesting the neighbourhood of Nusseerabad. However, no account was taken of these trifles, and the harassed party, ladies, children, and all, were once more sent forth upon what might be called without any metaphor 'a waste of waters.' This time they got three marches from Nusseerabad when they were ordered to halt, pending further instructions. These further instructions turned out to be an order to return; and back they went again, reaching the station on the 14th September. As on former occasions, they were warned that as their stay would be short, there was no need for them to take any measures for increasing the comforts, or lessening the discomforts of their position. The camels were again taken from them; this time they had paid for them in advance, having been forced to do so by the authorities; the money was returned to them, the hire of the cattle for the days they had been employed in marching and halting having been first carefully deducted.

Their patience being now pretty well exhausted, Colonel Shuldham, the senior officer with the party, applied to Captain Eden, political agent at Jeypore, for assistance; that officer at once responded to the call, and made every exertion to carry out the necessary arrangements; he procured camels and a trustworthy escort under a Thakoor, Poorum Sing; but all was not ready till the 11th November, when they made a final start, and after a long march, relieved by the kind attentions of Captain Eden and Captain Nixon, political agent at Bhurtpore, and by the unremitting exertions of Poorum Sing to get everything done that could conduce to their comfort and safety *en route*, they reached Agra on the 3rd December without mishap.

CHAPTER IX.

ORDER TO MARCH—DIFFICULTY ABOUT THE LADIES—INVITATION BY THE RAJA OF JODHPORE—SACK OF DEOLEE—START FOR JODHPORE—ILL SUCCESS.

THE march to Agra and a prospect of employment there or in the field would have been a pleasant change after the idle life we were forced to lead at Nusseerabad, had it not been that those who had families were fairly at their wits' end to know how to dispose of them. Ladies were not allowed to reside in the cantonment for some time after the mutiny; a good many were still at Beeawr, a few at Ajmere, and one or two adventurous spirits dared the Brigadier's wrath, and actually ventured on coming, contrary to orders, into the station and joining their husbands. When the order reached us for marching to Agra, and before we knew that our departure would be postponed, I went with another married officer on a kind of deputation to the Brigadier to seek a solution of the all-important question, 'What to do with our wives?' It was exceedingly undesirable that they should remain at Beeawr or Ajmere; at the latter place there was certainly an old fort, but little or no accommodation, and what room there was was very much required for European soldiers who formed part of the garrison. Beeawr was totally defenceless; we might have been excused just then for not having over much confidence in native troops of any class or kind, and we well knew that attempts had been and were being made to induce the local battalion to follow the example set them by their brethren of Bengal. What security was there that they would not break out as the latter had done, or that the little station might not be attacked by some of the numerous bands of mutineers that were occasionally passing upwards from the south on their road to Delhi, the great focus of the insurrection? Our troubles and anxieties were increased a thousandfold by the utter want of confidence in our own Government, whose proceedings had been from the commencement of such a nature as to destroy altogether any feeling of reliance upon its wisdom, or firmness, or prudence, we may have ever felt. Station after station had been allowed to drift into mutiny; proclamation after proclamation had been issued, not unfrequently of a contradictory tenor, when strong measures only were required to save India. The press had been gagged, and Lord Canning had given out that he had no confidence in the nationality of the small band of Englishmen then struggling to maintain the empire, and to save their lives, and alienated from him the whole European population. The natives openly insulted us, and firmly believed that our empire was gone, never to return: and no wonder. This utter want of confidence in our leaders, which was the natural result of their proved incapacity to meet the emergency, was perhaps the most painful, as it was the most disastrous, part of our position. There were one or two men here and there upon whom we felt we could rely, but they were few and far apart. Communication was difficult, nay, impossible. Henry Lawrence was one of these, and he was shut up in Lucknow, nor did we hear of his death till long after; his brother at Lahore was another, but Lahore was far distant; Edwardes and Cotton at Peshawur were others, but from such a remote corner of the empire news reached us rarely. Wheeler at Cawnpore we believed would do all man could to justify the high character for soldiership he had ever borne; and Colonel George Lawrence, who was invested by Mr. Colvin with the rank and authority of Brigadier-General, and directed to assume supreme military power, in Rajpootana, though not equal to his brothers, perhaps, in strategic or administrative talent, was the mainstay of British power in that province. He had never held high military command before, but I am sure that his advent to Nusseerabad, and his assuming supreme military power in the district, was hailed by all as a good omen, and we felt that whatever might happen under his leadership, we should do all that Englishmen could do to hold their own. He was a Lawrence, and there was something in the name; he had great experience, and had been well tutored in the school of political adversity, having been twice a prisoner in the hands of an Asiatic enemy; once in Affghanistan, and once in the second Sikh war. He understood natives, and understood what too many of our public men have forgotten, how to make himself feared and respected by them; above all, he had, as every one knew, indomitable pluck. Great fault was found with him for not being at the scene of danger earlier. When the Nusseerabad outbreak occurred, he was at Mount Aboo, but until any overt act of mutiny had been committed, he thought perhaps he was of more use in his proper place, the usual residence of the agents of the Governor-General for the States of Rajpootana, surrounded by the Vakeels from all the independent States, through whom he could hold communication with the chiefs. The Vakeels might certainly have accompanied him to the plains, and I cannot but believe that much mischief would have been prevented had he been earlier on the spot. But when officers assured their commandants, and commandants assured the Brigadier, that there was no chance of the Sepoys breaking out, we can hardly wonder that a man in Lawrence's position was deceived too. When the mutinous troops threw off the mask, and the die was cast, he hurried to the post of danger, and kept the helm till the vessel had weathered the storm. That he has hitherto met with no acknowledgment of his services from the Government is perhaps rather a proof of his capacity than the contrary.

When we asked the Brigadier if, in the event of our going to Agra, he would allow our wives to live at Nusseerabad under protection of the garrison there, he said, Not on any account; we then asked if they would be allowed to accompany us to Agra; he replied, Certainly not; could they retire towards Deesa and Bombay? that course was, he thought, out of the question; it was undesirable they should remain where they were. We couldn't fix it any way, as the American would say, and returned to our brother officers to relate the result of our conference with the supreme military authority of the place, for Lawrence was then at Beeawr, with certainly no fresh ideas on the subject. The knotty point was referred to the Brigadier-General, who got over the difficulty by recommending every one to remain in statu quo, at any rate, for the present. But I was anxious that my wife should leave Beeawr on the first opportunity, and accordingly, when an invitation came from the King of Jodhpore, through the political agent, Captain Monck Mason, as it did shortly after, for all the ladies who were unprotected and wanted an asylum for the present, to repair to his capital, where he would take measures to protect them till the return of the cold season should enable them to proceed to Bombay, I thought it best that my wife should join the rest in accepting it.

There were a great many pros and cons to be considered. Every day brought different reports and fresh accounts, calculated to make changes in our plans. The journey to Jodhpore was a difficult and troublesome one; the ladies were unprovided with the commonest necessaries of life, almost without any servants, and I was unwilling to trust my wife, in a delicate state of health, amongst strangers, and at a time when she most needed the protection that I alone could give her. By degrees the political horizon in our part of India cleared a little. Agra, the fort and garrison at least, was safe, and, could we reach that place, we should be able to deposit our families at any rate in security under the guns of the fort; but there was a long, difficult, and dangerous journey to make before we could reach Agra; the weather was most unseasonable for marching; we had no tents, scarcely any means of conveyance, and no money to get them with. It was like the American roads, whichever one you took, you regretted that you had not taken the other. At last the party at Beeawr broke up; it was determined to remove all the ladies;

part returned to Nusseerabad, the rest, among whom was my wife, set out on their journey to Jodhpore.

This place is the capital of the independent territory of Marwar—a territory stretching from the borders of the desert that separates Sind from Rajpootana to Ajmere, from Guzerat on the south to the sterile districts of Jaysulmeer and Bickaneer on the north and north-west. It is 330 miles in length from the south-west to north-east, and 160 in breadth, comprising an area of 35,672 square miles. It is a wild country, mostly desert; here and there are towns and villages, and a little cultivation, but camel breeding is the great resource of the inhabitants, and these animals find abundant pasturage in the desert plains. The king resides at Jodhpore itself, which is a large city, containing about 70,000 inhabitants. The city is commanded by a strong, and said to be impregnable, fort, built on the top of a hill that overlooks the whole country. Indeed, as you approach the capital, or stand on the summit of the hill on which the fort is built, and look upon the vast expanse of level plain stretching on three sides as far as the eye can reach, it is impossible to help feeling the resemblance of the situation to that of an island in the midst of the ocean. A range of volcanic hills, rocky and barren, rises abruptly from the plains to the height of 300 or 400 feet, on the first of which, facing the east and south, stands the fort. It is a very picturesque object from whichever side it is viewed; and the city is picturesque too at a distance, for the fact of water being tolerably abundant there led probably to the selection of the site, and the consequence is, that there is vegetation in and around the city, while all the country in the neighbourhood is a waste wilderness. On passing through the narrow streets of the town you emerge on the hilly ground beyond; a winding road leads between ruined walls, and temples, and houses, and gardens, mixed together in strange confusion, to the Political Agency, which is a palace formerly used as a country seat by the kings of Jodhpore, but subsequently devoted to the residence of the British political agent. It has a large garden laid out in native fashion, and full of splendid trees, surrounded by a high brick wall with a tower at each angle, while on the other side, and separated from the house by a good-sized garden full of fruit-trees, and well supplied with reservoirs and means for watering the ground, there is an open kind of alcove: a sort of building much used by Asiatics, from the window of which you look down a considerable depth upon a valley covered nearly all the year round with green grass, and interspersed with a few clumps of trees and large boulders that have been carried down from the sides and summits of the surrounding hills. The spot is called the Sur Sagur, and was originally intended for a lake. A stream of water meanders through this valley, and many years ago some chief who had plenty of money to spare, or means at hand for procuring labour, attempted to dam up the stream, so as to force the water to accumulate and form a kind of lake, half natural, half artificial. A natural elevation of the ground in the position on which the Agency now stands was taken advantage of, and the palace was erected on it, and the ground in the vicinity laid out in gardens; a flight of steps was made to lead from the alcove I have mentioned down to the level of the ground below, which was intended to lead to the water; but the water proved refractory, and would not remain. Owing either to want of engineering skill, or some radical error in the choice of the site or construction of the buildings, or some peculiarity in the soil, the plan failed; so the massive brickwork and masonry still remain, and the British Political Agency has not the advantage of a lake in its immediate neighbourhood. This sort of half artificial reservoir or lake is very common in Rajpootana, and it generally succeeds better than the Sur Sagur.

The Agency itself is a large massive building, chiefly of marble; it has three stories; the lowest, or ground story, contains a large room, half divided into two by arches; it opens out on to a flight of steps that lead into the garden. The second story contains much greater accommodation, and consists of six or seven good-sized rooms, and a spacious verandah, an immense height from the ground, from which there is a fine view of the fort and the surrounding country and villages. A long flight of steps from the outside leads on to the top of the house, where an additional room has been built by one of the former political agents, with a thatched roof. From the top of the house the prospect is magnificent.

The ancient feudal system that at one time prevailed all over India still obtains in Marwar, and may perhaps be seen as fully developed here as in any other part of Asia. The King or Raja, Takht Sing, is not a Marwari by birth, but came from

Guzerat, having been confirmed in the sovereignty he now holds by the British Government some years ago, when, the throne becoming vacant, the former Sing not having left a lineal descendant, there were several claimants to it, and the British Government, as paramount lords of Hindostan, had to decide on the merits of the respective aspirants to the regal dignity. Takht Sing was selected by the votes of the Thakoors, or chief men in the state, and he was accordingly installed; but he is far from being a popular sovereign, in spite of his having been elected; and the fact of his not being a Marwari of pure descent has probably more effect in rendering him unpopular than even his private character, which is tainted with the vice so common among Asiatic sovereigns—avarice. But though Takht Sing is not a Marwari, he is connected by relationship with nearly all the more powerful feudal chiefs, or Thakoors, as they are called: the principal of these are the Pokhurun, the Katchawun, and the Awab Thakoor. The king's authority over these independent chiefs is very limited, being much the same as that of the King of Scotland, in the earliest periods of its history, over the Highland chiefs, or of our own kings over the barons: and the consequence is, that a war between the Raja and one or more of his Thakoors was a matter of no unfrequent occurrence. The king maintains a standing army, so to call it, and when it is necessary to carry on military operations against a rebel Thakoor, these valiant forces are marched to the scene of conflict. Perhaps the disaffected chief, surrounded by his tenants and dependents, comes out to engage the soldiers of his liege lord, but more generally he prefers awaiting them in his fort or stronghold. The king's troops surround the place, or encamp outside, if it is too large to surround; and a very harmless kind of siege is carried on, which usually lasts for a month or two. But the worst manned artillery, with the worst ammunition in the world, will in time produce an effect on mud walls; the fortress gets battered, perhaps a breach is made, when, rather from the inconvenience of remaining any longer within his walls, than from any dread of the results of a general assault, the rebel chief offers terms: negotiations then succeed to active operations, and both parties being anxious to come to terms, they agree perhaps to let their *casus belli* be settled by the British political agent at the capital: his advice is asked, and his services, always ready to be exerted in promoting union, called for to arbitrate: and so the rebellious Thakoor returns to his allegiance, and the king's troops strike their camp and march back to the capital: the *entente cordiale* between them and their gallant foes having been pretty well maintained all along. An entire change must have come over the Rajpoots during the last three centuries, and we search in vain for traces of the daring and chivalrous spirit that centuries ago earned them undying fame in their conflict with the Mahometan invaders of Hindostan. The stories, however, of their prowess and extraordinary bravery in war, rest chiefly on the authority of the Persian or Mahometan historians, who would be inclined to exaggerate the courage of the Rajpoots for the sake of adding fresh laurels to the brow of the warrior who overcame foes so worthy of his steel; and in those cases (and they were pretty numerous) in which the Mussulmen were worsted, the disgrace of a defeat would be lessened in proportion to the valour of the enemy.

The Maharaja usually resides during the cold season in his fort above the city; the rest of the year he spends at one or other of the numerous country seats in the neighbourhood. He is very fond of sporting, especially of shooting wild pigs, and fishing. He likes to combine the pleasures of the chase with those of the zenana, so he has a platform built on the outside of one of his country palaces overlooking a part of the jungle, and here he sits ensconced behind the breastwork, in company with his favourite wives, and rifles ready loaded by his side. By and by the pig is seen wending his way through the bushes, in search perhaps of food, when the Raja takes aim, and being a good shot, generally succeeds in killing his pig, to the intense gratification of his fair admirers.

The attitude assumed by the independent powers of Rajpootana during the rebellion was of the most incalculable advantage to the British Government. Had they seized the opportunity to recover a portion of their former influence in Hindostan, and sided with the rebels, their influence, and the weight attached to their name and rank, and hereditary associations, would have been sufficient to turn the scale. Humanly speaking, all the rebels wanted to secure success to their cause was unity of action, and leaders of more influence than the Nana or the Begum, or any of the prominent characters of the war; wants which the independent chiefs of Rajpootana might have supplied; but they were faithful to their allegiance, and though in many cases unable to control their soldiers and subjects, they themselves never swerved from the path of duty. Holkar stood firm in Central India; Scindia lost his throne for a short time only, as the penalty of his attachment to the British Government; while the princes of Rajpootana Proper followed the example set them by the descendants of the founder of the Mahratta Empire and the kingdom of Gwalior. Most of them lent their troops to our Government, but the loan, though well meant, was not of much value; for the men would not act against the mutineers, except in very rare cases, though they were useful as police in keeping open communication, affording escorts, &c. Still there can be no doubt that the whole of the districts under their independent chiefs was very much tainted with the spirit of revolt and hostility against the English Government (for in their case it cannot be called rebellion), and had the siege of Delhi been protracted much longer, it is exceedingly doubtful if this feeling would not have manifested itself in a general rising of the people against their own sovereigns on account of their alliance with our Government. Had the immense and somewhat overgrown fabric of the British Empire fallen over, it would have dragged down with it all the inferior structures of petty dynasties that rested upon it, and involved them in common destruction with itself; and there can be no doubt, on the other hand, that the fact of all these surrounding and inferior buildings resting on their great centre, and contributing to its support while they maintained their own position, added immensely to the stability of the whole edifice of Government in Hindostan. It was for a long time the policy pursued by the British Government towards independent States, to insist on their keeping up a body of troops of all arms equipped and disciplined in the English fashion, and officered by English officers, which was called a contingent; the expense of the establishment being supplied by the State for whose protection the force was raised and maintained. These contingents were mostly recruited from the very same class of men as our own native army, and therefore it is no wonder that they followed suit, and mutinied very much as the regiments of the Bengal army had mutinied, killing the officers in most cases, and committing other outrages. The Gwalior Contingent was pre-eminent in this course of wickedness, and earned, perhaps, a greater name in its death than it had ever rendered itself entitled to in its life. Jodhpore was provided with a legion of this sort, which was quartered not at Jodhpore, as its name would signify, but a place called Erinpoora, seventy-eight miles distant. A company of the legion and a detachment of cavalry were stationed at the capital as a guard or escort for the political agent. When the mutiny at Nusseerabad took place, the legion, or a portion of it supposed faithful, was immediately ordered to march for the scene of disorder. Most providentially, Captain Monck Mason determined to send the detachment at the Agency to head-quarters, in case of its being wanted to aid in restoring peace, or acting against the rebels, determining to trust to the Raja for the means of protection and an escort, and to send every available bayonet and sabre that could be mustered into the field. It was not till afterwards that he learnt how the detachment marched through the streets of Jodhpore calling upon the astonished citizens 'To rise in rebellion against their king, for the British Government was no more.' The Contingent, as we afterwards learnt, was infected with the spirit of mutiny quite as much as any portion of the regular army.

The ladies, three in number, left Beeawr under protection of an escort of the Raja's men, and reached the Agency without accident; the only thing they had to complain of was the heat of the weather, and the badness of the roads, and a tremendous storm which overtook them the second day, and drove them all back to the resting-place they had last left. The rain poured in torrents, as if the windows of heaven had in very deed been opened, the lightning descended in vivid flashes to the earth among the frightened horses, and the thunder pealed over their heads in terrific grandeur, as if its deafening clash was heralding the universal destruction of the elements and all the material world that is generally supposed will usher in the advent of the Great Day. At Jodhpore they were received with the utmost kindness and hospitality; and the Raja sent his fair visitors, according to court etiquette, a dinner consisting of various kinds of curry and sweetmeats, and an allowance of two bottles of ale to each lady—that being, as he supposed, their daily allowance.

There were two other ladies at the Agency who had reached that asylum after difficulties and dangers far greater than those undergone by our party, Mrs. —— and Miss ——, the wife and sister of the officer commanding the Kotah Contingent, a force resembling in construction the Jodhpore legion, and quartered at a little station called Deolee. The Kotah Contingent took the field immediately the disturbances commenced, and after marching and counter-marching a good deal in the vicinity of Nusseerabad—one day being ordered up to Agra, and another being called for at Ajmere—it eventually reached the former place, and there mutinied. The circumstances attending the mutiny belong to the Agra chapter of the rebellion, and will not therefore be here related. The ladies who were left behind at Deolee in the now deserted station with a slender guard of their own men, for a long time remained in fancied security, unconscious of the dangers that were thickening around them. Brigadier-General Lawrence, however, was aware of their critical position, and sent out palanqueens and bearers from Ajmere to bring them away, with a letter urging Mrs. —— to leave the place immediately, and not to delay for the purpose of packing up and sending off her property. The admonition was not before it was wanted, for the Neemuch mutineers, after hovering about the country, threatening first one station and then another, made for Deolee, and had they not carried out the old custom they had been used to, of halting on Sunday, Mrs. —— with her sister and children would have fallen into their hands. As it was, they escaped all dangers, and after suffering the greatest possible inconvenience—if it can be called by no other name—from exposure to the fierce rays of a June sun all day, and great impertinence from natives in the villages through which they passed, arrived safely at Ajmere, and thence went on to Jodhpore. The Neemuch mutineers on reaching

Deolee found the place deserted except by the guard of the Kotah Contingent that had been left behind to protect it; so after gutting the houses and burning down the place, they went on, taking with them the 24-pounder, which was used for firing the twelve o'clock, and morning and evening guns, and having their ranks swelled by the guard of the Kotah Contingent and the budmashes belonging to the place.

The departure of the others for Agra being indefinitely postponed, I obtained leave of absence to visit Jodhpore a short time after the ladies had arrived there: an expedition I was the more anxious to make, my wife having met with a rather severe accident on her arrival, and dislocated her shoulder. We enjoyed to the fullest extent in those days that feeling of independence which results from want of property. I knew a lady, a philosopher in her way, who, on getting out of a railway carrriage at the end of her journey, beheld to her surprise the train proceed, taking with it to its distant destination all her baggage and her servants, who had neglected to get out at the proper place. Ordinary individuals, and particularly of the fair sex, would under these circumstances have fussed and fumed, rushed to the station-master for relief, telegraphed in hot haste to the next station, and then sitting down in the waiting-room, abandoned themselves to despair, or to a flood of tears. Not so my friend, who regarded with a look of exultation the train as it receded in the dim distance rapidly from view, and then gave vent to her feelings of happiness in being rid of the greatest torments of her life—her baggage and her servants. We comforted ourselves something in the same way; the mutineers had relieved us of the cares attendant upon the possession of worldly goods, and after all, there is a source of satisfaction in feeling that you can carry everything you have got in the world in your pocket. Poverty has its advantages, and in setting out on a journey we had no anxiety on the score of carriage. We required no camels, or carts, or beasts of burden to convey our slender stock of worldly possessions, no guard of faithful Pandies to escort it. The whole of my wardrobe could be tied up in a small bundle that one man could easily carry; indeed the greater and most valuable portion of it I could carry without inconvenience in my haversack. A lota (a small brass vessel for containing water, that all natives of the lower classes carry about with them) and a piece of cord long enough to reach to the bottom of a well, so as to enable me to get water on the road during my peregrinations, an umbrella, a pair of pistols, and a sword, completed my travelling apparatus; and mounted on a pony, a sorry beast lent me by a friend (I had sent my own on, so as to be able to ride two stages without stopping), I set out. But the Fates were against me, and at the first resting place I received an unwelcome missive from the Colonel of the regiment recalling me. An intimation had been received that the exodus for Agra was about to be commenced; so back I went. However, the Agra expedition was a will-o'-the-wisp; we did not march, and about a week after, I again set out for Jodhpore, selecting this time the Ajmere route, as before I had taken the Beeawr one. Jodhpore is about equidistant from Ajmere and Beeawr, that is, 120 miles, but the road through the former place is the most frequented.

For a long time after the mutiny, Captain Monck Mason had kept relays of bullocks on the road from Jodhpore to within about twenty miles of Ajmere, in the event of fugitives wanting to travel in that direction; and understanding that this arrangement was still available, it was my object to get from Ajmere to the spot where the bullocks were supposed to be located, and so go on, without having to halt upon the road.

It was a fine sultry afternoon in the beginning of July, that, ensconced in a vehicle called a bayley, drawn by two bullocks, I wended my way through the suburbs of Ajmere. A bayley is about the most uncomfortable kind of conveyance a man can possibly be tortured in. It consists of a small square cart, the seat of which always slants either backwards or forwards, with roof supported on four slender poles; it is impossible to sit upright in it, for there is nothing to lean against; lying down is equally out of the question, for there is no room wherein an ordinary-sized mortal can bestow his legs. Natives who can sit all day in an upright posture with their legs doubled up in some inconceivable way under them, vastly approve of this method of conveyance, and will ride the whole day and night quite contentedly in a position that would subject every Englishman in a quarter of an hour to the most excruciating cramps. There is no protection from the dust, and very little from the sun, and altogether it is about as unadvisable a mode of travelling as one could well meet with. But in the year of grace 1857 we were not particular. A year before, if any one had told me the time would come when I should consider myself most fortunate in possessing a lota and riding in a bayley, I should have either thought my informant mad, or that he was 'chaffing' me.

An escort had been given me of three sowars (horsemen) from the Raj troops, and a more villanous looking set of men it has scarcely ever been my fortune to behold. They were tolerably mounted, at least for Raj sowars, and armed with spears and swords, but no matchlocks—a little matter whereupon I had subsequently cause to congratulate myself. One of these worthies, the head man among them, was a grey-bearded individual, who looked as if he had indeed grown old in iniquity; the other two, judging from their physiognomies, must have been guilty of every crime in the calendar twenty times over. A fourth attendant, a volunteer on foot, armed with a large iron-headed stick or pole, accompanied the cortège. I was perfectly indifferent to the respectability or otherwise of my escort, so to call them, but it was probable they might be useful to me on the road in procuring supplies, should I require any from the villagers, but I cannot say I trusted to them much to befriend me in case of accident, or stand by me in the event of danger. They did not appear inclined to fraternize, but on the contrary seemed rather disposed to be sulky and insolent, so I left them to themselves, and was jolted along the uneven road at the rate of about two miles an hour, in silence as far as I was concerned.

The high road from Ajmere to Jodhpore one would suppose would have been pretty well known, but, strange to say, my Jehu, and the escort, and the volunteer on foot, whose express vocation was, as far as I could make out, that of a guide, all lost their way at least twice before we left the environs of Ajmere. This was not cheering, but I was pretty well indifferent to all external events, and had made a vast proficiency in practical stoicism since the 28th May. If we lost our way on the high road, close to the bazaar at Ajmere, it was not to be wondered at that my friends declared themselves utterly at a loss in which direction to proceed when they had emerged into the open country. At length the sun set, and, as the moon had not risen, the darkness of the night by no means aided my zealous guides in discovering the right road. We got into fields, bogs, quagmires, went over hedges, mounds, anywhere but on the road; the driver only returning answer to my oft-repeated inquiries if we were going right, 'He was totally ignorant even of our destination, and consequently not well informed as to the way that led to it.' At last, after being very nearly upset several times, I determined to abjure the vehicle altogether, and got out to walk; indeed, I had walked the greater part of the way as it was, for half an hour's torture in the cramping cart was as much as I could bear at once.

After we had been wandering about in a vague manner for a long while in total darkness, we came to a village, and here, thought I, we shall at any rate be able to get a guide. However, on our arrival, my accommodating escort quietly, but firmly, refused to go any further, and, as the driver of the cart followed suit, I found myself compelled reluctantly to halt for the night, having made, as I felt sure, but a very bad day's journey. Indeed, considering the way we had wandered, first one side then the other, then back, and then round again, it was fairly open to doubt whether I was a bit nearer my destination than before I set out. However, as they would not go on, there was no help for it but to stay, and I regretted a thousand times that I had not come on my pony alone, when I could, at any rate, have got over the ground as soon as I had discovered the road. Outside the village there was a public halting place, called a dhurrensala, for travellers; it consisted of a stone shed, raised from the ground, open on one side and closed on all the rest. To this spot I had my cart taken, and my escort proceeded to make themselves and their beasts snug for the night. I had hoped that when the moon rose, which would be shortly, they might perhaps be prevailed on to proceed, but it was soon apparent that nothing was further from their intentions. There were robbers, they said, on ahead, who would certainly destroy the whole party if we proceeded by night.

The arrival of the cortège caused a sensation in the village; for a crowd of men, all armed with sticks, making a great noise, came down professedly to have a look at me, and, seating themselves on the edge of the stone platform in front of the dhurrensala, enjoyed a good stare at, and a noisy discussion about the stranger. Not feeling very sure of my visitors' intentions, I displayed my pistols and sword rather ostentatiously, and lay down in my cart. The bullocks had been taken out, and the driver no longer sitting in front, I found, to my great relief, that a stretch of the legs to their full extent was at last practicable. By and by the villagers, departed; two chowkedars, or watchmen, from the village, attached themselves to my party, of course to take care of me. The moon rose by degrees high into the heavens, and I lay silent, in an attitude of rest, absorbed in thought, and really enjoying the quiet and soothing influence of the calm moonlight night. I had no inclination to sleep, but indulged in waking dreams, revolving in my mind the events we had lately witnessed, and forming plans, as far as I dared look forward, for the future. I had lain in this manner for a considerable time perfectly still, when I observed one of my unpleasant-looking friends of the escort come, as if casually, near the cart, and take a good look at me in passing; I lay perfectly still, and by and by he tried it a second time, and came much closer; he tried it a third time, and took a good long look at me. I had closed my eyes, and was to all appearance fast asleep. I then heard one of the others ask 'if the Sahib was asleep.' The inquisitive gentleman who had, as he thought, thoroughly investigated the point, replied, 'Yes, fast asleep, and even if he were awake, he cannot understand a word we say.' Oh, I thought, then I will keep my ears open. The old grey-haired man, who was much the best of the party, had lain down and covered himself up, and was fast asleep. The other two sowars and the watchmen from the village then sat down, and entered into a long conversation, speaking in rather an undertone, but, in the stillness of the night, I could hear every word they said, except when they dropped their voices, which they did now and again, and spoke in a whisper.

The language they used in conversation was a rustic dialect of Hindu, occasionally introducing Marwari words, which I could not understand; I paid attention at first merely from curiosity, thinking I should probably hear some unbiassed opinions expressed regarding recent events; and I was curious to know what these men really thought of public affairs. This, no doubt, was the reason why they had taken the precaution to see if I was asleep before they entered on a free discussion of the character and prospects of the English. But I soon heard words that made me anxious not to lose a syllable, and, without moving my position the least, strained my ears and attention to the utmost to catch what was said. They began by talking about the late disasters, and the overthrow of our Government, which they thought had been effected; and the events that had occurred at Agra appeared to have made great impression on them. They then proceeded to discuss a plan for killing me, and taking what little property, and it was little enough, I had. They also contemplated a general rebellion in their own country, Marwar; and one of them remarked that there were men ready to rise and join a rebel chief in every village in the country. But the part of their conversation that was most interesting was that relating to myself. They dwelt very much on the fact of my having pistols, of which they seemed to have a wholesome fear, one repeatedly bringing it as an objection against attacking me. The others tried to encourage him by observing that, after all, there were only two shots, and when they were expended they could despatch me with their swords.

They appeared to have postponed their charitable purpose for another opportunity, as well as I could make out, till we had advanced further on our journey; and so, after a long conversation, they lay down to sleep, leaving one of the watchmen sitting up, professedly to look out, but in reality to follow the example of the others in a sitting instead of a recumbent posture.

I deliberated with myself what I should do. The first thing was to get out of the cart, where, in case of attack, my movements would have been very much hampered, and the assailing party would have it all their own way. So I waited for a considerable time in my old position; then raising myself as if awaking from deep sleep, and getting out of the conveyance with my sword and pistols, spread my scanty store of bedding on the stone floor of the dhurrensala, and lay down.

I deliberated as calmly and impartially as possible on all that had been said, taking care to give full weight to the great improbability of men in their position concocting and carrying out such a scheme as murdering a solitary traveller. Had I been a political agent, or any one of importance, there would have been nothing at all singular in it; but of what value to these semi-barbarians was the life of a wandering subaltern of a mutinied regiment? The property I had was so small as hardly to tempt men to such a crime; and would they not be held answerable for my life on their return either to Ajmere or to their homes? On the other hand, the men had made use of certain expressions, which, take them any way I would, it was impossible to interpret in any other sense than that they really intended attacking me. It might be an object to them to take the life of any Englishman, and as for my property, small though it was, the pistols alone, which were such an object of dread to them in my hands, would be proportionably valuable in theirs. As for want of motive to such a crime, or any considerations of self-interest being likely to deter them from it, had I not lately seen numberless instances of men, as far as we could see, sacrificing all their worldly interests to gratify a whim or a passion, turning their arms against their own Government, attempting the assassination of their own officers, towards whom they could have no possible cause for ill-will? and I had expressly heard the Marwari horseman affirm that he knew disturbances would spread immediately into his own country, so that there would be little or no danger of their being apprehended. On the whole I determined at any rate to be on the safe side, and get rid altogether of any escort. From their previous behaviour it was clear that it would be useless to tell them to go back, as I had before repeatedly told them I would rather they returned and leave me to pursue my journey alone, when I found how unwilling they were to guide me or to afford me any effectual assistance; they would simply refuse, so I resolved to frame some excuse for getting rid of them one by one as I went along. Alone, and on horseback, I could pursue my way more expeditiously, independently, and safely. So I wrote a note in pencil to a friend (Captain Phillpotts, A.D.C. to General Lawrence,) at Ajmere, desiring him to send out my horse, and added a postscript, 'Don't let the bearer return.' It would be a good way I thought of testing the accuracy of my suspicions; if they were groundless, one of the men would not object to returning for my horse, but if correct, it was certain my orders would be disobeyed.

I then went and woke up two of the sowars, and told them that I had been so jolted in the cart, and it was such a wretched means of conveyance, I had determined to go no further in it; that I wanted my horse sent out, and one of them must return with the note to Ajmere to have it forwarded; meantime I should wait there till it came. They appeared very much surprised at my order, and after observing to one another that they were not going back to Ajmere to be punished, flatly refused to go, calling me a fool at the same time. This I pretended not to understand, but feeling secure in the possession of the dreaded pistols, which were concealed in my breast, so that I could draw them in a moment, I remained standing among them, calmly insisting on the order. They got very violent in their gestures and language, and held conversations apart, which I could not overhear, and at least half-an-hour was spent in this profitless discussion. They appeared unable to understand my motives, for the excuse about the horse they thought a sham; at last one of the watchmen (who also had taken an animated part in the previous conversation) said, 'This is it, the sahib has been awake all night, and not asleep, and overheard all we said.' The truth seemed to flash across the mind of the sowar who had been the most insolent and most violent in his language, and laying his hand on his sword as if to draw it, made a gesture to the others to attack me, calling out, 'Strike for——religion;' the very cry that had heralded so much bloodshed and so many crimes already in India. I remained perfectly still, but on my guard, watching every movement, and in a moment could have presented a pistol at my antagonist; whether it would have gone off is quite another question. I had reason to believe subsequently it would not. The attack, however, was never made; the other horseman laid his hand on his arm, and endeavoured to pacify his brother savage. But their behaviour only confirmed my resolution to get rid of my friends at all hazards, and again calmly but resolutely I insisted on the necessity of the note being taken, and added, 'If one of you will not go alone, all go together.' I should have been delighted with the arrangement. After a good deal more of this violent language on their part, and obstinate persistence on mine, one of the sowars suddenly consented to take the note on my asseveration that there was nothing in it but an order for my horse to be sent out, and on the condition that he was to return. I allowed myself to be guilty of deceit in this instance, thinking that the circumstances justified it; but it is a mistake—the inevitable law of right and wrong cannot be transgressed with impunity. A man may get out of a temporary difficulty by deceiving his enemy, and far be it from me to condemn any one for so doing, but in the long run I believe the old proverb holds good, and that honesty is the best policy. An Englishman who stoops to deceit does his country a wrong—for he lessens in a material degree the respect which is always accorded to men whose natural characteristics are honesty and love of truth. However, the note was taken by the sowar at last, and I saw him ride off with satisfaction. I got a little rest, and as soon as daylight appeared, I again awoke my accommodating escort, and informed them that having resolved to remain there till my horse arrived, and make the rest of the journey on horseback, it was my will and pleasure that the cart should go on, and I would overtake it, and one sowar must go with it. Here I met with the same sort of opposition as before, but it was more easily overcome. The order was so reasonable that they could not refuse to obey it; so after abusing me a little more in conversation, the old sowar harnessed his stud, and slowly and unwillingly set out with the cart. I was now quite at my ease; two of the sowars were gone, and the solitary one left was as likely to cut his own hand off as to attack me single-handed; and the gentleman with the iron-headed club went off with the cart, so I lay down quietly to wait for my horse. But it never came. The sun got higher and higher, still no horse appeared. I walked a little way along the road expecting to meet it every second; first I sauntered a few yards, then a quarter of a mile, sitting down on the bank at intervals; at last I found I had got so far it was no use going back, for the open country was as good a resting place as the dhurrensala, and when once I got my horse I should soon make up for lost time. By degrees I had wandered on I thought half way to Ajmere, and no signs of my having any other means of conveyance than my own legs appearing, I walked on, and astonished my friends by presenting myself before them about noon, very hot, very dusty, and very hungry.

CHAPTER X.

AJMERE—POKHUR—START FOR JODHPORE—MAIRTA—PEEPAR—ARRIVAL.

ABOUT a quarter of a mile from the walls of the Ajmere fort there was an estate, consisting of a garden and a grove of magnificent trees, under the shade of whose thick foliage and wide-spreading branches the traveller might find shelter during the hottest season of the year. The grounds were situated on the shore of the lake: a raised terrace of masonry had been built, overlooking the lake itself, and as there was generally a breeze blowing across the large expanse of water, the rippling waves sparkled merrily against the walls below, affording a sight and sound only to be properly appreciated by those who have resided long in the sultry plains of India. Upon this terrace stood a row of houses, at a considerable distance apart, of different sizes, but all built in the native fashion, improved by subsequent additions made for the convenience of the European residents, who had monopolized the place for their abode. In the largest of these, General Lawrence and his staff had taken up their quarters, and here I resided for a few days after my return. Ajmere had not presented such a curious spectacle for many years as it did during the season of 1857. The fort was held by a small body of the 83rd Queen's, and as these men were the first European soldiers that had been quartered there for a very long time, they were regarded by the inhabitants, and the frequent visitors from the surrounding districts that the emergency of the times assembled at the capital of the district, with feelings of wonder and awe. Some of the old Thakoors from the villages in the deserts of Marwar, who had repaired to Ajmere to wait on the Governor-General's representative, and to tender their allegiance, or to lend their services, and those of their retainers, to the British Government, in accordance with the Rajah's injunctions, used to watch the European soldiers engaged in sports, or in the performance of their military duties, as children in England do the wild beasts in a show. Public matters wore about as unpleasing an aspect at that period as they well could. In consequence of the wretched state of the country, the mails from the north and north-east came in irregularly; for many days, while the Neemuch mutineers were on the road near Agra, we received no news at all from the seat of Government in the North-west Provinces, which was generally believed among the natives to have been totally destroyed. Our sanguine hopes of having aid sent out from England, overland, had been dashed to the ground; the assurances given to the native chiefs and sovereigns of Rajpootana and elsewhere, that in six weeks after the news of the outbreak reached England, European troops would begin to arrive in numbers at Bombay, had to be contradicted by the same officers who had made them, relying, alas, in vain, on the national sympathy of the mother country, and the energy of Government. One after the other the waves of disaster had rolled on, station after station fell, regiment after regiment had mutinied, destroyed their cantonments, and marched to swell the hosts of our inveterate foes. Cawnpore had gone, though at the time we only received vague and uncertain rumours of the calamities that had fallen on that devoted garrison; but the natives knew it well: the whole of Oude, with the exception of the capital, had been wrested out of the hands of the British Government; the gallant little band before Delhi held their own bravely, but as yet had made no permanent impression on the besieged garrison; our native auxiliaries who still remained faithful to our cause, looked with anxious eyes on the weakened fabric of the British Indian Empire, tottering from the violence of the repeated blows dealt against it, well knowing that if it fell, they fell too; sedition was still rife, and active but secret enemies were busy in sowing the seeds of rebellion, and tampering with the uncertain fidelity of the few native troops we had got to depend upon; while, if we turned our eyes to our own Government, we beheld nothing but ridiculous vacillation and want of energy to meet the crisis. The population of Ajmere, which was chiefly Mahometan, was disaffected, and though, as a matter of history, the inhabitants of wealthy mercantile cities seldom initiate a rebellion, we knew that they only wanted an example set them to lend their aid in exterminating the hated race of the Nazarenes. So little was the confidence in the stability of the empire that Government paper had been selling at sixty per cent. discount, and one or two lucky individuals made a handsome profit by purchasing it at that rate. Efforts had been made to seduce the Sepoys of the Bombay army from their allegiance, and there was good reason to know that the Poorbeeahs (or men recruited from the Bengal Presidency, chiefly Shahabad and Oude) would be only too glad to join the common cause, but that they were held in check by the men of other races in the ranks with them. The Jodhpore legion (Poorbeah) had been overheard talking open mutiny when they marched into Nusseerabad a month ago, but had not yet declared themselves. Within the fort all was bustle and activity: the fortifications were undergoing repairs, a large workshop was filled with carpenters and wheelwrights, all busy making new gun carriages, or repairing old ones; shot and shell was being piled in heaps at convenient spots; wells were being sunk; artisans and labourers of every class were being employed in some part of the premises, and every precaution was being taken to make the tumbledown old place capable of standing a siege, should matters eventuate in the unhappy necessity of holding out the place as a last resort. Whatever ideas the natives may have entertained regarding the fate heaven had in store for us, they must at any rate have been impressed with the idea that the unbelievers had lost neither their energy nor their confidence in themselves.

One day during my short residence at Ajmere we made a party to Pokhur, a place of Hindoo pilgrimage alluded to above, about ten or fifteen miles from Ajmere. The General was our host, and the necessary arrangements for a party of Englishmen's 'sine qua non' for enjoyment—plenty of provender—having been sent out, we started early in the morning, mounted on horses, ponies, and camels, and all well armed, to enjoy our pic-nic. Seldom had I witnessed a more picturesque scene than that presented by our cavalcade. Our course lay along a stony road winding round the hill, at the foot of which the city of Ajmere is built; thence we emerged into a broad valley above the lake, intersected by a winding stream, which in the rainy season turns the ground into a marsh. The sun rose as we cantered across the valley. The varied costume of the officers, and of the escort of Rajpoot horsemen taken by the General as a guard of honour, made a pleasing foreground to the picture; on the right was the lake, sparkling in the rays of the rising sun; behind the city and suburbs of Ajmere—the high brick wall looming out from among the trees and foliage of the surrounding gardens and orchards; and on all sides of us were high, barren, wild-looking mountains, the highest of which, called Taraghur, 'the Abode of the Stars,' was crowned with a conspicuous place of Mahometan pilgrimage. After crossing the valley we ascended a very steep causeway that led over the hill, pitched with huge stones, many of which had been worn so smooth and slippery that a horse could scarce keep his footing, in other parts so rough that our ponies and camels had the greatest difficulty in ascending it. But the descent the other side was far more difficult than the ascent; at the bottom was the sandy bed of a river, which ran for a considerable distance between beautifully wooded hills of considerable elevation. The scenery the whole way was very pretty, and very unlike that barren, uninteresting country one sees so much of in the plains of India. Pokhur is a curious place, and well worth visiting; there is a large pond or lake lying in a basin among the hills; the banks are studded with buildings, old temples, summer-houses, and gardens, and in the centre a ruined fane, which formerly stood out of the water, and has been partially submerged, owing either to the soil underneath having suddenly given way, or to the effect of volcanic phenomena, and is accordingly regarded by the superstitious natives with great veneration. The town seems thickly populated, and, judging from the enormous number of children we saw, the population is in no danger of diminishing. We put up in a kind of summer-house overlooking a large flight of stone stairs where the pilgrims resort for the purpose of bathing in the sacred waters, which is set apart for European visitors, whose amusement, I believe, generally consists in watching the naked urchins, who are hopping about the steps, now in the water now out, now climbing the roof of the neighbouring buildings, and all clamouring for 'baksheesh,' jabbering, chattering, laughing, and gambolling about like an enormous family of monkeys. We made no exception to the rule, and a copper pice (a coin, value about three-farthings) thrown into the water, was sufficient inducement for hundreds of these amphibious creatures to throw themselves eagerly after it, dive down, and scramble for it among the weeds at the bottom of the lake. The fortunate possessor would at length emerge with the prize between his teeth; half of them would turn to the shore, and half remain, treading water, till another pice was thrown to a little distance, so as to be clear of the band, and down they went again, diving, swimming, struggling, scrambling, like so many fish. Excitement rose to the highest when it became known that the 'burra sahib,' the great man, had with extravagant munificence, hitherto unrivalled, offered eight annas, or a shilling, to any boy who leapt from the topmost parapet of an apartment, a height perhaps of thirty feet or more, into the water. Places like Pokhur, that are held sacred in the eyes of the Hindoos, are resorted to by thousands, and the crowds of people about showed that the disturbances had not turned aside the usual stream of devotees. The General had some business to do there, I believe; at any rate, our visiting the place at the time must have had a very good effect, for if a small band of English gentlemen could go on a pleasure party to a place essentially a hotbed of fanaticism, and the head-quarters of Hindoo superstition, it was a pretty good proof that the prestige which had for so many years attended the British officer wherever he went, and invested him with a certain degree of imaginary sanctity and awe in the eyes of the vulgar crowd, had not yet died out. If we could trust ourselves among the armed crowds, among the fanatics, fakeers, devotees, and Sepoys in disguise, that swarmed about the streets and the suburbs of Pokhur, it was plain that the English had not yet been driven out of India, or had any expectation of being so. Before we returned, we visited, by invitation, a garden belonging to the chief man of the place, of which I cannot give a very good description, except that it was so thickly studded with trees, that all we could do was to walk with our heads downwards in single file, one after another, along the narrow path, creeping under the branches or pushing them aside, which, on account of the luxuriance of the vegetation, it was necessary to do at every step. We had a pleasant ride back to Ajmere, by the same road we had come, in the cool of the evening.

I was anxious to be on my way to Jodhpore, and no visible change in public affairs having resulted from the bad news received a few days before of the disasters at Agra, where our troops had to retreat in presence of the mutineers, and where all the residents were shut up in the fort, and besieged, as the phrase is (though a siege generally implies the presence of two parties, one outside and one inside the walls, and in this case the former was wanting, for the enemy retreated as rapidly as our own men) the General made me over by a kind of imaginary writ of 'habeas corpus' to a dependent of the Jodhpore Vakeel, who became answerable for my safety, and was bound to deliver me alive and sound at Jodhpore in three days. I mounted the camel provided for me, and, attended this time by an escort of five men, better-looking ones than I had before, set out once more. It was about two P.M. in the middle of July, and the clouds which had partially obscured the sun's rays for a few days past, and induced me to forget the intense heat at the time of the year, having cleared off the very day I started, the heat was overpowering. We made about eighteen or twenty miles that evening, and put up at nightfall in a village where the people received us kindly enough, owing to the imposing presence of my guide, Achal Sing, who appeared, like a coachman of one of our best coaches in the old days, to know everybody on the road, and every one to know him. A charpoy (rude bedstead) was brought out into the street of the village, and I sat down, every motion, every act being watched by crowds of men, women, and children, with as much interest as a rhinoceros would excite among the inmates of an English farm-house. A large party of travellers were putting up in the same village besides ourselves, and were reclining at full length on the ground, their bundles under their heads, and their matchlocks leaning against the wall behind them. By and by the cattle were driven in, and I passed the night in pretty close proximity to a very large mass of cows, calves, buffaloes, ponies, and camels, who took up their abode along with me in the centre. The heat was intense. The blazing sun had been pouring its burning rays all day upon the little confined spot, and had set some time ago, leaving the earth and the mud walls of the houses thoroughly heated, and capable of refracting a good deal of caloric all the night. Not a breath stirred through the sultry evening air, and to improve matters, the wayfarers lit enormous fires all round me for the purpose of cooking their food, which, though it increased the heat, had the effect of keeping off the swarms of musquitoes and insects that were buzzing about in myriads. The exposure to the sun during the day had brought on a slight attack of ague, and I experienced that very uncomfortable creeping, half-shivering cold sensation which betokens the presence of fever in the system. I tried to eat and drink a little of the food I had with me, and smoked a cheroot, determined to ignore the presence of so inconvenient a companion in my present circumstances as an attack of fever, and to the surprise of my companions, who, though natives of the country, felt the heat so much that they were forced to strip themselves to the skin, covered myself with a piece of felt—the only thing I had to serve me for bedding, great coat, cloak, and many other purposes besides for many a long day—and tried to sleep.

We started early next morning after an unrefreshing night, and made about thirty miles by ten o'clock, when we reached the city of Mairta, put down in most of the maps in large and conspicuous letters, as if it were a place of great importance. It is one of the khalsa towns (as they are called), that is, the peculiar possession of the sovereign, and not, as many places and districts are, held by a Thakoor, or noble, as a fief. It is a walled town, and from a distance has an imposing appearance. The heat was overpowering even by nine o'clock, and, as may readily be imagined, I had gained as many particulars as possible regarding the place we were to put up at, and the fare and quarters I was likely to find, from my companion, old Achal Sing. His account (and he was by no means an impartial witness as to the excellence of everything in Marwar, for that dry, dreary, desert country he thought the finest in the world, and was as proud of it as Pat is of the Emerald Isle) led me to expect the most hospitable reception from the magnates of the place, and splendid quarters to put up in, like those M. Huc seemed so fortunately to find always during his wanderings in China; so that when I entered the gate of the city, and rode through the principal street, and beheld it half peopled, the houses more than half in ruins, even the wretched little bunneahs' shops exhibiting all those signs of poverty and lack of business that are so characteristic of Eastern cities which have been depopulated by misrule, and allowed to fall into ruin through neglect and tyranny on the part of the rulers of the land, my heart rather sank within me, for I was dreadfully tired and unwell. At last we reached a large enclosure, surrounded by a high wall, with a lofty gateway as an entrance, which at one time had been a fine large serai; on one side there was a house, or range of rooms, one story towering above another to a great height, the whole surmounted by an open, airy-looking domicile, consisting of a domed roof, supported by thin, and not inelegant stone pillars. Had it been stormy weather, one would scarcely have ventured up there, but thinking I should certainly get what little air might be stirring, I managed with some difficulty to discover the way up, and with still greater difficulty to accomplish the ascent, for the stone steps were all in ruins, and the whole place looked as if a very gentle shock of an earthquake, or a good gust of wind would send it about my ears.

Residents in India, more particularly travellers, are held in estimation by the natives exactly in proportion to the size of the retinue, the quantity of baggage, and cattle, &c., they take about with them. This is the case all over the world. In England a solitary portmanteau or a carpet-bag carries weight with it, especially if it be new. In Wales even, and other parts of the country where it is so common for tourists to travel on foot during the summer months, it is extraordinary what a different reception the possession of even an unhappy portmanteau will ensure its owner at any of the principal hotels, to that which a walking-stick and knapsack secures. Had I travelled through Marwar with camels, and tents, and servants, and horses—such an establishment as officers are in the habit of taking about with them wherever they go—I should have been recognised as an officer of the British Government, and treated accordingly; while here I was the possessor of only one seat on a camel, the animal not my own, with no baggage but a small wallet containing my very slender wardrobe, so slender, that I had actually been reduced to what, under other circumstances, would have been, to say the least, the undignified necessity of borrowing a pair of unmentionables and a very old shirt from a friend, and not returning them. But the state of poverty to which the mutineers had reduced us was a stern reality, from which there was no possible way of escaping, and I had made up my mind to disregard appearances, and not look for the wonted respect we had been in the habit of receiving from the hands of natives and subordinates till fortune should smile on me again, and the British Government recover its position, and enable its officers to recover theirs. I was somewhat amused by the apologetic, and at the same time assuring air with which my friend Achal Sing used to tell every one that I was not what I seemed, that I was an 'Amir' or gentleman among my own kith and kin, and though I went through the country with no 'dhum dham' (an expressive word, that I cannot translate better than by kicking up a dust), I was entitled to respect; and to do them justice they generally believed him; though it required a considerable degree of faith, for appearances were decidedly not in favour of the truth. I was fortunate at Mairta. The rumour of an English traveller having arrived at first attracted a small crowd under the shade of the gateway, which situation was exactly opposite to the rickety, airy position I occupied, to gaze at me. By and by, it reached the ears of the magnates of the place—most likely Achal Sing went and told them—and I had a visit from one of the kotwals, or native magistrates. This man had been at Ajmere some time before, where I had accidentally met him in the quarters of the fort commandant, and though we had not on that occasion exchanged a syllable (and he was a sulky-looking fellow I thought), he appeared overjoyed to see me. Mairta was honoured by my presence, he was proud; his brother, the hákim or head man of the place, was proud; the moonshees and writers were proud; all that they possessed was at my disposal, the resources of Mairta should be ransacked to supply my wants; and first of all I should be 'shampooed.' Now, shampooing is a process against which I have always entertained perhaps a very foolish prejudice. The idea of a native standing over one, clawing, and pawing, and muddling with one's limbs and muscles, is a thing I never could bear even the thought of. I begged to be excused; I pleaded national habits—all was of no avail; the barber was summoned forthwith; I was forced to lie down, and be subjected to the operation. It certainly had a soothing effect; but the great man's influence was more satisfactorily exerted in procuring some limes which my parched lips were longing for. I always like making my own sherbet, as in squeezing the juice out of the fruit it is apt to run over the hand, and trickle down the fingers into the glass or vessel used as a receptacle. But my new friends would not allow it, they would make the sherbet for me; so I resigned myself to circumstances, and lay still on the charpoy, surrounded by these uncouth, yet kind mortals, for the crowd increased every moment, and the *élite* of Mairta hastened to see the white man who had appeared so unexpectedly; as if he had dropped from the clouds, and only alighted half-way after all, on the summit of the highest building in the place. They assured me, which was scarcely possible, that I was the only European who had ever visited their city within the memory of the oldest inhabitant. The political agent had passed through once, but he was not visible—they were not permitted to enter his presence, squat on their hams, and have a good look at him as they could at me. While the barber shampooed me, one held the lota or brass cup, one squeezed the limes, another held limes ready for squeezing, another took charge of the sugar, and another of the water; between them all I managed to get a good draught of refreshing, though not over-pure sherbet.

Natives are very inquisitive, and the questions I had to answer were innumerable. At last, as soon as I could decently make such a request, I begged to be left alone to take some rest, and my friends departed, the kotwal promising to have some rice and a kid curry cooked for me and sent up in the evening; when he assured me the hákim would come and see me, and sundry other of his brethren.

I managed to enjoy that greatest of blessings occasionally, solitude, till the afternoon, when, after bathing, I had another visit from my friends, and by and by the hákim arrived, and brought his own carpet, which was spread beside my charpoy, where he sat, and commenced talking, while I ate as much of the curry and rice as I could, which was not much, for I had little appetite. They were anxious, however, to see the stranger eat, and had timed the meal to suit their afternoon visit; so I ate my dinner in public, like the Kings of France in olden days.

At last night came to my relief, and my importunate friends departed. How I enjoyed the comparative coolness of the night air, and the delightful quiet and repose after the heat and bustle of the day! In the elevated position I had chosen, I seemed actually raised for the time above the trouble and turmoil of the world; one by one the groups of people below loitered away to their homes, or lay down to rest in a remote corner of the building, for it was the public resort for travellers. The noisy crowd of worshippers that had thronged the court-yard of a Hindu temple below me, singing, and playing on drums, by degrees dropped off, and all relapsed into silence. The stars came out one by one, and, under the soothing influence of the calm night air, I lay and gazed at them. I thought of home, and recalled the incidents of the past fortnight, till one idea mingled with another, my perception of external things grew more and more indistinct, and I fell asleep.

We were off by moonlight next morning, an hour or so before daybreak, and, after a tedious journey of about forty miles, reached Peepar, another walled town about the same size as Mairta, but belonging to a Thakoor who was away. My reception here was consequently more doubtful than yesterday's. I had fallen out with Achal Sing, too, on the road; he wanted to stop at a village we passed about sunrise, which would have been making only half a stage, and involved my spending another day in the desert wilds of Marwar. And though he yielded to my importunity and orders to proceed, he did so unwillingly, and we lost a good deal of time by the discussion. It was consequently very late before we reached Peepar; and that I was not struck down by *coup de soleil* was indeed extraordinary. No words can describe the intensity of the mid-day July sun in a desert, where there is scarce a patch of green or a tree to relieve the eye from the painful glare and refraction of heat from the white, glittering soil. I believe I half lost my senses, for I abused poor Achal Sing most unmercifully, which, considering how completely I was in his power, and how much my comfort depended on keeping him in a good humour, was, to say the least, unwise; he said little, but jogged on patiently, and told me afterwards that the sun had affected my head on the road, and I did not know what I was saying.

At Peepar, after some little delay, we dismounted in a yard surrounded by a brick wall, a kind of half fort, half serai. There were numbers of horses picketed in a long shed or stable on one side, on the other side was a long, double-storied building, the only human habitation in the place, in the lower story of which I could see a number of Rajpoots loitering and lounging about, something in the same way that ostlers and boys do in the yard of a large village inn, on a sunshiny day, in England. Though the Thakoor was absent, I was informed by Achal Sing that the building I have mentioned was nevertheless tenanted by Thakoors; and when I asked who the men were that I saw standing about, he told me they also were Thakoors. I had certainly come into the country of Thakoors, so I went up to introduce myself. What became of Achal Sing I don't know; he always disappeared somewhere on these occasions. On arriving at the place, which seemed half stables half a barrack, I was invited up-stairs, and on entering the upper story found myself in a long, rectangular apartment, open on two sides, and closed on the other two. There were about half-a-dozen men or more in the room, in all stages of undress, some lying, some sitting on charpoys, and some asleep. I understood them to be retainers, and probably relatives of the absent Thakoors of the place. They received me courteously, but not very respectfully, and no wonder; my appearance was not in my favour. They admired, however, my sword and pistols very much, and seemed to have a wholesome dread of the latter, being afraid they would go off in their hands while they were examining them. My head was aching dreadfully from the effects of the sun, and I would have given the world to have been able to lie down quietly in a dark room and get some sleep, but I soon saw that there was no privacy to be got here. I should have to sit, eat, drink, and probably sleep, too, in public, besides running the gauntlet of innumerable questions from a crowd of inquisitive visitors. It was intensely hot, and the glare was most distressing, but there was no help for it, so I lay down on a charpoy which they gave me, on the side of the building where there was the most shade, or, to speak more correctly, the least sunshine, and set to work to make some sherbet with the limes I had taken the precaution to bring from Mairta.

My hosts, meantime, gathered round me; those that were asleep woke up and joined the group, which was increased momentarily by a number of little boys, who came in to see the Feringhee stranger, and gratify their curiosity. The conversation, after I had replied to numerous questions as to my name, rank, destination, &c. (natives do not look upon questions of this kind in the same way that we do), turned upon public matters, and I was astonished to find how well informed these semi-barbarians, living as they were in a half-ruined town in a desert, and so far removed, to all appearance, from any communication with our provinces, seemed to be with the events that were passing in the rest of India. I wondered that they had ever heard even of the names of many of our stations which had been destroyed by the mutineers, and which they mentioned as having rebelled (phirgaza) against British authority. Agra, they told me, had been swept from the face of the earth; not a brick remained standing on another. I expressed my unfeigned astonishment at such a remarkable event, and asked how they knew it. They said they knew it, and everybody knew it—it was a common report. I burst out laughing, and told them they were very much deceived; that all that had happened at Agra was that a few bungalows had been plundered and burnt, but as for the European population, they were quite safe inside an impregnable fort. They alluded in conversation to the king, calling him 'Badshah,' which was the term employed in former days, during the Mogul Empire, to designate the King or Emperor of Delhi, to whom all India more or less owed allegiance. It is a word signifying a higher rank than Raja, Sultan, or any of the other significations of regal power. The instant the word escaped their lips, I looked up, and, in a tone of astonishment, said, 'Badshah!—what Badshah?' 'You know,' they replied, with a very expressive look. I said, 'No, I don't know any Badshah.' Still they would condescend to no explanation, so at last I added, 'Oh, I suppose you mean the Delhi Badshah.' They nodded assent. 'Pooh,' I answered, 'if you mean him, he is a miserable decrepit old man, just put on the throne by the Sepoys, who want to make use of his name to justify their mutiny and subsequent crimes.' It is difficult to judge by physiognomy, especially when dealing with Asiatics, so I would not venture to affirm that I was credited; but they certainly appeared to believe me, at all events behaved with more respect than they had previously evinced. By and by the mutiny came upon the *tapis*. I asked them if they knew why the Sepoys had thrown off their allegiance. 'Yes, we know well enough, and so do you,' they added, with a knowing wink and a half grin. I said, 'I suppose you mean to say that you believe it was true that we attempted to tamper with their religion?' 'Yes, that was it,' they answered; 'we all know that.' 'It is false,' I said; 'will you believe me if I swear?' and, lifting up my hand towards heaven, I took an oath by the sacred name of God that it was all totally false. 'Now,' I added, 'do you believe me?' 'Yes,' they said, 'we do.' I merely mention this conversation, as it will go a little way towards showing the general state of feelings and opinions among the natives regarding the rebellion; and, travelling as I was without state or ceremony, they treated me without much respect, and spoke with infinitely less reserve than they would have done had I seen them under other circumstances.

Before leaving the subject, I must mention another conversation I had with a native. A little subsequently to this, when travelling in Sind, I was riding one night in company with some sowars belonging to the Sind police, and more from want of some topic of conversation to beguile the time than anything else, began talking about the officer commanding their regiment, who I knew was universally respected by his men. 'Ah!' an old fellow said, 'he is a fine officer; we all like him. *He,*' laying great emphasis on the word, for the sake of making an offensive distinction between their service and mine—for they all knew who I was—'never would do anything to interfere with *his* men's religion, and so ruin (bigār) the regiment.' He implied in his tone, which I cannot transmit to paper, as plainly as if he had said the very words, 'We don't do things in your Bengal fashion in this part of the country.' And he was not far wrong either.

The attitude assumed by Achal Sing on these occasions was sufficiently amusing. He regarded me something as Barnum would have done had I been a dwarf or a mermaid. Without any sympathy with my wish for privacy or desire for repose, the more I was surrounded with visitors, the better he was pleased; the notice I attracted seemed to him a source of unfeigned gratification, exactly in the same ratio in which it was disagreeable to me. I was his pet dancing bear, and he was the showman. So he would bring his huge carcass into the room (for he was an enormous man, with his broad chest and thick muscular limbs—a regular Hercules), and seat himself on his haunches, with his back against the wall, rest his chin upon his knees, and regard with a smile of satisfaction the crowds of sight-seers by whom I was surrounded, and the evident excitement my arrival among them had caused. At the same time he seemed to think it incumbent upon him to watch over me as if I had been a child entrusted to his care, and tried to impress on his fellow-countrymen the importance of the responsibility imposed upon him in the protection of my person.

During the course of the day I had a visit from a Mahometan bone-setter, among many others. By that time I had got on very good terms with the Rajpoot retainers; Achal Sing's solemn asseverations that I belonged to a higher class than my external appearance would denote had had some effect, and either from that or from some other causes they began to treat me with more respect than they had evinced at first. I saw at once that the Mahometan bone-setter was no favourite, and that it was rather a bold stroke that he had made in venturing there to see me. I received him as affably as I could, but his manners were offensive, and his language disrespectful, so I determined to be even with him, and watched my opportunity. He told me, among other things, that twenty-five years ago a party of three European gentlemen were travelling through Marwar, and one of them had met with an accident near Peepar, and broken his leg. The party had no surgeon with them, and my informant was called in; he set the broken limb, and nursed the unfortunate traveller for six months, for his companions had gone on, and left him behind. He was well rewarded for his services, and mentioned all the particulars of the event. On subsequent inquiry I found that his statement was perfectly true: that a party of English travellers, whose names I forget, had passed along that route about the time mentioned, and one of them had met with an accident, and had been detained.

He continued to press me with questions and seemed inclined to make a butt of me. The rest of the company took no part in the conversation, but sat and listened, till the bone-setter, who thought himself a bit of a wag, tried to exercise his art at my expense, but I turned the tables against him, and raised a shout of laughter from all the rest of the audience at his expense, and he very soon left off teasing me.

I had urged on Achal Sing the necessity of getting another camel here, the beast which had brought us thus far being worn out, and so tired that we had no help for it but to make the remainder of the distance in two days instead of one. This was a great disappointment, as my conductor told me the last thing at night he had been unsuccessful in trying to get a fresh camel. In the middle of the night he came and awoke me—a most unusual proceeding, as it was generally a difficult matter to stir him up, and I had never started without a good deal of trouble on this head. When he called me, thinking we had only half a stage to go, or about twenty miles, I told him I would not get up then; as we were going so short a distance, we would start at a later hour. When I descended, however, at the usual time to the court-yard, I found two camels ready caparisoned. The second he had got during the night, and intending to give me an agreeable surprise, had not acquainted me with the pleasing intelligence. I would gladly have started two hours before; however, we set out, and about nine o'clock came in sight of Jodhpore. The first glimpse the traveller gets of it from a long distance it presents a most picturesque appearance, bounding as it does the horizon, and seeming, in comparison with the wide expanse of perfectly level ground all round it, much more elevated, and a much more imposing place than it really is.

I had changed camels, and had another driver, a young man, one of the Thakoors, as he called himself; he had a small black eye, and a merry expression in his face, and as we drew near the end of our journey, the distance diminishing every step as we jogged across the plain, our spirits rose; and my new companion soon evinced symptoms of extraordinary hilarity. 'How long is it since you have seen your meensahib?' he asked. I told him. 'And does she expect you?' he said. I replied that she did, though without knowing the exact hour of my arrival. 'And wont she be glad to see you?' he continued. 'I hope so.' 'Ah, wont she be glad to see you!' he exclaimed; 'Hi! Hee!' accompanying each exclamation by waving his stick with a triumphant air round his head, and bringing it down on the camel's side, to the tune of 'Hi, Hee.' The stubborn beast caught the enthusiasm of its rider, and no wonder, seeing the practical manner in which it was evinced, and stepped out at a good fast trot, my guide continuing his flourishes of the stick and ejaculations as we sped over the sandy plain under the burning sun. Achal Sing actually awoke from his customary lethargic state—the result of perpetually renewed doses of opium—and trotted along by our side with a grin on his broad countenance at the antics of his more volatile brother Rajpoot.

CHAPTER XI.

RESIDENCE AT JODHPORE—POSTAL LINES—VISIT TO THE KING—COURT ETIQUETTE—ATTEMPT AT MUTINY THE SECOND AT NUSSEERABAD—ÉMEUTE IN THE AJMERE GAOL.

IT is possible that this unpretending narrative may fall into the hands of some who have experienced great vicissitudes of fortune during their lifetime. There may be some who have been reduced suddenly from a state of comfort and affluence, as regards the good things of this life, to one of utter, or almost utter destitution. During the period which has been embraced in these pages there were thousands in this country who underwent a similar trial. The mutiny and rebellion burst upon us like a sudden storm. We had all sails set, and were going along merrily before the wind, unheeding the threatening aspect of the horizon, and the clouds that were gathering around us. Warnings we had, or might have had, for it is easy to be wise after the event; we paid no regard to them till the storm was upon us, and it was too late to shorten sail. With a thunderclap that resounded throughout India, and made many a face grow pale, it burst over our heads. The sea arose, and, amid the war of contending elements, our bark heeled over on its side, the timbers strained, the masts bent before the gale, the canvas was rent, and the rigging tossed wildly about at the mercy of the storm. There was no firm hand at the helm, and had there been, the violence of the tempest would have almost prevented its agency from being felt. How families were driven houseless into the jungles, how ladies brought up in all the delicacy and refinement of modern civilization were suddenly forced to work with their own hands, prepare food for themselves and families, sleep on boards or stone floors, or wander through thorny jungles, exposed to the rays of a tropical sun, carrying or dragging their children with them, their bare tender feet cut, and bleeding from sharp stones and briers, has been recorded over and over again by abler pens than mine.

From hardships such as these we had been mercifully preserved, but no one, unless he has gone through an ordeal of the kind even far less terrible, can possibly realize the feelings with which one returns to the comforts and habits of life which previous custom had rendered a second nature. For nearly two months we had been living, as far as external conveniences of life go, in a most wretched way. True, we had enough to eat and drink, and a roof to cover us, and thankful we were for them. But we were huddled together, all of us, in one house; the heat was very great, and we had none of the appliances for cooling the air to which we were accustomed. We fortunately possessed a table and a few broken chairs, which, supported by bits of wood to act as legs, served, with the aid of empty boxes, to accommodate our party. The instant the viands were placed on the table they became black with flies, and it was almost impossible to avoid consuming a good many of these troublesome creatures with our food. Our wardrobe was reduced to the narrowest extent possible. A few tailors, and some coarse cloth were with difficulty procured in the bazaar, and some of us had managed to get clothing made up. The English residents in the neighbourhood, or in places where the outbreak had not effected a total destruction of property, kindly collected as many things as they could for the ladies and gentlemen, and sent them to be distributed. It was not a time to be particular about the fit of a coat or a pair of trousers, and some of us presented rather a curious appearance. The ladies had had a distribution of this kind when at Beeawr, and it was, so we heard, a curious exhibition. There was a large heap of miscellaneous garments of the genera described in outfitters' advertisements as ladies' under-clothing, deposited in a room. Dr. —— made lots, and the ladies drew, and each made her selection according to her turn. One lady, a Radical in her way, refused to submit to the arbitration of fortune, and seizing a quantity of what appeared to be the best assortment, fairly made off with them, amid the confusion of the unfortunate bystanders. *Punch* would have made a good picture of the scene, but the best of it was that Dr. —— was obliged after all to come down upon the group like a 'Deus ex machinâ,' and settle the dispute, he being of the other sex, and therefore an impartial judge.

On reaching Jodhpore, after the wandering, beggar-like, hand-to-mouth way in which I had been roughing it, I found myself, something like the victim of magician's wiles in the *Arabian Nights*, suddenly transformed into a gentleman again, and surrounded as if by the touch of a fairy's wand with all the pleasing concomitants of civilized life. Our kind hosts, Captain and Mrs. Monck

Mason, had given not only a house, but a comfortable home to the ladies and children who found refuge under their hospitable roof, and extended the same kindness to every wretched husband who found his way across the desert to the oasis of comfort, quiet, and luxury—the Political Agency—on a visit to his family. To find oneself decently dressed, in a comfortable drawing-room, and in ladies' society again, in a spot so secluded, and as it seemed so far removed from the troubles and turmoils, and noise and discomfort of a half-furnished barrack, in a place exposed to attacks from rebels and wandering hordes of mutineers, was like coming into a new world. It was a happy family circle, and to hear the merry laugh, and music and singing, and the chattering of children's tongues, you would have supposed—as was indeed at the time the case—that at last you had reached a spot where mutiny and rebellion had not interfered with the easy flow of domestic life. And for some time it really seemed as if we were destined to be a happy exception to the general rule that had involved so great a portion of India. But a cloud was gathering over our heads, though we saw it not, and before very long, in our small circle, the voice of mirth was to be turned to mourning, and the merry laugh to tears.

In consequence of the disturbed state of the country great difficulty was experienced in securing the safe transit of the mails; indeed, it was often impossible, though the accidents and delays which occurred in this department of the public service were much fewer than might have been expected. By degrees, however, one road after another became stopped. The road between Calcutta and the

Punjaub was interrupted by the state of the districts about Mirzapore, Mynporree, Meerut, and Delhi. The mail road between the Punjaub and Bombay ran through Agra, Indore, and Mhow; this, too, after a time, became unsafe, in consequence of the bands of rebels hovering about the country between Mhow and Agra. Another line of road from Ajmere and Nusseerabad to Bombay took the direction of Pallee, Erinpoora, and Deesa; from thence a branch led up to Mount Aboo. Communication was kept up between Ajmere and Agra pretty regularly, as the road lay through the states of independent chiefs in alliance with the British Government; and as this was the most direct and the nearest route by which communication could be kept up with Kurrachee—a place that was daily growing in importance, in consequence of its being a harbour and a landing place for European troops, and the seat of Government of the North-West Provinces—Mr. Frere, the Commissioner of Sind, conceived the idea of establishing a post line across the desert, between Hyderabad in Sind and Jodhpore, from whence communication was easily extended to Ajmere, and so on to Agra. Mr. Frere's views and instructions were ably carried out by an officer named Lieutenant Tyrwhitt, who held the office of Deputy Collector of Meerpore. This appointment placed him in charge of the whole desert between Hyderabad and the frontier of Marwar, though Meerpore, where his head-quarters were, was only about two or three marches from Hyderabad. During the summer months the heat in the desert is such as to render travelling not only inconvenient but dangerous, but Lieutenant Tyrwhitt was not to be daunted, and he set out in the burning month of May, and rode up attended by a few followers all the way to Jodhpore. Resting at certain distances, and calling around him the chiefs of the surrounding tribes, he struck a bargain with them, by which they engaged themselves to keep three camels at each station, about ten miles apart, for the conveyance of the mails. A considerable expense was incurred by this means, but Mr. Frere was one of those men who do not shrink from responsibility, and who recognise the importance of individual energy and the necessity of departing from the routine of established regulation in times of great emergency. Sir J. Lawrence was another, and it was to men of their stamp that we may say, humanly speaking, we owe the retention of our Indian Empire. Captain Mason, the political agent at Jodhpore, eagerly co-operated with Mr. Frere, and his active subordinate, Lieutenant Tyrwhitt, and the plan was extended beyond the limit originally designed, by a line of camel dâks, as they are called, being established between Jodhpore and Bhawulpore on the Sutledge, by which means communication was easily kept up with the Punjab, and a line of road open that was not likely to be affected by the movements of the rebels, who would hardly penetrate so far into the desert. Another mounted post was established between Jodhpore and Ajmere. The former place thus suddenly became the centre of communication between some of the most important parts of our Eastern Empire. A deputy superintendent of the line, Mr. C. Hewitt, who is now dead, took up his residence near the

Agency, and made it his head-quarters, from whence he set out on a periodical inspection of the line, and was ready to go to any point where the presence of a supervising officer was requisite. These lines were begun in the latter end of May, but the several branches were not completed till the end of June or beginning of July, and it was some little time before the various streams of communication, so often thwarted in their progress, began to find out there was an open channel for them, and turned their course accordingly. Now, however, the influx of work upon the poor little post-office establishment at Jodhpore, presided over by a native writer on a salary of twenty-five rupees a month, was so great as utterly to bewilder the methodical old gentleman, who had never before had anything more to do than start off a bag of letters once or twice a day by the regular runners, and receive and distribute a few English letters to the political agent, his family, and the few European residents attached to the agency, and the Maharaja's court, and a small quantity of native correspondence in the city. The Jodhpore lines, as they may be called, as they all centred there, were enormously expensive. Three camels were maintained at each post, two for work, and one spare one in case of accident, and for expresses, and for each the sum paid by contract was sixteen rupees per mensem; but the money was usefully spent. It was of the last importance to keep up communication, and whatever roads throughout North and Central India were stopped, the Jodhpore lines were always open and in working order. But supervision was required, and as there was no immediate prospect of the unattached Bengal officers going to Agra, and I was therefore unemployed in any capacity, Captain Monck Mason easily procured the sanction of the Governor-General's agent to my being placed in charge of the Jodhpore post-office. I gladly accepted the task, and was soon deep in the postal department's rules and regulations. At times as many as eight mails arrived during the day, not small letter-bags such as are usually seen on the backs of runners in India, but regular camel-loads, and often as many as two camels were required at once to bring on the bags, or rather sacks of letters. The packets were deposited in a part of the verandah of the agency that was enclosed to serve for a post-office, distributed and started off again on their route, either to Sind across the desert, or to Ajmere, Nusseerabad, and Agra, or to Bhawulpore and the Punjaub, or to Bombay *viâ* Pallee and Erinpoora.

At one time letters and despatches from Calcutta to Meerut had to be sent across the country to Bombay, thence to Jodhpore, thence to Lahore *viâ* Bhawulpore, and from Lahore down to Meerut, and for a very long time the only communication with the army before Delhi was by this roundabout route.

The work kept me well employed all day, from six o'clock in the morning till late at night, though of course with intervals of rest; and very often during the night expresses would arrive, and have to be forwarded immediately; but it had at any rate the charm of novelty to recommend it, and there was a satisfaction in feeling that one was doing something, in however humble a way, to keep the rickety old wheel of the State machine going.

Shortly after my arrival at Jodhpore I accompanied

the political agent on a visit to the king. The raja was at the time residing in one of his country-houses or seats, a few miles from the capital. We dismounted from the elephants in the neighbourhood of the royal demesne, as the walls of the palace were so low in comparison to the surrounding hilly ground (for it was built in a kind of nook or crevice in the hill), that any one mounted on the back of an elephant could see over the wall, and no profane eye might thrust itself into the sanctum sanctorum of the royal zenana. A short distance from the entrance the ministers used to meet the agent, and walk before him as far as the door of the palace, where the king received us, and after shaking hands, conducted us—leading Captain Mason by the hand—to his sitting apartment, which was an open room, tolerably nicely carpeted, with a pillow or gaddu (a round kind of bolster covered with handsome velvet) at one end. We left our shoes at the door, the king's feet being slipperless as well as our own.

Asiatics being so fond of ceremony, it has been deemed necessary to settle by treaty with the independent chiefs of Rajpootana, and of other parts of India, too, I suppose, every minute particular connected with the ceremonies to be observed on the occasion of visits paid by the political agent to the king or raja. On arriving at the capital it is customary for the agent to wait on the king, and the king is called upon to pay one return visit to the agent at the agency, after which he is represented by his ministers. A special clause in the treaty between the British Government and these proud descendants of the ancient royal houses of Rajpootana provides that the agent shall take off his shoes at a certain distance from the seat, and of course he always does so, wearing, however, his hat, and the king must come a certain distance to receive him, dropping his shoes as he steps on the carpet at the same spot as the agent. I frequently visited the Maharaja with the political agent, and as these visits were all very like one another, a description of the forms observed at one will answer for all the rest. After we had seated ourselves cross-legged on the ground (I say cross-legged, but the phrase is a generic one, signifying that we sat on the ground and disposed of our legs somewhere, I hardly knew how or where, I generally sat on mine alternately), the king reclining on his gaddu, an emblem of sovereignty, and the ministers standing in a respectful attitude a few paces in front, some commonplace observations were exchanged, the king inquiring politely after the health of the agent and of his friend, and the agent expressing equal solicitude about that of his majesty, the ministers also sharing in the anxiety, and appearing quite relieved in their minds when they found that all were in the enjoyment of good health; a remark or two on the weather was then hazarded perhaps by the agent, perhaps by the king, in the answer to which the ministers again cordially coincided, in accordance with the precepts given by Persian laws of etiquette:—

'If at noon the king asserts that it is midnight, you are to say Behold the moon and the stars.'

These little matters having been amicably settled to the satisfaction of all parties, a momentary silence ensued (during which I generally found it necessary to change my leg, the one I doubled up underneath me being so cramped as to be no longer available for a seat without subjecting myself to excruciating tortures), and the ministers, after casting a glance at each other, made a deep salaam to the raja, and retired to another part of the room, where they remained just within call till the audience was over.

The king and the agent then conversed on weighty affairs of the state, or whatever the particular object of the visit might be, till it was time to retire, when the king, instead of clapping his hands to summon his slaves, as royal personages ought according to the *Arabian Nights*, used to call the obsequious ministers in a much more matter of fact way, by ejaculating 'Qui hy,' 'Is anybody there?' (the phrase always used in India, at least in the Bengal Presidency, when you want to summon a servant, as it is not the fashion to use bells). A number of attendants then appeared upon the scene, among them the ministers, who took up their former position. Some servants then came forward, one carrying a number of garlands and necklaces made of the flowers of jessamine, fastened artistically together, and another with a small silver salver, on which stood two little vessels of silver, shaped like egg-cups, in each of which there was some kind of scent or perfume. The salver was held out to the king, who moistened the forefinger of each hand in one of the little cups, and gently rubbed the shoulders of the agent, who put himself in a convenient posture for the reception of the honour, and then did the same to the king. This ceremony was new to me, and I did not understand it when first it was enacted in my presence, as I had never seen it at any court of an Asiatic prince before, and I fear I wriggled myself into position rather awkwardly, my cramped limbs refusing to act in so unusual a manner; but as soon as it became apparent that I had merely to follow suit, I managed to bedaub his Highness's shoulders politely enough. After this, the king threw the jessamine garlands round our necks, and the political agent having done the same to him, we arose and walked, accompanied by the raja, to the place where our shoes were deposited, and having resumed these useful appendages, we stalked in procession behind the ministers, who placed themselves in the van, between rows of courtiers—for a large crowd of these hangers-on thronged the precincts of the palace—adorned with the garlands round our necks, like bulls being led to sacrifice, as I have seen those animals depicted in ancient illustrations of Virgil's works, and the writings of other classic authors.

While great and stirring events were taking place in other parts of India, our days at Jodhpore passed quietly away; it was a period, however, full of anxiety, for, as the agency had become the refuge and asylum for so many families, the consequence of any untoward political event would be the more deplorable. The king was stanch in his alliance; he had no regular army anywhere near the capital; the troops he had were engaged mostly in British territory, and what with want of discipline, and wretched equipment, were pretty well powerless for good or evil alike. The greatest cause for disquietude was, however, in the proximity of the Jodhpore legion, a portion of which was at Nusseerabad, and the remainder and head-quarters at a place called Erinpoora, about eighty miles from Jodhpore. Before describing the events which took place there, it will be necessary to allude briefly to an occurrence at Nusseerabad that proves the temper and feeling of the Bombay troops, which had now succeeded those of the sister Presidency in the garrison of the place. There had been no lack of reports and rumours respecting the fidelity of the 1st and 2nd Bombay Cavalry. The whole of the former and a portion of the latter were now quartered at Nusseerabad. No doubt attempts had been made to tamper with the men, and seduce from their allegiance not only these, but many other regiments in the Bombay army. That these attempts met with so little success is only another proof among the many that might be adduced of the superiority of the system that prevailed in Bombay over that of Bengal; the train was laid, the match applied, but the material was not combustible as it was in the Bengal regiments. About eleven, some say fourteen, of the troopers of the 1st Bombay Lancers had gone off with the mutineers to Delhi; and it was hoped that the regiment had then been weeded of all its disaffected characters, and that, in fact, there were no more in the ranks who wanted to mutiny or sympathized with the cause of the King of Delhi. The trial was made, however. One day in the month of August a commotion was caused by a trooper galloping down the front of the lines occupied by the 1st Lancers, calling out hastily on the men to rise. Now this was a very common stratagem among the mutineers. During the revolt there were several instances in which a single individual had been able by conduct like this to create the utmost confusion in a regiment, to cause the men to arm themselves, and assemble in a disorderly manner on parade, and then, by the efforts of the designing characters among them, the confusion was kept from being allayed. Their officers were first disobeyed, then insulted, and if the plot succeeded so far that they were fired upon, and some of them killed, the thing was done, the regiment was compromised; there was nothing left but to complete the ruin of their character, plunder the station, and march to Delhi. The attempt to work on this plan, which had so often been found successful, showed how deeply the design was laid; but the result proved that the effort had been made without correct calculation as to the support it was destined to meet with, or the number of men that were prepared to rise. Instead of turning out, rushing for their horses and arms, and assembling tumultuously on parade, as had been the case in other instances, the men seem, for the most part, to have remained quietly in their lines. The fanatic, however, was pursued, and finding that he met with no encouragement in the cavalry, he rode down to the infantry, a wing of the 12th N.I., and did the same there. The men passively sympathized with him; at any rate, they did not seize him, as they ought to have done, and refused when called upon to give him up. The Brigadier had by this time come upon parade, the guns were called out, and the fanatic, finding his attempt had failed, fired at the Brigadier with his pistol or carbine; he was shot by an artillery officer, and died subsequently in hospital. The whole, or a portion of the detachment of the 12th N.I. were disarmed for their conduct in refusing to give up the culprit, and some four or five of the ringleaders afterwards hanged. The result, however, proved that this portion of the Bombay army, at any rate, was not disposed to mutiny, though no doubt most of the

Poorbeeah Sepoys would have been glad to do so had they dared, and to join their fellow-countrymen now in arms against the British Government. That this affair at Nusseerabad was not an isolated act, committed by an individual on the chance of success, is probable from the fact that the same afternoon an *émeute* in the gaol of Ajmere took place. It appears that on the morning in question a gap had been found in the wall which surrounded the gaol compound. The prisoners under sentence were confined in an inner enclosure, access to which was gained through two wicket gates, the first leading into an inner court, and the second opening from that again into the place of confinement. About four in the afternoon a number of prisoners appeared at the wicket, and begged to be allowed the usual indulgence of proceeding to a short distance from their place of confinement. No sooner was the wicket opened than a rush was made by the whole body, the policeman on duty cut down, and his sword snatched from him; the guard at the outer wicket was overpowered in a similar manner, and the prisoners were free, for nothing now prevented them from getting out but the external wall, which had a large gap in it. So they armed themselves with axes, or tools, or anything in the shape of an offensive weapon they could find, and started off, followed by as many of the other prisoners as felt any desire for freedom. The alarm, however, was given—and in those days people were always in a tolerable state of preparation—every one, European and natives, kept his sword and pistol by him. The mounted police lost no time in getting ready, and started in pursuit. The Brigadier-General, whose quarters on the lake were about three-quarters of a mile from the gaol, mounted, and, accompanied by his staff, joined in the pursuit. The police, however, had started before the General got down there, and, after going about half a mile, he met them returning, having killed and wounded some sixteen or eighteen, of whom some survived; about twenty-five were recaptured and brought back, and about a similar number managed to effect their escape altogether. The city people remained quiet the whole time, and there was no attempt whatever at co-operating with the prisoners. It is scarcely likely that this event, and the attempt to incite the native troops at Nusseerabad, both of which occurred on the same day, and almost at the same hour, were not the result of some preconcerted plan. If they were not, the coincidence is remarkable.

It was about this time, though I am unable to recollect the exact date, that an event occurred which was calculated to excite the native mind, ever prone to be affected by superstitious influences. We were visited by one of the most tremendous storms it has ever been my lot to witness. It came on at night; the thunder pealed incessantly, the wind howled, and the rain fell in perfect torrents. Captain Mason was sleeping, as was his custom, in the verandah, which, as I have before said, was at a great elevation from the ground. An apartment, a large vaulted room, paved with stone, was on the ground floor, raised a few feet above the garden. Suddenly, when the rage of the elements seemed at its highest, an explosion took place, the effect of which no words can describe. It seemed as if the earth and sky had split asunder, the whole house shook, and everything in the room, the house above us, and ourselves, too, seemed for a moment to be involved in destruction. I leapt out of bed and half across the room by the same effort, involuntarily, but had scarcely touched the ground with my feet, when another explosion, if possible more tremendous than the last, again shook the earth. I went to the door and looked out into the pitchy darkness. The rain was pouring down with increased violence, but nothing was to be seen. At the other side of the room, outside another door, several natives were sitting, who had been disturbed by the storm. I went and asked them what had happened, but they were as ignorant as myself. One of them said the house had been struck by lightning, which I was beginning to think must have been the case. At first we fancied the upper part of the agency had been thrown down, and that we could hear the fragments of the verandah above, and the upper story falling, but on listening attentively nothing was to be distinguished but the ceaseless dash of the rain, and the splashing of the torrents of water from the drains above. It was not till next morning that we learnt what had taken place. At about the most elevated part of the fort there was a Hindoo temple, a place of great sanctity; it was built on the wall, and its spire shot up towards the sky—a tempting bait for lightning. This it seemed had been struck, and the building shattered, but the destructive element did not stop here. It ran down the wall, and exploded an immense subterranean store magazine of powder, of which there were one or two in the fort. The whole thing of course blew up in a second with a tremendous report:

the wall was thrown down, large pieces of rock on which it was built, of immense size, being hurled through the air to a distance of two miles: houses were crushed, and blown up too, for the neighbourhood of the fort wall was pretty thickly populated, a great number of houses having been built resting on it. No one knew, till morning light revealed the awful consequence of the catastrophe, how much injury had been done, nor even then was the full extent laid bare. It was several days before they could give anything like an approximate guess at the number of lives lost. The most exaggerated statements, as usual, were circulated, but by degrees thousands diminished to hundreds, and at length it was found that not much more than two hundred had been killed outright. The number of maimed and wounded was of course immense. The raja gave away large sums of money for the relief of widows and orphans, and disabled men, and urged on the work of clearance as energetically as possible. He sent a message to the political agent in the morning to say, that although Heaven had preserved his kingdom from the calamities of rebellion that all other surrounding kingdoms were suffering from, yet it was not intended that he should escape altogether, and this was the way that he received his share of the troubles that appeared to surround every one.

The disaffected of course took advantage of it to prove their own assertion, that sooner or later the anger of the gods would be visited on the head of the impious sovereign who remained true to treaties made with unbelievers. The raja, however, himself was not affected by these fancies, but immediately began inquiring into the theory of lightning conductors, with a view to getting one erected for future security. The phenomenon of the storm would have been worthy of record by M. Arago. Captain Mason distinctly saw, at the time of the explosion, a ball of fire bound over the wall of the agency garden, where it burst among the trees at the same moment as the tremendous report was heard. There was no doubt that the temple was first struck, and this was followed almost instantaneously by the explosion of the magazine. What connexion the ball of fire had with these phenomena it is impossible to say. The effect of the shock on the atmosphere was so great as to burst open the window of Mrs. Mason's room, and throw some bottles that were standing on the sill to the other side of the apartment, besides breaking the window panes. The effect the accident had on the minds of the natives I have described. For ourselves, it made us feel how vain and futile were our attempts to provide for our own safety by adopting this plan or that, by going here or there to reside, by calculating chances and weighing probabilities; for the passions of the human heart and the thunderbolt are alike instruments in the hand of Him who ruleth over the kingdom of men.

CHAPTER XII.

MOUNT ABOO—ATTACK OF THE MUTINEERS—OUTBREAK AT ERINPOORA—LIEUTENANT CONOLLY—ESCAPE—MARCH OF THE LEGION—REBEL THAKOOR—JUNCTION AMONG THE ENEMY.

FOR the particulars of the mutiny of the Jodhpore Legion, as described in this chapter, I am indebted to Captain Hall, the officer commanding, and Lieutenant Conolly, Adjutant of the legion.

Mount Aboo, the favourite summer residence of the families of officers who are quartered in the neighbourhood, was garrisoned at the time I am speaking of by two parties of the infantry of the legion, altogether about sixty strong. There were in addition about thirty or thirty-five sick and convalescent men of H.M.'s 83rd Regiment, who lived in the barracks and hospital; there were a few officers residing there, but the greater part of the community were women and children—the families of officers and soldiers whose duty called them to the post of danger in the plains. Among others, the family of Brigadier-General Lawrence were at Aboo at the time.

The first intimation we received that anything serious had occurred, came from a letter written by the raja's vakeel at Erinpoora to the king; almost simultaneously came a letter from Lieutenant Conolly, reporting the mutiny of the legion at

Erinpoora. The latter arrived one day when we were all seated at dinner. It was put into Captain Monck Mason's hands; he glanced at its contents, and every one saw by the expression of his face that he had received bad news: still it was necessary to keep up appearances, both for the sake of the ladies, and to prevent the native attendants from getting exaggerated notions of our position. We went on with the meal as usual, but it was scarcely over, when a message arrived from the king, saying that he wanted an immediate interview with the political agent, to communicate some news of importance. Captain Monck Mason went to the king in the evening, and found him and the ministers in a state of the deepest dejection. We had become fully aware of the real facts of the mutiny from the perusal of Lieutenant Conolly's letter, but were not prepared for the startling announcement made by the raja, who persisted in maintaining its credibility. The vakeel had written to tell him that Mount Aboo had been attacked previously to the mutiny of the legion (which we knew was the case, as Lieutenant Conolly had mentioned the incident in his letter, but without detailing the result), and that every soul had been massacred. This was terrible news, and it was plainly possible that it might be true; we knew that there was no garrison at Aboo, except a few sick men, that there were scarcely any officers, and that the ladies and children, living apart from one another as they were, might have been overpowered and slaughtered by even a small band of resolute ruffians with the greatest possible ease. It was a terrible blow, and the raja and his court were so much affected by it, that they sat in silence, not uttering a word for a long time after Captain Monck Mason had arrived and taken his seat. At length the gloomy intelligence was communicated to him, and he at once said he did not credit it. A despatch was immediately sent off to General Lawrence at Ajmere, who was plunged into the deepest anxiety at the disastrous intelligence, nor was it till three days afterwards that his mind was relieved, by hearing that his family was safe. The escape of the helpless residents at Aboo was, however, a narrow one; while the attempt made by a large party of armed men on a small body of invalids, and women and children, was one of the most dastardly and cowardly episodes of the whole mutiny, fertile as it was in acts of treachery, deceit, ingratitude, cruelty, lust, and every crime that the meanest and worst of the human race alone could commit. There are some crimes that have a stamp of greatness in them, for the authors or perpetrators of which we cannot help having a feeling akin to respect; there are others which excite our contempt and disgust for their very meanness as well as guilt, and it is in crimes of this kind that the Indian mutiny abounded.

The Jodhpore Legion consisted of artillery, cavalry, and infantry. The artillery, two nine-pounders, was drawn by camels, and manned from the infantry. The cavalry consisted of three troops, each troop having a rassaldar (native captain), a naib rassaldar (a native lieutenant), one kote duffadar (pay-sergeant), six duffadars, one standard-bearer, one trumpeter, and seventy-two troopers. This branch of the legion was one of the best mounted and best equipped bodies of irregular cavalry in our service. The excellence of their horses was a constant subject of comment among officers altogether unconnected with the regiment.

In the infantry, there were eight companies of Poorbeeahs. In each company there were eighty Sepoys, a subadar, a jemadar, and the usual proportion of non-commissioned officers. Besides these, there were three companies of Bheels, each constituted as above, but only numbering seventy men. The Bheels, it should be observed, are a race inhabiting that part of India, and had of course no sympathy whatever with the Oude Sepoys, or Poorbeeahs, in the movements lately made. The Bheels are in a semi-barbarous state, many of them without any culture at all, and very much addicted, like all semi-savage races, to predatory and unsettled habits.

The usual proportion of men, viz., fifteen per troop and company, were absent on furlough at the time of the mutiny; some of these never joined, though a few of the sowars gave themselves up to General Cortland in the Hissar district. The Jodhpore Legion belonged, as I have before observed, to the same class of troops as the Gwalior and Kotah contingents and other forces of a similar kind located in many parts of Rajpootana and Central and Southern India. Maintained by the sovereigns of certain independent States, in accordance with treaties made between them and the British Government, they were officered from the British-Indian army, equipped and drilled on the English system. The object with which these forces were established was, on the side of the British Government, to secure itself and its subjects from annoyances arising out of political disorders in neighbouring territories, while the independent chiefs agreed to pay the expenses of these establishments ostensibly for the sake of the additional security thus afforded to their own power and thrones; in reality, because they could not help themselves. The men were mostly recruited from the same part of the country as that which the Bengal Sepoys of the regular native army came from, and the battalions thus employed, though under various designations, were, in fact, a part and parcel of the Bengal army. They were officered on what used to be the system of the Bengal irregular troops, that is to say, each regiment would have merely its (European) commandant, second in command, and adjutant, all officers of the line, taken from their legitimate duties with the corps on whose rolls their names were borne, and enjoying higher salaries than they would have received in their own regiments; the appointments to these corps, legions, and contingents were much sought after, and highly prized by the army in general. The duty was light and pleasant, the post considered an honourable one, and the pay good.

On the 19th of August, a company of the infantry branch of the legion which had formed a portion of the detachment at Nusseerabad arrived at a place called Auadra, which is two miles from the foot of the ghât or mountain pass leading up to Aboo. This company had been sent for with a view of holding in check a rebel chief, called the Rowa Thakoor, in that neighbourhood. A troop of the cavalry of the legion had arrived some days before, and were distributed in small parties in the different villages to protect the road from Deesa to Aboo.

Aboo is the highest peak in the Aravelli chain, which extends from the Vindhya range of mountains, till it merges in the rocky hills around Delhi. Being at its most elevated summit 5000 feet above the level of the sea, the site was fixed upon as a sanitarium in 1847. It is forty miles from Deesa, a military cantonment garrisoned always by a European force, in Guzerat, and the territory of a Mahometan prince, called the Nawab of Pahlumpore, at whose court a political agent from the Bombay Government always resides. Aboo is a very sacred place in the eyes of the Hindoos and Jains especially, which sect have a magnificent place of pilgrimage and worship upon the mountain. 'Beyond controversy,' says Colonel Tod, 'the most superb of all the temples of India, and there is not an edifice except the Taj Mahal that can approach it.'

On the afternoon of the 20th, Captain Hall was at Auadra giving orders for the distribution of a detachment to certain villages which were to be occupied. This party had marched in heavy rain from Erinpoora, and men, and tents, and baggage were all well soaked, but the former appeared in good spirits, and there was nothing to show that they intended misbehaviour, much less mutiny. After making all necessary arrangements, giving his final orders, and spending half-an-hour or so in conversation with the native officers of the detachment, Captain Hall returned towards Aboo; on his way he met a havildar from the Aboo guard, named Gozan Sing, a Rajpoot, who said he was going to see some of his comrades in the detachment. It was afterwards discovered that he had been deputed to manage the attack which was to come off the following morning.

The European force on Aboo, as has been observed before, consisted only of about thirty or thirty-five men of the 83rd Regiment, who had been sent to the sanitarium for the recovery of their health. Of these, a corporal and four men were posted at the school, and the remainder were in the barracks, which were a long distance from the rest of the settlement, out of sight of any of the houses, and in bad weather out of hearing.

The morning of the 21st of August was thick and hazy, and there was nothing to tempt people out of their beds; for residents in this cool climate are not forced, like those who live in the plains, to rise early and take their daily out-of-door exercise before the sun gets up. Under cover of the dense fog, and bent on their unholy enterprise, the band of murderers who had been left the evening before at Auadra by Captain Hall crept up the hill. It was a glorious work they were engaged in, the gods favoured them, and veiled the light of heaven with such a thick haze that they could crawl like serpents, unobserved to the very door of the building where their intended victims lay sleeping, unconscious of all danger, but relying on that Providence which had watched over the safety of so many of their countrymen during the late disturbances. The first thing was to overpower the handful of sick and invalid soldiers that occupied the barrack, and the work of slaughter among the defenceless women and children, deprived of their protectors, would be comparatively easy. This business they would take first, and having despatched this, they would then enjoy the luxury of crime. They near the barrack, and look stealthily through the haze. Are the soldiers stirring? No, not a sound—all silent as night, and almost as dark; the solitary sentry cannot see two yards before him. Now then is the time; a volley poured through the doors and windows cannot fail to accomplish the destruction of all within. Their muskets are all loaded—no need to betray their proximity by the ringing of even one ramrod—they are ready—the word is given, and the astonished soldiers start out of their sleep, awakened by the unwonted sounds of musketry so close to them, and the still rarer spectacle of bullets pouring through the windows and doors, and even the slenderly built walls of their temporary barrack. What can it be—a mutiny? they are attacked. Again and again ring out the sharp reports of the muskets discharged close to them, and by unseen hands. They fly to their arms—true to their natural instincts as English soldiers—they have loaded in a trice, and an answering volley from the barrack, fired in the direction the shots came from, tell that the little band of heroes, though weak and sickly, have got their arms, and know how to use them. The result was singular but satisfactory; one mutineer fell, and the rest—ran away.

Among the very few officers at that time residing on the hill was Captain Hall, commanding the legion. It was a great point with the mutineers to effect his destruction, as if he were killed, the number of gentlemen able to bear arms would be diminished by one, and the loss of one among so few would be severely felt; so, while the main body were engaged in what they thought would be an easy destruction of the soldiers in the barracks, a party, headed by subadar Mihrwan Sing, a jemadar adjovdia, marched silently through the mist to Captain Hall's house, and extended their line along the front of it. By word of command from the leader, they fired a volley through the windows and doors, just as the others had done into the barracks. Captain Hall and his family were aroused from sleep, like the soldiers, by strange sounds of the cracking of glass, and splintering of the woodwork of the doors. The house was raised from the level of the surrounding ground, so most of the shots struck high; and as the mutineers did not venture too close, or to surround the building, an escape was effected from the rear into the school. The state of the weather prevented the small guard at the school from hearing the firing or the alarm which was sounded at the barracks, but turned out and loaded the instant they became aware of Captain Hall's position. Shortly afterwards, a party arrived from the barracks and gave an account of what had occurred there.

Mr. A. Lawrence, of the Civil Service, son of Brigadier-General Lawrence, who was residing with his mother and sisters at Aboo, heard the firing, and ran towards Captain Hall's house to find out the cause; he was seen, fired at, and severely wounded in the thigh.

The alarm was speedily communicated to the other residents. Captain Hall and Dr. Young, the medical officer of the depôt, took five men with them and went off in the direction of the Sepoys' lines, and after some sharp firing, drove the rebels down the hill. The dense fog prevented much loss being inflicted, and the damp caused many of the muskets to miss fire. Owing to the small number of men present, any attempt at pursuit was deemed useless and unadvisable, but measures were immediately taken to collect all the English residents at the sanitarium in the school, the church hard by being used as a hospital. It was probable that the mutiny would extend to Deesa, and that another attempt would be made upon the little isolated band of Europeans on Mount Aboo; so they lost no time in fortifying the school, and making the best of their position, determined to fight it out to the last.

The whole work was done by the small party of the 83rd, whose excellent conduct throughout the crisis was brought to the notice of Government.

It was not likely that the quiet little station of Erinpoora, where the head-quarters of the legion were stationed, would escape the general conflagration. The lines occupied by the eight companies of Poorbeeah Sepoys faced the south, with the mainguard to the front in the centre, flanked, as is generally the case, by the bells of arms; to the right of these lines, and a little to the front, stood the bazaar where the Sepoys purchased their daily food; to the left were two little bungalows, occupied by the quartermaster-sergeant and the gun-sergeant; to the left of these, the magazine and the two 9-pounder guns attached to the legion; to the left again stood the bungalow occupied by the sergeant-major; and in front of these, extending at right angles to the row of buildings already mentioned, were the cavalry, and to the front of them the Bheel lines. The hospital was at the rear of the sergeant-major's bungalow; and to the rear of the whole space of ground thus occupied, were the officers' houses and compounds; the commandant's being in the left centre, or in rear of the quartermaster-sergeant's and gun-sergeant's bungalows, the adjutant's to the left of the commandant's; on the right was the house belonging to the second in command, and beyond this the medical officer's. The rear guard was immediately behind the compound belonging to the second in command, Captain Black, at this time absent with the detachment at Nusseerabad; and to the rear of the whole was a winding nullah, or dry bed of a stream, intersected by the road to Pallee, running due north.

The only European inhabitants at this time at Erinpoora were Lieutenant Conolly, the adjutant of the legion, and some of the sergeants attached to the legion, with their families, whose names I do not know.

The mutineers from Aboo, who gave out as they descended the hill, after their discomfiture at the hands of the few resolute men they had attacked in so dastardly a manner, that they had massacred the whole European population in the sanitarium, did not reach Erinpoora till the 23rd, but the fame of their glorious deeds preceded them, and what was more probable, their comrades at Erinpoora were aware beforehand of their intentions, and prepared to co-operate.

The first intimation of the intended outbreak appears to have been conveyed to Lieutenant Conolly by one of his men, named Macdoon Bux, who received a letter from the Mount Aboo party, detailing what had occurred. As soon as there was light enough to see, Lieutenant Conolly, on the following morning, mounted his horse, and rode towards the parade-ground. Here there were not wanting symptoms to show that the spirit of mutiny and disorder had infected the troops. The gunners were running to their guns, and shouted to Conolly to keep off; he then rode straight in the direction of the Bheel lines, and had consequently to pass the cavalry parade-ground. Here he was disgusted at seeing the sowars, who were considered more stanch than the infantry, galloping about in a disorderly and irregular manner. He called to the woordee major (non-commissioned staff officer), and told him to get the men under arms, but not to move; but orders were no longer attended to. He then reached the lines occupied by the Bheels. These men, as has been before remarked, had no sympathy with the mutineers' cause, and were therefore thought trustworthy; they were indeed ready and orderly, but the guns were loaded, and the whole of the remainder of the legion under arms, and the Bheels, even with the best intentions in the world, were powerless to act. Conolly ordered them to remain in their present position, and galloped off towards the infantry, to see, as a last resort, if it was possible to induce any of them to return to their duty, but they were mad with excitement, and would listen to nothing. He then determined to try the effect of persuasion on the gunners; and being joined by the woordee major of the cavalry, and a few sowars, he rode at a foot pace towards the artillery. On his approach, the gunners shouted to him to keep off; he raised his hand, and kept advancing, when they wheeled the guns round, pointed the muzzles at him, and held the portfires ready. He halted, turned his horse's head, and changing his direction, rode again towards the guns, taking them in flank. Upon this, several of the mutinous sowars galloped down in front of the guns, between them and their officer, and pointing their carbines at him, threatened to fire, crying out, 'Go back, go back, or we will fire;' some six or seven Sepoys also at the same time levelled their muskets at him. There was a short halt, when Conolly called out, 'What are you all at?—are there none on my side?' A few sowars, among whom was one named Nusseeroodeen, and another named Elahu Bux, then rode up, with the object apparently of protecting him. The Sepoys had by this time began plundering the houses in the cantonments, and as nothing else could be effected, Conolly, with the small party still faithful to him, repaired to the cavalry lines, and sent for the sergeants and their families. These poor people, terror-stricken and alarmed, had already commenced their flight on foot—a vain and useless measure, which could have had but one result, viz., their destruction. Here, then, the little band of Englishmen and women were collected in the cavalry lines, utterly helpless, surrounded by bloodthirsty villains, every instant plunging deeper and deeper into their career of crime, from which there was no stepping back, and becoming more and more intoxicated with the unbridled indulgence of their passion for plunder, lust, and rapine. Now was felt the influence which one man possessed of strong moral courage can exert over others.

An angry and noisy discussion ensued between the troopers. Many of those who had hitherto befriended Conolly and his little band of associates seemed inclined to desert them in their extremity, and leave them to their fate: what that would be, there was very little room for doubt. But a rassaldar named

Abbas Ali came forward, took off his turban, and laid it at the feet of the more boisterous mutineers, and declared that no hand of violence should be laid upon one of the captives till his life had first been sacrificed. Another, named Abdool Ali (and their names deserve to be recorded), did the same, and, by the courageous conduct of these stanch friends, Conolly's life was, humanly speaking, saved. Macdoon Bux, too, was willing to do his best; but, for some reason with which I am unacquainted, he was very unpopular among the mutineers, and had no influence whatever with them. Abbas Ali's example, however, was subsequently followed by several of his comrades and subordinates, and, although they would not allow Conolly to leave them, they, to the number of forty-five, swore either to save his life or die in his defence. He then endeavoured to persuade them to leave the place; but this they refused to do, with the strange inconsistency so often observed among the mutineers at the time. They offered, however, to let him ride off and save his life, but he could not leave the poor sergeants and their families to their fate. While he remained, his influence among the men might avail to save the lives of the whole party; had he resolved to save his own and sacrifice theirs, he might have done so; but this was a course of action not to be thought of for a moment by the noble-hearted British officer. With his companions in misfortune he would die or live, as it pleased Providence to ordain. The sowars, indeed, offered to take the children, but said it would be impossible to save their parents.

After a few hours had been spent in this way, the artillery brought their guns down upon the cavalry lines, and threatened to open fire upon the little party of fugitives and their defenders if all the horses in the lines were not immediately brought out and picketed under the guns. There was no help for it; indeed, the men did not seem inclined to resist; so they took all the horses away, and picketed them on the parade-ground, close to the artillery, as desired. When evening came, and that long, long day drew to a close, the captives,—for such they now were,—were brought out on the parade-ground too; a small tent, called a rowty, was pitched, and in it they passed a wretched, sleepless night—three men, two women, and five children.

Next morning, the band of murderers from Auadra and Aboo marched into the station in a triumphant manner, and were greeted with a salute. They told the story of their deeds, which they, no doubt, misrepresented strangely, and after being dismissed, came in knots of fives and sixes to stare at the English prisoners; but the faithful sowars kept jealous watch over them, and would not allow them to be maltreated. Mihrwan Sing, subadar, who seems to have taken a very prominent part in the infamous proceedings, came and gave vent to his feelings in a most undignified manner, walking about and shouting at Conolly that 'Captain Hall was a liar, and so was he.'

That evening they consented to let the sergeants and their families go, and at first declared they would give Conolly his liberty too, but on this point they subsequently changed their minds; so his companions, for whose sake he had risked his life, were to be suffered to depart, while he remained alone prepared for the worst. The Sepoys then demanded that he should be given up to them, but Abbas Ali, well supported by his men, stoutly refused, so they went and consoled themselves by setting fire to all the houses in the place, and completing the plunder and ruin of the once favourite little station. The sergeants and their families, though they had been promised their liberty, were still kept captives; and they sat up the whole night watching from the door of their tent the conflagration of the houses where they had passed so many happy days.

Next morning, all except Conolly were allowed to go; and Mihrwan Sing, promoted to the rank of General, ordered a march. Conolly was mounted on his horse, but carefully guarded; as he rode along, however, he could not help being amused at the strange scene presented to his view. The remainder of his adventures, and the account of his escape, will be best given in his own words, extracted from a letter to Captain Black.

'Such a scene of confusion I never saw; some Sepoys firing at Bheels, they shot seven poor wretches on the parade-ground, who, I declare, were only looking at the novel scene. During the day we halted. The first day we marched to ——, and a greater rabble never crossed country than our once smart legion; not a Sepoy hardly saluted me. I was taken to Abbas Ali's tent at ——, and the infantry were a little behind, when a tremendous row commenced. Some Meenas made a rush at the carts; the infantry thought it was an attack; away went the cavalry to see to matters, cut up a few Bheels, and, seeing no one else, pulled up to look about them. Another row and rush towards where I was standing near my saddled horse. I can't say I was desperately alarmed, for all hope of life I had cast aside some hours before, when we marched. The rush towards me was caused by some amiable Sepoys taking the opportunity to make a run at me. Abbas Ali and his men saw it, and were soon between us; but I cannot enter into details of self; once again they attempted to get at me at Doola. What made them so mad was, that my strenuous attempts to seduce the cavalry had been made known to Mihrwan Sing, and he swore I should die. At Doola they had three or four rows—councils they called them—aboutme. At last, Mihrwan Sing and the other beauties, seeing Abbas Ali would not give me up, said I might go solus. Next morning, they sent again to say, no, I should not go. However, Abbas Ali and his men surrounded my charpoy all night; we none of us slept, and on the morning of the 27th, when the force was ready, the guns were loaded, the infantry shouldered arms, and I was brought up. I was told to ride to the front; poor Dokul Sing, the havildar-major, and some others, ran out blubbering; Abbas Ali and Abdool Ali, rode up on each side, made me low salaams, and told me to ride for it; that not a sowar should be allowed to interfere with my retreat. My three sowars, who, I have forgotten to say, had stuck to me as if I had been their brother since the very beginning, by a preconcerted plan, were ordered to see me off a little way. I could not help giving a farewell wave of the hand to the infantry in irony; they shouted and laughed, the band struck up, and that is the last I saw of the legion. I rode right in to Erinpoora with three sowars; I came straight here, and the people seemed ready to eat me with joy. The names of the three sowars are, Nusseeroodeen, second troop; Elahu Bux, third troop (the man who used to ride my grey); and Momin Khan, first troop. They left everything behind, and, I must say, are three as fine fellows as I wish to see. By-the-by, the cavalry said if I would agree to turn Mussulman, to a man they would follow me. Very kind of them. They offered me money when I was coming away, and also on the march. I took twenty rupees from Abbas Ali; now I wish I had taken my pay: they twice offered it. Now is our time, the legion is divided. Jawan Sing, golundaz, and his party, about seven other golundaz (gunners), will play the infantry a trick if they can. I have told Jawan Sing I will myself give him 500 rupees if he breaks with the infantry. Abbas Ali, the havildar-major, and Abdool Ali, are in danger on my account, and they are kept with their men under the guns night and day. I feel most glad to think I did them as much harm as I could. Macdoon Bux had a musket put to his breast for letting me ride with my sword on. I was a bone of contention. I have this morning sent a sharp kossid to Abbas Ali, telling him, for his own sake, to try and communicate with Mason, who, I believe, is at Pallee, and to whom I have written to try and communicate with Abbas Ali.'

Abbas Ali, as Conolly had advised, did communicate with Captain Monck Mason, who was, however, at Jodhpore, and not at Pallee at the time. The terms the rebel rassaldar offered were, to desert with a large body of his own men (cavalry), and the guns, and bring the party into Jodhpore, provided he and his comrades were pardoned, and reinstated in the service of Government.

We had a long and anxious discussion as to whether it would be right or not to accept these terms; but unfortunately Captain Monck Mason's hands were tied by one of those injudicious orders, so many of which were issued at the time by Lord Canning, who, residing at Calcutta, and surrounded by counsellors who knew little or nothing of the state of Upper India, and were notoriously unfit for the emergency, could not by any possibility judge what course of policy it was best to pursue in remote parts of the empire, separated from the seat of Government by an immense distance, and with communication often stopped for months together. An order had shortly before been issued that no officer was, on any pretext whatever, to make terms with mutineers as long as they had arms in their hands. This precaution was undoubtedly necessary in some instances, where incompetent men might have done the State incalculable injury by an injudicious exercise of independent authority; but exceptions ought to have been made; and certainly an officer who was considered fit to hold the responsible position of representative of the British Government at the court of an independent sovereign, should have been entrusted with power to do as he thought best in an emergency of the kind alluded to.

The responsibility of acting in the face of an order of this sort is very great, for all depends on the result of the policy pursued. Had Abbas Ali's terms been acceded to, and disaster followed, Captain Monck

Mason's prospects in the service would have been ruined; had matters turned out well, he would have had the satisfaction of doing the country a service, but he was sure, notwithstanding, of incurring the displeasure of his superiors, from Lord Canning downwards. There was no time to refer to a higher authority, and at length it was determined to be on the safe side, and a message was sent back to say that the political agent was precluded from accepting the terms Abbas Ali had offered, by a recent stringent prohibition from the Governor-General, but that if he (Abbas Ali) would act as a faithful soldier and servant of the British Government, and weaken the cause of the rebels by deserting, as he proposed, there was no doubt that his case would be viewed leniently by the Governor-General, and he would probably receive an unconditional pardon, and a suitable reward, but to treat with rebels in arms was forbidden.

There can be no question that, as a general rule, the British Government could not, without great injury to its prestige, and without initiating a ruinous precedent, so far lower itself in the eyes of its enemies, and of its allies, as to treat with rebels actually under arms. But it is impossible to establish any broad general principle of action upon which Government officers, in high and responsible posts, are bound to act in an emergency like that which had befallen us, without running the risk of doing the State a great injury. With large and distant provinces in rebellion, communication intercepted, and all that remained of the British empire being small and isolated bodies of men, forced to act in a great measure independently of each other, while every day produced some unlooked-for change in the features of the rebellion, which, for all we knew, had only begun to develope itself, the best course for the Governor-General to have pursued was to have sanctioned and encouraged as much as possible the exercise of independent and irresponsible power by officers in important posts, who had sufficient talent, energy, and courage to remain at them, instead of tying their hands, and fettering them by rules and regulations passed in Government House, Calcutta. Abbas Ali's case certainly deserved consideration. He had rebelled, it is true, but he had saved the lives of Conolly and of all the European residents at Erinpoora. He had seen his error, and was anxious to atone. Had his request been attended to, there is no doubt that he could have succeeded in doing what he promised, namely, inducing a large party to secede from the rebel cause, and bring away the guns by which they made themselves a terror to the whole country.

There was another reason, however, which had some weight in Captain Monck Mason's deliberations, and that was, whether it would be safe to trust a strong party, even of professedly repentant rebels, with guns at the capital. It was no small source of gratification to the raja and to us that the company of the legion which had been quartered at Jodhpore had been sent away some time before the occurrence of these events, and it seemed impolitic to bring a much larger and stronger party back again to the very spot where, of all others, they could do most mischief; for our safety at Jodhpore consisted mainly in the fact of our being without regular troops. A small party of sowars belonging to the cavalry of the legion had been left behind to act as orderlies, &c. There were not more than ten or fifteen, but it was deemed advisable to disarm them. The ministers undertook to do this, aided by the armed rabble which formed the garrison of the fort, and protected the Agency and palace. Such an utter contempt did the disciplined soldiers of the legion feel for the raja's troops, that it was doubtful if, even isolated as they were, they would yield up their arms quietly to a force numerically very much superior. It was kept as secret as possible, but they got wind of our intentions somehow; their horses were ready saddled, and the instant the move was made, they mounted and rode off, pursued by the king's sowars. One or two offered resistance, and one, I believe, was eventually killed, but the greater part escaped, after riding right through the city, and joined the main body of rebels then marching upon the Pallee road towards that place, in the direction of Beeawr and Nusseerabad.

The consequences of Abbas Ali's request being refused were very serious, and to none more so than to Captain Mason himself.

About midway between Pallee and Erinpoora was the territory and stronghold of an independent chief, called Awah. This Thakoor had been in rebellion against the raja for a long time past. The original cause of discord was the interference, as he considered it, with his feudal privileges. Sir H. Lawrence, who was agent for the Governor-General for the Rajpootana States before he went to Lucknow, had throughout his public career made it an especial part of his policy to protect as much as possible the oppressed lower classes from the encroachments of the upper. He acted on this principle from a sense of duty—a feeling that guided all the actions of this great and good man. But it may fairly be questioned whether in some cases he did not push this policy—a policy founded on the lessons of civilization and the Gospel—a little too far, especially in those instances where the state of the country, long-established prejudices, and customs, and habits, suited only to races in a semi-barbarous state, militated against the introduction of any system of modern social progression or Christianity. He looked upon it as the peculiar duty of the British Government to civilize and regenerate India, and ardent as he was in the cause of all that could promote improvement, or extend the blessings of good government to oppressed and subject races, and raise the people from the state of degradation into which centuries of misrule and tyranny had thrown them, he exerted his influence, as agent and representative of the British Government among the independent provinces of Rajpootana, to carry out reforms which had been effected, as far as they could be effected, already in our own provinces, and with the best results.

One of the old feudal customs of Rajpootana was that no artisan or serf, as the lower class might well be called, could leave the territory of his own immediate chief or Thakoor, and go and settle in that of another, without permission. These men formed in fact part of the property inherited by the feudal lords from their ancestors, and were regularly attached to the soil. Sir H. Lawrence was determined to put a stop to a custom that rendered the condition of the lower classes so analogous to one of slavery, and directed the various political agents at the different courts to exert themselves to break down this remnant of barbarism and barrier against the march of civilization, with all possible firmness and forbearance. Two men, money-changers or money-lenders I believe by trade, attached to the territory of the Thakoor of Awah, had become involved in debt, and determined upon shifting their quarters—further residence in Awah being inconvenient, owing to the importunity of their creditors: they accordingly packed up their goods and chattels one fine morning, and went off to a neighbouring estate, where they settled themselves to their trade, confiding in the power and influence of the Governor-General's agent to protect them from any evil consequences that might result from their transgression of an old-established feudal custom, under which their fathers and forefathers had lived for countless generations. The Awah Thakoor resented this interference with his privileges; he looked to his own raja for support, and would not acknowledge the right of interference on the part of the officers of the British Government. The raja of course would not put himself in opposition to the paramount ruler of Hindostan, and the proud and unyielding Rajpoot chieftain threw off his allegiance, refused to pay his revenue, and entered on a course of open rebellion. Other circumstances occurred to widen the breach between the king and his unmanageable subject, and the dispute had been some time standing when the Jodhpore Legion mutinied, and marched up the road towards Pallee; on their way they had to pass through the territories of the rebel Thakoor, and within a few miles of his fort.

As it was well known that ever since the beginning of the disturbances which spread over India like an infectious disease, the Thakoor of Awah had been collecting arms, men, and supplies in his fort, strengthening the place, and exhibiting other symptoms of a warlike intention, we no sooner saw the course taken by the legion than we concluded at once that the whole plan was preconcerted, and that the mutinous soldiery would go straight to Awah, and place themselves under the orders of that chief. It was indeed said that he had sent letters to the men of the legion before they mutinied, calling upon them to rise and to join him, but the story is, I suspect, without foundation. However that may be, the camp of the mutineers was standing for several days in front of the walls of Awah before they and the rebel Thakoor made common cause. It was said they could not come to terms; and it was supposed that the Thakoor was afraid to admit so strong a party of armed men inside his fort, which would be placing himself completely in their power, without having some guarantee for their good behaviour. On the other hand, the mutineers had much to gain by placing at their head a chief whose name, family, and position in the country would give them a prestige, which they could not otherwise possibly hope to have. The Raja of Marwar was unpopular; his fort and palace were supposed to be rich in hoarded treasures, jewels, and other things most acceptable to an armed rabble thirsting for plunder; many of the other Thakoors in Marwar were disposed to join any leader who raised the standard of rebellion, and set up a usurper on the throne, and, just as I had overheard the sowars saying a month or two before, there was not a village in Marwar that would not lend its quota of men to aid a rebel cause. All these circumstances were arguments for them to remain. Delhi, the focus of rebellion, was a long distance off, and it was more than probable they would have to encounter British troops on their way thither, and so they determined to stay, and see whether it was not possible to come to some favourable terms with the Awah chief.

One morning, while this was going on, I went into the verandah (the place where Captain Mason used to receive his native visitors and transact business with them, the whole of the interior of the house being given up to the families residing there), and saw a stranger just rising from his chair preparatory to taking his departure. He was a fine-looking man, though clad in no prepossessing costume—for he had ridden many miles that day, and had many more to ride—but his appearance and bearing were martial, his look was proud, and as he made his salaam on leaving, there was a kind of sorrowful yet defiant expression in his countenance that could not pass unnoticed. This man was a Rajpoot of good family, an emissary from the Awab Thakoor, who had just ridden in from the rebel chieftain's fort to have a last interview with the British political agent, and make a last offer of terms on behalf of his master before he decided to throw away the scabbard, enlist the mutineers of the legion, and wage open war with the raja. If certain conditions were acceded to, his lord, he was empowered to say, was prepared to return to his allegiance, would keep his gates closed against the mutineers, and, if co-operated with by either a British force or the king's troops, would open fire upon their camp, which was within gunshot of the walls. But unfortunately, as in the case of Abbas Ali, Captain Monck Mason was unable to accept the terms offered, or to treat with rebels in arms. In this instance the Thakoor steadily refused to hold any communication with the king, and the latter had not empowered Captain Monck Mason to hold any friendly communication with him, or to offer or accept any terms; so that the only answer that officer could give was, that he had no authority whatever to treat with the rebel chief, whose quarrel was as yet with his own sovereign and not with the British Government, and as the king's resolution had been taken, and frequently expressed, to hold out no hopes of reconciliation unless the Thakoor threw himself upon his mercy, confessed his error, and made the only practical reparation he could, by paying his arrears of revenue, now amounting to a considerable sum, no communication whatever should pass between them. The messenger received his answer and withdrew; five minutes afterwards Captain Monck Mason bethought himself of something else he had to say, and sent to recall him, but he was gone. We very shortly after heard that the two parties had come to terms, and that the mutinous Sepoys and the rebel chief were determined to stand or fall together.

CHAPTER XIII.

PROGRESS OF THE MUTINEERS—ANAR SING—ROUTE OF THE KING'S TROOPS—DEATH OF THE POLITICAL AGENT—POSITION AT JODHPORE—RETREAT OF GENERAL LAWRENCE.

AS soon as it was known that the mutineers of the legion intended marching through the territory of Marwar, the raja made every exertion to stop their progress. He declared positively that they should never get safe out of (if once they entered) his dominions. But though ardent himself in the cause of the British Government, his feelings were not shared in either by the populace or his soldiers. The infection had spread even to the undisciplined rabble that went by the name of the royal troops; and as they had been known openly to declare on a previous occasion, when first called upon to act against the Nusseerabad mutineers, that they sympathized with them, and thought them justified in adopting the course they had taken for the protection of their religion and caste, which they believed had really been threatened by the British Government, it was not likely that they would act heartily against the enemy to which they were now opposed. There was an additional reason certainly for their good behaviour on this occasion which did not exist in the last; they were now called upon to fight in the territory of their own sovereign, and by his order, and under their own leaders, against a foreign force, whereas they had before been summoned to assist an allied power beyond the limits of their own country.

The raja had a famous soldier and most trustworthy servant in Anar Sing. This man held the highest military post in the raja's service, that of killadar, or commandant of the fort and palace; he was also general-in-chief of the royal army. The raja had brought him from Guzerat when he first came to ascend the throne of Marwar, and being thus partly an alien, that is, not a regular Marwari, Anar Sing was less popular among the soldiers of Marwar than he otherwise would have been, at the same time that he enjoyed on this account a greater share of his master's confidence. And this very trust which the king reposed in him would have been sufficient of itself to arouse a feeling of jealousy among the nobles, even if he had not been partially a foreigner. He was a tall, well-made man, with that peculiarly martial bearing so characteristic of Rajpoot chiefs of high descent. Nor did his appearance belie his character, for in action he was bold and undaunted as a lion. Captain Monck Mason, who had known him intimately for many years, had the highest regard for his character. He had seen a good deal of him, too, in his military capacity, as he had been out with him on one or two expeditions against rebel Thakoors and Dacoits. On one occasion they had hunted to earth some leaders of rebels or robbers, or both, of whom they were in pursuit; the outlaws took up their position in an underground hole or apartment, to which there was but one opening, through a small door; here they were determined to sell their lives as dearly as they could, and, being well-armed and desperate, there was no doubt that many lives would be sacrificed before they were overpowered. Anar Sing was not to be deterred by any idea of danger, and waving his sword in the air, with his shield well poised on his left arm, he made a dash at the entrance, and in one moment would have been engaged in deadly conflict, against great odds, with the outlaws. But his life was too valuable to be sacrificed thus rashly, and Captain Monck Mason, who was happily close by, seized the daring chief by the arm, and by main force held him back. What the soldier would have attempted to accomplish at the risk of his life, the British officer succeeded in doing by diplomacy; he held a parley with the chiefs inside the door, and induced them at length to yield without further bloodshed.

The raja at first conceived such a contempt, in which we all shared, for the disorderly rabble, as we believed the mutineers to be, that he would not suffer Anar Sing to leave his post in the fort, and take the head of the force that was already in the field. But it soon became apparent that the legion, though without its European officers, was a great deal more than a match for the king's troops led by any inferior chief, so Anar Sing was sent, reluctantly enough, by the king, though he himself, unconscious of treachery, and naturally fond of fighting, gladly accepted the post assigned to him, and led the king's troops against the legion, then encamped under the walls of the Awah fort.

Several days elapsed without any decisive steps being taken. The Rajpoots have a way of fighting now very different from former days, if history be true, and would not leave the beaten track which the custom of the country has rendered a second nature, for all the ardour of their general or the impatience of the political agent. In vain we waited for intelligence of an attack; day after day the post brought in the regular despatches from the army for the king, but no news of active operations. At first the royal troops entrenched themselves at Pallee in a favourable position, in which the enemy would have attacked them at a disadvantage; but the latter had no idea of doing anything so unwise, and as the mutineers would not come to the king's troops, the latter were obliged to go to them. They broke up their camp, left their entrenchments, and took up a position in close proximity to the rebel camp. Here, in accordance with all the maxims of Rajpoot warfare, they began to entrench themselves, and waited for something to turn up. The delay was unaccountable, though subsequent events threw some light upon it. General Lawrence at last got impatient, and wrote a very severe letter to the raja, a copy of which was also sent to Anar Sing, in which he upbraided the king with lukewarmness in his alliance, and taunted the army with their cowardice for not having effected anything, saying they were dancing attendance on the rebels like orderlies. This letter had the desired effect of bringing matters to a crisis, but it stung Anar Sing to the quick, and wounded the feelings of the brave old chief, who determined not to survive the disgrace should he be unable to accomplish the destruction of the enemy. At the same time a British officer, Lieutenant Heathcote, the deputy-assistant quartermaster-general of the Rajpootana field force, was sent to the royal camp to give the advantage of his advice, and add the prestige and weight which the presence of a British officer among native troops always carries with it.

As the two forces were close to one another, this officer at the first glance at their position strongly recommended pickets being posted in front of the camp to give the alarm in the event of a sudden attack being made, and retard the advance of the enemy until the rest of the troops were under arms. The officers with the force promised ready compliance, but the pickets were never posted, or, if posted, betrayed their trust; the latter supposition is the most probable. Anyhow, one morning, just before daylight, the hour usually selected by Asiatics for sudden attacks, or 'chappaos,' as they are called, the whole camp was thrown into confusion by a sudden advance of the enemy. Anar Sing called his men to their arms, and took up his post with the guns that were in position in the most exposed part of the field. But he was ill supported; his men, either from cowardice or treachery, fled in confusion, after a show of resistance which neither the example or persuasion of Anar Sing or Lieutenant Heathcote, who exerted himself in restoring order and trying to induce the men to stand, could turn into an effectual attempt to hold the entrenchment. The rout was complete. Lieutenant Heathcote was forced to mount his horse and gallop from the field. Anar Sing, surrounded by a small, very small band of kindred spirits, sold their lives as dearly as they could, and were cut down at the guns, the whole of which, with the camp equipage and military stores, such as they were, fell into the hands of the enemy.

The king was deeply distressed at the death of his favourite officer. We paid him a visit two days afterwards, and he could not allude to his loss without shedding tears. He had, he said, eaten nothing since the disastrous intelligence was brought to him, but had spent the time in pacing restlessly up and down his apartment, till he yielded to the solicitations of his attendants, and endeavoured to console himself by drinking two bottles of beer!

For some time after this the rebels and mutineers had it all their own way. The Thakoor exerted himself in strengthening his fort; the king's troops were scattered, and it was evident that they had no intention of doing anything. It was not till the middle of September that Brigadier-General Lawrence was able to take the field with a small force consisting of 150 men of H.M.'s 83rd, three horse artillery guns, weakly manned, a portion of the Mhairwarra battalion, and the 1st Bombay Lancers. A large force of the king's troops were to have co-operated with him, but their behaviour on the previous occasion showed that they were not to be trusted.

Captain Monck Mason resolved to go out to camp, and encourage the Raj troops and their officers by his presence. We expected that the affair would soon be over, and many indeed thought that the rebels would not remain in their stronghold till the arrival of the British troops, but would evacuate it, and take themselves off to the hills. It turned out, however, to be one of those numerous cases in which the fault so common among British officers was made, viz., that of despising their enemy. The king was most averse to Captain Monck Mason's going; he had a strange presentiment that some great disaster would ensue if the political agent left the capital, and made such strenuous and repeated exertions to dissuade him from the expedition that he once or twice almost changed his mind, and determined to remain at Jodhpore. He decided, however, at last, upon going, but had he not done so, a letter which was on its way from General Lawrence ordering him to repair to the camp, would on its arrival have settled his course of action. As it was, he started without knowing that he had been sent for. The king did not lose all hopes of dissuading him till the very last, and sent the ministers down to him late in the evening to convey a last remonstrance. I was present at the interview. Mason was inexorable, laughed at the idea of danger, and said that he should be back again in a day or two after witnessing the destruction of the rebel fort, and the defeat of the mutineers. The ministers shook their heads as they rose, saying, 'Awah is not so easily taken.' The last time I ever saw or spoke to Mason was a little later on the same evening before his departure, when he gave me final instructions, leaving me in charge of the Agency, and adding, as if he felt a presentiment that the advice might be needed, 'If anything happens, or you get very bad news, see to the protection of the Agency, and double the guards.' We heard nothing directly from him or from the camp for two or three days, but on the 19th September, as I was sitting in the office, it was announced to me that the ministers had come to see me. I knew that they must have some intelligence of great importance to communicate, otherwise the king would not have sent them to me, as I had no authority to transact business with them, and no political powers whatever. They were by my desire ushered in, and seated as usual on the occasions of their visits to the political agent. As soon as the attendants had left us alone, one of them, the spokesman, informed me they had been sent to communicate intelligence of such a distressing nature, that they could neither tell it, nor I hear it. It at once flashed across my mind something must have happened to Mason. I said, 'Captain Mason Sahib?' He replied by a nod of the head, and added, 'Yes, he is killed;' at the same time producing a letter from the vakeel in the camp, he proceeded to read the contents to me. A good deal of mystery still hangs about the circumstances that immediately led to the death of this gallant officer. The account communicated in the letter, and which was corroborated in a measure by further investigation was, that as Captain Monck Mason arrived in the neighbourhood of the fort, he dismounted from the camel he was riding, and proceeded a short distance on foot. Brigadier-General Lawrence's force was then engaged with the enemy, and (artillery) firing was going on. It appears he inquired of some one he met on the ground the direction in which the Brigadier-General was to be found, and went off towards the spot indicated, saying he was going to speak to the General, and would return to the place where he left his camel and attendants. He only took one pistol with him in his belt. He had not gone many yards before he was fired at from behind the bushes with which the ground was covered, and wounded in the breast. He retired, and sat down, and almost immediately after, a charge was made of a large body of the enemy's horse upon the wounded officer, who was immediately cut down and killed. His death was described in the letter as the result of the merest accident. But it is scarcely possible to believe that an officer to whom a skirmish or an action was no new thing, who was in full possession of his faculties, should so completely have mistaken the direction he was going in, as to have walked towards the enemy instead of towards the British position, especially when firing was actually going on. At the same time there was ample evidence to show that the spot where he fell had just before been ridden over by the General, accompanied by his staff; the enemy had selected that time, too, for making a flank movement upon the British right, and may have come accidentally upon the wounded officer. But by whom was he wounded? and how came the enemy's sharpshooters so far in advance of their position, and on the ground which the General had only just left? Whichever way the truth may lie makes, perhaps, but little difference now, for Captain Monck Mason died on the field of battle in the execution of his duty, as many as noble and brave, though none more so, had fallen before him, and have fallen since. The raja's idea was that treachery had been employed, as I heard him myself subsequently express that opinion.

My position was a painful one. I had no authority to act in any political capacity, yet it was certain that the intelligence of Captain Mason's death would occasion a great deal of excitement in the city and neighbourhood, and might be followed by most disastrous consequences. The distressing news would have to be communicated to Mrs. Mason and her children, the latter now orphans, and the more distressing it would be, as it was so totally unexpected and unlooked for. Still, was there not a chance that the intelligence was false? It was native intelligence, and that is proverbially untrustworthy. This was a straw to cling to, but nothing more. On a previous occasion, when disastrous news had arrived from Awah, of the rout of the king's troops and the death of Anar Sing, the regular dispatch had been preceded by vague rumours that assumed a greater character of exactitude every minute, and though we tried to disbelieve them, they proved but too true in the end. At any rate, I thought it better to delay to the very latest moment making public what had been reported, both because there was a shadow of a chance that it might turn out to be an exaggerated report in the end, and because I hoped in the evening to receive intelligence of a complete victory having been gained by General Lawrence over the rebels, which we never doubted for an instant would be the result of his operations. People were evidently very much excited, though the ministers declared positively not a man knew what had happened, and that it had been kept a profound secret. I saw by one glance at the face of the first man who entered the office that he knew well enough what the ministers had come for, and what they had to tell. The news of the victory, I thought, would counterbalance in a great measure the bad effect which the death of the political agent under such suspicious circumstances must necessarily have on the public mind; and so, begging the ministers to maintain the strictest silence on the subject, at any rate till the dispatch expected in the evening arrived, I dismissed them. I sadly felt the want of some one to talk over matters and consult with, but there was no one. Mrs. Mason, whom I should have gladly consulted in every other emergency, and whose views were always the clearest and most correct, was the person from whom I most of all wished to conceal the truth; my own wife's health was in such a precarious state, that I dared not disturb her by even hinting at the disaster, and, to make the matter worse, Mrs. Mason, who had some presentiment or suspicion that intelligence of some kind had reached me, repeatedly asked if I had heard anything. I was forced to tell her that reports had come in, which, however, were not authenticated, and that we were quite certain to hear in the evening. At last that long day drew to a close, the dispatch had not arrived, but rumours came in plentifully as usual, in advance of the true report, and revealed more or less of its real character that was bad enough; instead of the news of the victory I was hoping for, came a report of a total defeat; they went so far as to say that Lawrence had been totally routed, and driven helter-skelter from the field. This I disbelieved; but it was quite plain that the operations had been unsuccessful, that the public mind was deeply agitated, and that the natives could scarce conceal their real pleasure at hearing of this additional blow that had been dealt to the already fallen prestige of British power.

That evening our party, with the exception of Mrs. Mason, who suspected something was amiss, and myself, were particularly merry. Captain Mason and Captain Denyss, one of his oldest and most intimate friends, were expected shortly, and great was the glee expressed at the anticipated meeting.

It was scarcely bearable; the merry laugh grated on my ear, the sprightly jest, so sadly out of tune with a heavy heart, jarred against my feelings; for he, the noble-hearted soldier, the doting husband, and the loving father they were laughing and talking about, was at the moment lying a lifeless corpse in the jungle. I rose and went to the office, on pretence of business, really to escape from conversation so unsuited to the time. Meanwhile, however, more accurate intelligence had arrived from the field of battle, brought in by numerous messengers, fugitives, and others; the thing became bruited abroad, and though we had yet received no letter, the servants all got hold of the story of Captain Monck Mason's death. As a matter of course, the ayah hinted to Mrs. Mason that something had occurred. The secret could no longer be kept: I was subjected to a searching, though short examination, and the truth, as far as I knew it, was revealed; still there was a hope, for till I had seen it on the authority of an English officer, I would not believe it. Half an hour later the expected letter arrived. It was from Captain Denyss, who accompanied General Lawrence on the occasion, and was intending to come over to Jodhpore, where his wife was residing. The same messenger brought letters to the widow, condoling with her for the loss she had suffered. The account given in the native letter which had been shown to me in the morning was mainly corroborated by the description given in Captain Denyss'. Lawrence had indeed been unsuccessful, but not to the extent reported; he had not taken the fort, but had retreated out of fire, and encamped before it. The rebels had shown fight well, and with the small force at his disposal, the Brigadier-General thought he would not be justified in attempting to storm the place; it was as much, indeed, as he could do to protect his baggage with the whole of the troops under his command. Whether he ought ever to have set out with such a small force is another question; or whether, having once taken the field, it would not have been better to have sacrificed his baggage or anything rather than leave the work undone, is another: it is certain that the failure had a very bad political effect, and I believe that if Lawrence had been left to himself, and not yielded to advice, he would have gone at the place at all hazards, and captured it. As it was, he remained a day or two in camp before it, and then returned to Nusseerabad and Beeawr, leaving the rebels triumphant.

The annals of Indian history record very many instances of places much stronger than Awah being taken by British troops against greater odds than those which Lawrence had to contend with. The real truth of the matter was, that he had to keep a sharp look out on friend as well as foe; with the exception of the few, very few white faces in his camp, he had not a soldier with him he could really trust. The men may have behaved well since, but at that time any general officer who trusted native troops of the line would have been highly culpable. Lawrence's position was a painful one. If he had delayed to take the field at all, there was no calculating the bad effect such inaction would have had on the country; if he took the field, he would have to march against a strong fortress and a powerful garrison with a mere handful of reliable troops.

His own instinct would have led him to make a rush at the place and take it at all hazards, and had he been acting in any subordinate capacity there is no doubt he would have done so; but he was not only a general officer in command of the troops in Rajpootana, but Governor-General's agent as well, and in this double character the responsibility of any step he took was infinitely increased. The small band of English soldiers he had with him was almost all that was available for the protection of the whole province; even had success attended his efforts, it would be necessarily accompanied by much loss, and the little band of Englishmen might have been so weakened as to be unable any longer to uphold British dominion in Rajpootana. Any great disaster then would have been followed by the loss of Ajmeré, the defection of all the independent chiefs, and probably the mutiny of the Bombay army. Few men have been placed in a more awkward position, and none ever made a retrograde movement in presence of an enemy more unwillingly than Brigadier-General Lawrence.

I may as well here give a brief conclusion to the story of the Jodhpore Legion. Soon after Brigadier General Lawrence's ill-starred expedition, the mutineers and the Thakoor seem to have had some dispute; at any rate, they separated, the former marching towards Delhi, and the latter remaining to bide the brunt in his stronghold. At Narnoul, on the borders of the Shekhawattee country, the legion was brought to action by Brigadier Gerrard's force, one of the pursuing columns detached after the fall of Delhi, and totally defeated. Brigadier Gerrard himself was killed; the cavalry of the legion fought well, but were cut up by the Carabineers, and that is the last that has been heard of them; the survivors probably dispersed, and went to their homes. Abbas Ali, the ressaldar, was pardoned by Lord Canning, as a special case, and after some time returned to Erinpoora, where he was residing in April this year, 1859, while his old officers were trying to get him reinstated in the service. He left the mutineers soon after they marched from Awah, and hid himself in the Bikaneer territory till he heard of his pardon. The three sowars who proved so faithful to Lieutenant Conolly were promoted. That officer, I may add, remains Lieutenant Conolly, still adjutant of the second Jodhpore legion, which has chiefly been called into existence since. The subsequent fate of the fort of Awah is thus briefly described in the *Friend of India*:—

'The campaign of retribution did not commence till January, 1858, when Colonel Raines, arriving from Deesa, marched with a reinforcement from Nusseerabad against Awah. These consisted of detachments of Her Majesty's 83rd Regiment, of the 10th Bombay N.I., of the 1st and 2nd Cavalry, and of the 2nd Sind Horse, with fourteen guns and mortars, the whole under command of Colonel Holmes, 12th Bombay N.I. This force numbered about 1800 men, 700 of whom were cavalry. After five days' siege operations, the cavalry being disposed so as to prevent escape, a breach was pronounced practicable, and the assault fixed for the next morning. Unfortunately a most fearful storm raged during the night, when it was impossible for sentries, placed at a few paces apart, to hear, much less see each other. During the storm the enemy evacuated the place, and were only heard by one picket, that of the 1st Lancers, who killed eighteen and took nine prisoners. Next morning the cavalry pursued, and took 124 prisoners, and among them twenty-four of our Sepoys, who were tried and shot. The remainder were handed over to the officiating political agent, Major Morrison, who was with the force. Six brass and seven iron guns were found in the fort, with a large quantity of ammunition. The defences were of great strength, and consisted of two lines, both well loop-holed. After destroying the palace and fortifications, the troops proceeded to Nusseerabad, where, at the request of General Lawrence, a force was assembling from Bombay to retake Kotah.'

CHAPTER XIV.

PARTY AT JODHPORE INCREASED—MURDER OF MAJOR BURTON—ANXIETIES—ESCORT ARRIVES—START FOR SIND—BALMER—DESERT TRAVELLING—OMERHOTE—HYDERABAD—KURRACHEE.

A DEEP gloom was cast over our once cheerful party by Captain Monck Mason's fate. He was a universal favourite; from the king down to the lowest servant about the Agency, all seemed deeply to feel his loss, and to sympathize most fully with his afflicted widow and her bereaved children. The king sent a message to Mrs. Mason to say that he would never rest till the head of the Awah chief was suspended over the gate of his fort.

A few days after the sad event, our party was increased by the arrival of Captain Denyss and Lieutenant Bannerman, the former commandant, and the latter adjutant of the late Kotah Contingent, which mutinied at Agra on the 5th of July, and contributed so much to the assistance of the rebels on that occasion. Major Morrison, who had been political agent at Bhurtpore till he was forced to leave it during the disturbances, was sent as officiating political agent to Jodhpore. The unexpected delay in taking Delhi—unexpected, that is, to all at a distance, who were unable to appreciate the difficulties with which the gallant band outside its walls were surrounded—produced the same effect in Rajpootana as it did elsewhere: it shook the confidence still placed in our cause by the native princes, kept the animosities of our enemies alive, and turned the population more and more against us. Central India was in a terrible state of disorder, and day after day the most alarming rumours were brought in, and diligently circulated by designing persons. Still we remained unmolested in the Agency, watching, it is true, with the greatest anxiety the signs of the times and the progress of events, but trusting that we had seen the worst, and that the news of the fall of Delhi, when it came, would have a great effect in quieting the public mind. The express came at last, at midnight—the hour important expresses generally chose for their arrival. I awoke Captain Denyss, to tell him the good news, and to let it circulate as speedily as possible through the household. It was forwarded on at once, and the intelligence reached Bombay first, by the Jodhpore and Kurrachee route. The raja fired a salute next day, which was Sunday, but it was a feeble one, and being only twenty-one guns—a royal salute after the English fashion—sounded as quite a secondary way of heralding a great event, compared with the native custom of firing a hundred guns for the smallest object of rejoicing.

Like most other crowned monarchs and regularly constituted authorities, the king had been getting uncomfortable of late. He had begun, and not without reason, to distrust his men, and had some days past, on Captain Monck Mason's departure, moved into his fort. Here, as long as his own guards were faithful, he was perfectly secure, for against a native force, or an Asiatic enemy, his fort was impregnable, though it would not have given us much trouble to take it.

One day in October we were startled by the intelligence of the treacherous assault on Major Burton, political agent at Kotah, and the murder of that officer, his two sons, and the medical man attached to the agency. In many of the published accounts of this transaction, the Kotah Contingent was described as having enacted this tragedy, but this was a mistake into which certainly no Indian writer ought to have fallen. The men who attacked and killed Major Burton were the king's regular troops—a body of soldiers entirely distinct from the Contingent, which was drilled and commanded by British officers, and which mutinied, as before related, at Agra, on the 5th July. Major Burton had returned with his two sons to Kotah, from Neemuch, where they had been residing, upon the assurance of the raja that a residence at Kotah would not be attended with danger, and from a desire to be at his post. The day following his return he was surprised by hearing a great noise, as of a multitude approaching from the direction of the city towards the Agency. At first he supposed it was a procession coming out to welcome him back, but he was soon undeceived, for it turned out to be a large body of the king's troops coming to attack the Agency. They brought guns down to bear upon the place. Major Burton and his two sons retired to the top of the house, where they defended themselves for several hours against the host of cowardly assailants, but were at length overpowered, and cut to pieces.

It was not known at the time to what extent the

raja was answerable for this crime, though, from the course the Governor-General has pursued towards him subsequently, it is to be inferred that his statement was supposed to be credible—that he was powerless in the hands of the rebels, and a prisoner in his palace. But the effect of the intelligence of this new outrage against the person of a British political agent was very apparent in the insolent conduct of the natives at Jodhpore. They could no longer doubt but that the officiating agent there, and his guests, would likewise fall victims to the spirit which was abroad, and that the Agency, the prize so long coveted, would be given up to plunder. The king was especially uneasy, and made no secret any longer of his fears, that his position was as insecure as ours. He told us indeed at one time that we might safely trust the men he had given us for the protection of the Agency, but at other times he said he did not know whom to trust; and on allusion to the Kotah tragedy, he remarked that it would be very hard to treat the raja as guilty of complicity, when he was helpless in the hands of the disaffected: plainly implying that a similar scene might be enacted at Jodhpore, and he all the time as innocent and as powerless as his brother raja of Kotah. Our source of anxiety was solely the large number of ladies and children dependent upon us for protection, one of the former of whom was not in a fit state to be moved without the most serious consequences. It was difficult to determine, too, in what direction we should proceed, supposing it had become necessary to leave the capital. On the south and east the road was dangerous, owing to the extended influence of the rebel Thakoor of Awah, whose fort was only a few miles off the high road, between Pallee and Deesa: to the north-east also, in the direction of Ajmere, the road was infested by bands of rebels, and equally unsafe; on the other two sides stretched an almost interminable waste—part of the desolate tract of Jessulmere and Bikaneer, and the wide range of desert country that separated Marwar from Sind, and ended southward in the runn of Cutch. Several of our party were anxious to return to Ajmere; one lady to join her husband at Beeawr, and Captain Denyss, who had lately been nominated to officiate in a political capacity at Neemuch, wanted to repair to his new scene of duties, and take his family with him, as Jodhpore was no longer a desirable place of residence. Any of the male portion of our party could at any time have ridden across country, either to Ajmere or Aboo, or in any direction, but it was most desirable to remove all the ladies and children who were capable of travelling, and this caused our embarrassment, for the risk of travelling slowly, with a camp and camp followers, bag and baggage, as we must have done had we marched altogether, taking our families with us, was so great, that it would have been the height of imprudence to have attempted it with no more trustworthy escort than it was in the power of the raja to provide.

My own movements were uncertain. The mounted postal lines, which during the height of the disturbances in the North-west had been so useful, had of late begun to lose their importance. Delhi had fallen, and order was in some measure restored, and communication re-opened throughout the country from the Punjaub to Delhi and Agra, even down to Cawnpore and Allahabad. The establishment for the conveyance of the mails across the desert, from Jodhpore to Sind or Bhawulpore, was maintained at an enormous expense, and it had been decided to keep it up only so long as it was absolutely necessary. The work in the office declined, and there was every prospect of its reverting soon to the original position which it held before the outbreak, when it was managed by a native clerk, or baboo, on a salary of twenty-five rupees a month. I resolved therefore, as soon as my wife was able to travel, to leave Jodhpore if possible, and, after seeing my family as far on their way towards Bombay as I could, to join the first Queen's regiment I should come across, and go up the country with it.

Mr. Frere, the Commissioner of Sind, who had throughout the trying time kept himself in constant communication with us, and had done all he could to render our position as safe as possible, had commissioned Lieutenant Tyrwhitt, deputy collector of Meerpore, before alluded to, to march up across the desert to Jodhpore, with a strong escort of Sind police, Beloochees, &c., and bring away Mrs. Mason and her family, and as many of the other residents as wished to accompany them to Hyderabad and Sind, from whence transit to Kurrachee and Bombay was easy. In consequence of the aspect recent affairs had assumed, Lieutenant Tyrwhitt made some addition to his escort, and pushed on with all the zeal and energy for which that most efficient officer is famed. He marched at the rate of forty miles a day, as far as Balmer—120 miles from Jodhpore—and leaving part of his detachment there—all the men, and horses, and camels that were knocked up with the rapid travelling—hurried on with all possible expedition to the capital. It is impossible to speak in too high terms of the character and zeal of this officer. Inured by constant habit to every kind of hardship, and leading a roving life, constantly travelling from one part of his immense desert district to another, he exhibited powers of endurance and an untiring energy that was perfectly marvellous. He was almost worshipped by the rude and savage denizens of the desert, who could never cease when they once began to sing the praises of their favourite 'Sahib.' His word was law, his slightest wish attended to, his anger dreaded. In the immense influence he had over natives, he resembled the late Major Hodson, more than any one else; and whether sitting round the fire with his men, or the chiefs of some of the desert tribes, and passing the pipe from mouth to mouth, or in kutchery, hearing evidence and settling disputes, or scouring the country in search of a dacoit, or cattle-lifter, or training a camel, or acting as keeper of the course at the Hyderabad races, or entertaining jovial and congenial spirits with the song and jest at mess, he was equally at home, and was the most popular character in the whole country, both with Asiatics and Europeans, from the borders of Marwar to the Indus.*

---

* As an instance of the miscellaneous nature of the duties an officer in Tyrwhitt's position may be called on to perform, I relate the following occurrence. During one of his night marches to Jodhpore, one of his men received a kick from his horse,

As soon as this officer had arrived with his advanced party—who encamped just outside the walls of the Agency—active preparations were set on foot for our departure. The journey was a long one, 360 miles through a desert, where there was no road, water was scarce and bad, and only found at long intervals, and wheeled conveyances had never penetrated the wilds. The raja, who was by no means sorry to see us depart, for he must have felt considerable anxiety on our account, his honour being in a manner pledged for our safety, and his own position having latterly become so precarious, lent us every assistance in his power. He supplied all the ladies with shagrams (two-wheeled carts) and bullocks; he furnished us with camels, and lent Captain Denyss the elephant which had always been attached to the Agency for the use of the political agent and his guests: he also provided a large escort, but the men were sulky and unwilling, and they and their charge were soon mutually glad to part company.

The only obstacle to my leaving, my wife's inability to travel, having been meantime removed, we determined to accompany the rest into Sind, and our hurried preparations having been completed, on the

---

which broke his leg. The fracture was a compound one, and the casualty consequently serious. Tyrwhitt halted his detachment, dismounted, and cut off a piece of the stem of one of the stunted shrubs with which the ground was covered. Out of this he speedily made a splint, set the broken limb, bandaged it, and left the patient in the nearest village. We had a medical officer with our party who examined the patient when we passed the village, and said no professional man could have set the limb better.

30th October the caravan set out; our party consisted of Mrs. Mason and three children; Captain Denyss, his wife, and three children and sister, who were bound for Neemuch; Mrs. Caunter, whose husband was at Beeawr, 120 miles from Jodhpore, exactly in the opposite direction, but who was forced to accompany us in this roundabout route to her destination, and two children; myself and wife, with a little baby six days old; Dr. Young; Captain Hardcastle, one of the assistant agents to the Governor-General for the States of Rajpootana, who, after ten years spent in his political duties, was repairing to his native land with his constitution completely shattered, and who died, shortly after he reached Europe, at Baden; and Lieutenant Bannerman. Lieutenant Tyrwhitt assumed charge of the whole party, and was indefatigable in his exertions, seldom taking more rest than two or three hours out of the twenty-four. The carts, of which there were ten, were arranged in a long line, Mrs. Mason's leading; a party of mounted police led the van, cleared away obstructions, and—no easy matter always—found the road: flanking parties, mounted on camels and horses, rode at the distance of a few yards from the cavalcade on each side, and the rear was brought up by a strong party of police. My wife was forced to travel in a dooly, and consequently was kept in the rear, where the dust was almost suffocating, and at times so thick as to endanger the life of the little child; but it was necessary to push on, for we had to make long journeys, and, being short of bearers, it was as much as we could do, by promises of rewards, coaxing, and threats, to keep them up to the work, and get them to keep pace with the bullock carts; for had they once begun to lag behind, it would have detained the whole party, and our only chance of getting over the journey was to accomplish each stage during the night, for the sun in the day-time, though it was the month of November, was exceedingly hot, and the bullocks would have been knocked up after the first three marches had they been forced to work in the daytime. It is a strange thing that these animals are so susceptible to the influence of the solar rays. To look at the Indian bullock or buffalo, one would suppose them capable of undergoing any amount of exposure, at all events, if not fatigue, but just the contrary is the case; and if it is necessary to keep them in good working order, they must march at night, and halt during the day.

The first night we made upwards of thirty miles, and reached our encamping ground about half-an-hour before daylight; the few tents we had with us were pitched, and we lay down, some on charpoys and some on the ground, to take what rest we could. About noon, intelligence was brought us that a large body of horsemen had been seen in the neighbourhood, following us up with hostile intent; their number was stated to be not less than a hundred. Our energetic Meer Kafila, who, as well as his men, had been busy, with scarcely two hours' intermission for the last twenty-four, no sooner heard the news than he took a party of mounted police and sallied forth on a reconnoitring expedition. The story he found corroborated by what he gathered from the villagers, but it seems the horsemen, who were followers of the rebel Thakoor of Awah, did not seem inclined to come to close quarters, at least, just yet. They were probably following us up, and trying to find out the strength of our party, and what sort of watch and ward we kept, before they committed themselves to an attack. Their alleged object was to seize the ladies and families, and keep them prisoners as hostages; but Tyrwhitt was not likely to let them catch him unawares, and the strictest look-out was kept for the rest of the day. Towards evening, as the sun grew low, we dined, and after dinner orders were given to march. Tents were struck, bundles packed (for being almost all of us refugees who had been impoverished by the mutineers, we were not over-burdened with a very extensive amount of property), we moved off the ground about sunset, the same order of march being observed as the night before. The flanking parties and the rear-guard were on the *qui vive*, but nothing occurred to disturb us.

On the 4th November we reached Balmer, the first place of any importance upon our route. It is situated on the Sind and Marwar boundary, and in former years boasted of a military cantonment or outpost, occupied by a detachment of irregular troops. Two ruined bungalows, formerly inhabited by the officers, are still standing. There is a large village here, and supplies and water are good, and tolerably plentiful. From this place a road branches off to Deesa, and here we expected to part company, Captain Denyss and family, Mrs. Caunter, and Dr. Young proceeding to Deesa, and thence to their several destinations, and we continuing our journey to Hyderabad. But it was found on inquiry that the road was impracticable for wheeled conveyances, besides being unsafe, so our companions were destined to go yet further out of their way. Dr. Young, however, left us here, and taking a small party of mounted police from Tyrwhitt's detachment, started for Mount Aboo.

As we were now about to leave the Raja of Jodhpore's territories, we were to exchange carriage at this place, and make one or two other arrangements which involved delay, and we were not ready to move till the evening of the 7th. We had, however, enjoyed the halt. The invalids benefited greatly by the rest thus afforded them, and the shelter of the tumble-down old bungalows was not to be despised. I was wrong in calling them ruins, for the walls were still standing, and the roofs upon them, too; only through one, at all events, the sky was plainly visible. We had a guitar with us, strange to say—a relic that had by some extraordinary freak of fortune been preserved to us when everything else was destroyed—and we used to sit round a blazing wood fire in the evenings, for though hot in the day it was cold and chilly at night, while the guitar was passed round from one to the other, and the echoes of Balmer were astonished with the unwonted sounds of ladies' voices in songs, duets, and trios. It was a curious scene, and so the wild Beloochee sentries seemed to think, as they stood at a little distance from the group, their figures just discernible in the gloom beyond the range of the fire-light—rendered doubly intense by the contrast between the bright flames of the burning logs and the pitchy darkness of the moonless sky—pacing up and down in the short walk, while the red light of the fire glanced now and again like fireflies from the polished surface of their naked swords.

This good practice of a bonfire was hereafter inaugurated as a part of our regular proceedings; and every halt we made the guitar was called into requisition.

Our usual course was to start at sunset; on a longer march than usual, a little before. We made always three halts during the stage, one about 10 P.M., when Tyrwhitt's attentive myrmidons would have a blazing fire ready, and plenty of tea, which we drank out of large brass cups, the small allowance of crockery—three broken teacups, I believe—not being sufficient; this, with sandwiches and biscuits, served us for a good meal; and after resting for about an hour, sometimes more, the ladies got into their carts and conveyances, and went to sleep; the gentlemen mounted their horses, camels, or the elephant, and on we went again. The second stage was not unfrequently a sleepy affair. We halted again about one or two, when the party round the fire was considerably smaller than on the former occasion, as the ladies mostly preferred not being disturbed. After this, the third stage would bring us to our destination or halting-ground till next sunset, when off we started again. During the day the heat was so great, and the flies were so troublesome, that it was next to impossible to get any sleep, and as it was difficult to get any during the night, the reader will easily perceive that, however delightful such a journey may appear in description, there was, at all events, this very serious difficulty in the way of our enjoying it as thoroughly as we no doubt ought to have done. We were differently situated in this respect. Tyrwhitt appeared to have the faculty of doing without either rest or sleep. One of our party had brought a vehicle called a 'rut,' partly for the accommodation of faithful domestics, and partly for his own. This conveyance consists of a small cart exactly like that I have previously attempted to describe, called a bayley, only that it possesses the doubtful advantage of a cover—in shape and size like a huge extinguisher—which gives it something the appearance presented by Juggernath's car in the illustrated histories of India usually devoted to the instruction of youthful minds, and renders it topheavy, and very liable to be overset. The seat, or body of the cart, in which the occupant has to sit, or sustain himself as best he may, is about two or three feet square at most. Of course there are no such things as springs (what springs could have survived such a road?), and the machine went along, jolt, jolt, swaying first to one side, then the other, a combination of motions which, under any ordinary circumstances, could not have consorted, even by the wildest flights of imagination, with the idea of rest. It is one of those hidden mysteries to which I have long ago despaired of ever finding a clue, how two men, one particularly remarkable for length of limb, could by any possibility have managed to stow themselves away in this Juggernath-looking conveyance. Yet it is equally certain they did so, and not only that, but managed to sleep, different extremities and divers portions of their limbs protruding from underneath the bottom of the extinguisher-shaped covering, intertwined and commingled in the most unaccountable posture imaginable. Not being provided with even the doubtful convenience of a rut, I had not this resource open to me, and enjoyed what sleep I might, at one time on my pony, at another on a camel, and occasionally was lucky enough to be able to court the drowsy god rolled up in a howdah on the elephant's back. The instant we reached the halting-ground, and my wife's dooly was safely deposited, and the ayah summoned, I looked out for the spot where I was least liable to intrusion from man or beast, and threw myself recklessly down and slept, till the glare of the sun's rays, and the bustle of the camp, aroused to life and work, warned me of the inutility of attempting such a course of conduct any longer.

The tract of country we were travelling over is called the desert, and certainly it does not belie its name, but we did not see its true character displayed till we got beyond Balmer. The features were pretty much the same here; regular ranges of sand-hills of very considerable elevation; not soft, yielding sand, but complete hills covered with brushwood, except in places. They were said to be the result of the sand having collected, and formed a nucleus, as it were, or a foundation for the superstructure; the soil, however, becoming hardened by moisture from the dews of heaven, and by the growth of stunted shrubs that extend everywhere in the utmost profusion, and intertwine their roots beneath the upper surface of the ground.

The accounts I have read of the deserts in other parts of the world, such as Africa and Arabia, suit so well the features of the track I am attempting to describe that it is evident that the same causes were in operation in both instances, which resulted in the phenomena we now see. My theory may be wrong, but it is my belief that these hills or ridges, called sand-hills of the desert, are the result of aqueous action on the surface of the land, which at a former epoch was probably submerged, and, either from the uplifting of the soil, or the subsidence of the water, was subsequently rescued from the sea, and formed a portion of the dry land. The water in running off would hollow out for itself channels, the direction of which would be determined by the nature of the soil, and the intervening portions which, from being of a harder and more unyielding nature than the rest, would be avoided by the water, remained at their former elevation, and the whole operation resulted in a series of parallel ridges and depressions, or hill and vale. Anyhow, it was tedious and toilsome work getting the carts over these 'bits,' as they call them in the desert; and had it not been for Tyrwhitt's unceasing exertions, and the extraordinary influence he exercised over both men and bullocks, I verily believe we should have been there to this day.

On moonlight nights our caravan looked most picturesque, and I often cantered off the road, to the summit of the rising ground at a little distance, to watch it winding along below me: the wild-looking escort on their camels and horses, covered with gaudy trappings; the matchlocks and steel, wherever visible, glittering in the moon's rays; the long line of carts wending their way in single file; then the flanking parties, mostly on camels, and the quaint 'ruts,' with their pyramidal coverings, the motley group following in the rear, amid which the elephant towered like a large ship among a fleet of little boats, all passed below me like a panorama, while ever and anon the sound of laughter or the chorus of some rollicking song, swept through the clear, bright air, and fell, mellowed by distance, on the ear; while all around, far as the eye could reach, stretched an interminable waste of desert, stunted shrubs, and undulating ground, unblessed by a single spot of verdure or cultivation, or a single trace of human habitation. There is something glorious in the intense solitude of the desert, a feeling akin to that one experiences on the sea shore. There is a charm in the very luxury of desolation, a music in the very intensity of silence, not even the wailing howl of the jackal being there to interfere with the solemn stillness that reigns over everything. One can easily imagine how it was that in ancient times, when men thought it a duty to leave the only place where they could do their duty—that is, the busy world, where man meets man in the daily struggle of life—and waste their intellectual energies in contemplation, they chose the solitude of the desert for their resort. There is little indeed to admire during the day, when the unclouded sun lights up everything with a distressing and monotonous glare, but at night, when the stars shine brightly through the clear atmosphere, or the moon sheds her gentle rays upon the scene of solitude, a man can feel the littleness of earthly things, for there is nothing external, at all events, to intervene between his soul and God.

The soil is in most places covered with the stunted shrubs and dwarf bushes before spoken of; at others, with a soft or shifting sand, and occasionally we passed large tracts in which wild colocynth grew in abundance. Here and there the soil is indurated clay, and at intervals intersected with deep and precipitous ravines, most troublesome to caravans like ours, where wheeled carts take the place of mules and camels, and ladies and children are inside who must not be disturbed if it can be helped, still less upset. In other places the ground is covered with a thorny species of grass, fatal almost to the heedless wayfarer, whether mounted or on foot. So sharp are the thorns or spikes of grass, that they would penetrate at the slightest touch the thickest corduroy, and, if a little force is used, even the leather of a boot or shoe. The dooly bearers especially found it most annoying, for they generally ran along on bare feet; and though they put on their shoes, their legs were still exposed, and suffered exceedingly. Had it not been for a wee narrow path, which those who were carrying the dooly could just manage to keep upon, while the rest followed in single file, it would have been impossible to proceed: the men would have been all lamed in a single night. It may give some idea of the sharpness of these spikes of grass, when I say that even the elephant could not kneel down on it to receive his burden; it penetrated the thick skin with which that animal is covered, and the mahout was forced to look about for a bare spot to allow the creature to kneel on before we could mount.

Elephants are almost, if not quite unknown in Sind, and the greatest excitement was caused by the appearance of such a gigantic beast in our train whenever we came to any inhabited place. While encamped near a village or town, the people used to turn out in crowds, and throng the spot where the elephant was tied up all day long, watching its motions, and seeing it devour its food with as much and more interest than children do at home on a first visit to a zoological garden. At a place called Allyarka Tanda, which is a tolerably large town, with a good many inhabitants, it was most amusing to see the crowd which collected round us at starting. I was alone in the howdah, and behind the rest of the party, and made my exit from the place with certainly three-fourths of the whole population following me for near half a mile.

We had to regulate our halting places by the water, which was procurable—sometimes tolerably good, but generally brackish and muddy—only at intervals of from twenty to thirty miles. The longer marches were very tedious affairs. Several times we started at sunset, and did not reach our ground till next morning at seven or eight A.M.,—once as late as nine; and when the starting hour arrived, I have often been so utterly wearied out from want of rest, that it was only by a great exercise of the will that I could summon energy enough to mount. We had a good rest, however, at Balmer, and again at a place called Gudra, some four or five days further on. We halted a day there, and pushed on again to Omerhote. Here there is a fort and a gaol; the unhappy prisoners were turned out of their comfortable quarters to make room for us, and as we were forced to halt here for three days, the accommodation thus provided for us was most thankfully accepted. I and my wife and child occupied a cell with adjoining court-yard, and we may consider we have at any rate earned distinction, if nothing else, for it is not every English lady that has spent some days in the Omerhote gaol. This place is mentioned in Sir C. Napier's life; but it has acquired far greater fame as having been the birthplace of the great Emperor Akbar, who was born under a tree in the neighbourhood of the fort, while his father Humayoun was flying a houseless fugitive from his enemies. The natives still venerate the spot, and show the tree under which the great Emperor of Hindostan struggled into existence.

The next place of note we reached was Meerpore, a large city, and the head-quarters of the civil officer of the district, Lieutenant Tyrwhitt, who has a house and large garden, with a farm-yard and all the other accompaniments to a country residence in India. Meerpore is only about two days from Hyderabad during the dry weather, but at the time we were there the water from the river which overflows the country at this season, had rendered the road impassable, and we were obliged to make a long detour to avoid it; this we only just succeeded in doing, for it had reached the very edge of the road, and in some places spread over it, and was rapidly advancing. No little inconvenience was caused during the night on this account, for the water unexpectedly came down lower than Tyrwhitt had calculated on, and we were again forced to deviate still further from our direct route. However, our toils and wanderings were destined to have an end, and as we drew nearer and nearer Hyderabad, the prospect of soon reaching our (temporary) destination made us forget all the minor inconveniences and troubles attendant on such a journey, and cheered our flagging spirits.

On the morning of the 30th, about eight A.M., we came in sight of the fort of Hyderabad, and hailed the unwonted spectacle of a European sentry mounting guard at the postern gate with feelings which only those can appreciate who have seen so much as we had of native soldiers, and been so long at their mercy.

At Hyderabad we were most hospitably received by Captain Lionel Dunsterville, deputy magistrate in Sind, and his wife, and every attention was shown us by the officers and residents at the station.

The climate of Sind is better appreciated than it used to be; probably drainage and other sanitary measures adopted in localities occupied by European residents have had a great effect in rendering it less obnoxious than it was in former years to the European constitution. The day after our arrival, the 1st December, a cold, bracing north-east wind was blowing across the elevated plateau upon which the station of Hyderabad is built, and the weather was just as cold and healthful as any I have ever felt in the Punjaub, to which province, in point of climate, Sind is very much assimilated.

The officers of the Bombay army received their less fortunate brethren of Bengal with every kindness and attention, nor can I speak too warmly of the open-hearted hospitality of the Bombay army, whenever it has been my good fortune to fall in with any portion of it, and that was not seldom. In former days an honest and honourable rivalry existed between the two armies; we each had our own peculiar customs and system of discipline, and in those days I could without a blush uphold in argument the honour of the army and Presidency to which I belonged; now, however, matters were changed, and I appeared among them a living, tangible, walking testimony to the inefficiency and rottenness of the system I had so often stood up for. There was no denying it—the Bengal army had gone, irretrievably gone, as it deserved to go, and as everybody ought to have known it would go, and what could I say for it? I was prepared for a little bantering at the first Bombay mess I went to, but the subject was too serious to joke about, and too many of those I saw around me had lost dear relatives and friends, victims of the great mutiny. Once, and once only, was the subject alluded to in an offensive way, and that was by an artillery officer at Kurrachee, but my answer (in the same spirit as that of the remark which called it forth) was ready: 'Your men were just as bad as ours, for they had all the will to mutiny, but wanted the pluck.' And as regards the Poorbeeah portion of the Bombay army, I believe this was the case. But it was owing to the system that it did require more pluck to mutiny in the Bombay Presidency than in Bengal. Nor let it be supposed that the experiment had not been tried. At Kurrachee, at Hyderabad, at Shikanpore, the epidemic broke out, but it was met by vigorous measures, such as were too often wanting in other parts of India, and suppressed ere the spark had burst into a flame. It was owing to the vigour and energy displayed by the Government of Sind as well as that of the Punjaub during the rebellion, that our Indian empire was, under Providence, preserved; a character of Government that stood out in striking contrast to the indecision, vacillation, and delay manifested in other parts of the country. In Bengal and the North-west Provinces, while the authorities thought, debated, consulted, the officers in Sind and the Punjaub acted. While in Bengal and the North-west any officer, in however high a position, who, feeling himself equal to the crisis, extricated himself from the folds of red tape that bound him hand and foot, and acted on his own responsibility, was blamed, rebuked, disgraced, and even the proclamation of a Lieutenant-Governor was annulled; in Sind and the Punjaub, an officer who did his duty and served his country well, was sure of the support of his superiors, encouraged, praised, rewarded. While in Bengal and the North-west rebellion was comparatively a safe game to play at, in the Punjaub and Sind it was held down by an arm as prompt to arrest as to punish. While in Bengal and the North-west all the independent Europeans in the country were alienated from the Government, thwarted in their efforts to do good, rebuked for their offers of assistance, and degraded so far as to be ranked in the same class as the natives who were in open rebellion, in Sind and the Punjaub they were encouraged to rally round the seat of Government, and to lend their utmost aid in suppressing the revolt, while they were incorporated with the ruling class now engaged in the deadly strife of races. The present generation will perhaps not acknowledge the services of the men who saved India. The letters in the *Times* and powerful connexions may tend to keep the laurels for a time where they have placed them, and where they are not deserved, but history will not fail to do justice to the men who have proved themselves equal to the emergency, and who behaved, in a time of unprecedented anxiety and danger, not with an apathy and silent inaction, mistaken sometimes for calmness and self-confidence, but who, with the courage and energy of true Englishmen, threw themselves into the breach, trusting in the God whose service they are not ashamed to confess before men while engaged in the performance of their duty.

Hyderabad was formerly a place of great importance, being the residence of the chief Ameers of Sind. The plateau upon which it is built is about a mile and a half long, and 700 yards wide, the height about eighty feet; the river is four or five miles from the town and cantonment, and there is a very tolerable road leading down to its banks. On the opposite side is Kotree, a pretty little place, the head-quarters of the Indus flotilla, whose commander-in-chief or commodore has a fine house and garden on the banks. The journey to Kurrachee occupied about two days, and we were fortunate in getting a passage in a new steamer, the 'Frere,' which had only made one voyage from Kurrachee to Kotree. It was Saturday evening when we drew near the harbour of Kurrachee, and right glad were we to find ourselves in the still water, for it was blowing hard, and the sea rising, and the motion of a flat-bottomed steamboat in a pitching sea is unpleasant to such land-lubbers as we were. Going ashore that night was out of the question, so we made ourselves as comfortable as we could on deck, the ladies occupying the cabins and saloons below.

I know no place which has altered so much as Kurrachee within the last seven years. I first visited it in 1849, immediately after the second Punjaub campaign, and had I been taken blindfold and put down in the middle of the station, I should scarcely have known where I was. When I visited the place again in 1855, a handsome church had just been erected in a commanding site, whose tower is a safe landmark for mariners approaching the coast, and distinguishable from a long distance. The houses of the residents have been very much improved, and the general appearance of the station vastly changed for the better. But it is towards the harbour that the alteration is chiefly remarkable. The landing-place is three miles from the town, which must be passed on the way up to the cantonment; a mole and road connecting the two have been constructed at the cost of 30,000*l*. There are always a large number of native boats, or 'patimans,' as they are called, lying at and near the pier, and there is all the bustle and animation of a busy seaport town.

When I was at Kurrachee there were three native regiments there, one of which had been disarmed. A wing (the left) of H.M.'s 7th Royal Fusiliers had just arrived, and was under orders to proceed up to the Punjaub immediately. My services having been already placed at the disposal of the Sind Government for employment with any body of troops in want of an interpreter, I was, immediately on my arrival, posted to the 7th Regiment in that capacity, and had just four days to complete the requisite arrangements for so long a journey, procure the necessaries which I had been deprived of so long that I had almost learnt to do without them, and send my family to Bombay.

Christmas-day, 1857, was anything but a merry one to many, and it certainly was not so at Kurrachee, which was full of people, all, the strangers at least, unsettled and uncomfortable. Troops were landing constantly, and being pushed up to the Punjaub as fast as they could go; families there were in numbers, both of the upper and lower classes, officers' and soldiers' wives and children, all alike in one thing, separated from fathers and husbands; widows and orphan children on their way to England; wives whose husbands had just left them for the seat of war, uncertain whether to remain there, and wait till the war was over, or to go back to England or to Bombay; and others who had come out expecting to find their husbands waiting for them, and destined to disappointment. Several regiments had left England in the ordinary course of relief, only having heard of the beginning of the outbreak, and supposing it would be all over long before they reached the shores of India. The officers had brought their families with them. No sooner, however, had they landed, and learnt the real state of things, than they had to take a hurried parting from their wives and children, and send them back in many cases in the same ships in which they came. One regiment I heard of—at a time when every English soldier with a musket and bayonet in his hand was worth his weight in silver almost—had brought out its women and had left its arms in England, by mistake.

Once more I was bound for the Punjaub. It seemed as if fate had linked my fortunes to the province in some extraordinary manner. For once during eleven years' service my regiment had been stationed out of the country of the Five Rivers, and here I was, after two months' sojourn with it at Kurrachee, under orders again for the Punjaub.

At twelve o'clock on Christmas night, the hour when our friends at home begin to get the merriest, the wing of the 7th Royal Fusiliers paraded in the barrack square. There was a little delay while the final preparations were being completed: at last the bugle sounded the advance, and I once more commenced my wanderings.

CHAPTER XV.

CONCLUSION.

HOWEVER much further investigation may be needed to elucidate the direct cause of the mutiny, we can, I think, form a pretty correct judgment even now of its effects upon the country and our position in it. Undoubtedly this is much stronger than it ever was before. Not only have we got rid of a dangerous portion of the native army, which would some time or other have imperilled the existence of the empire, but the natives have learnt a lesson they will not easily forget; not that they have been treated harshly, not that as Englishmen we have forgotten ourselves in the hour of revenge—for I suppose never before in the history of the world was so slight a punishment inflicted on a conquered nation in proportion to the offence—but they have found out how difficult it is, even with everything in their favour, to drive the English out of India. They had enormous arsenals, well stocked with military stores, almost inexhaustible in quantity, and of the very best sort, provided by ourselves, in their possession; they had an immense force of artillery, and guns almost without number; they had nearly the whole of the late Bengal native army, provided, be it recollected, with English arms, accoutrements, and ammunition. They took us by surprise when the European force in India, was at its lowest limits, and at the very first outset got possession of many of our most important forts and strongholds. Above all they had Delhi, and the advantage of the prestige afforded to their cause by the fact of a descendant of the house of Timour being seated on the throne. Should a second outbreak occur, as some predict, how differently would they be situated? The country has been pretty effectually disarmed; if any heavy pieces of ordnance are in existence at all, they must be carefully concealed, buried under ground, where rust will soon materially injure them. Our important arsenals and forts are in the hands of European soldiers; and the present native army, if it mutinied, as it very possibly may attempt to do, would not be of any value scarcely compared to the last. Fears are expressed in many quarters that the Sikh army may attempt to recover the Punjaub, but this is hardly likely as long as the traditionary policy of the Punjaub Government is carried on—a policy instituted by Sir Henry, and acted on by Sir John Lawrence. The power that holds Peshawur, Amritsur, Lahore, Sealhot, Mooltan, and Kurrachee, may well be considered to have the Punjaub safely in its grasp. Nor even have we much to fear as a nation from religious fanaticism. A great deal has been said of our utter helplessness if assailed by the whole population: men have taken the trouble to demonstrate how, if each native in the country contributed a handful of sand, they might bury the whole European inhabitants of India under a sand-heap; and so no doubt they might—if the latter let them do it. But if nothing else has been proved during the rebellion, this much has been set beyond a doubt, that the natives of India are by many, many degrees an inferior race to the Anglo-Saxon; they never can compete with them, they never can resist them. That we shall have *émeutes*, mutinies, disturbances, and occasional massacres (only on a small scale, it is to be hoped) for many years, perhaps for all time to come, is only to be expected—such things betoken the normal state of India—but I do not see any human probability of our ever being forced to abandon the country, or of our being destroyed in it. The fetters were upon India before the outbreak of 1857; now they are riveted. There is an end to all mundane calamities, and even the period of Lord Canning's administration must one day draw to a close, and India, relieved of the incubus that now oppresses all her faculties, and almost deprives her of vitality, will be able to raise herself and breathe again, and a state that shall have survived five years of such misrule as we shall have seen when that time comes, can be safely considered capable of surviving anything.

I call the outbreak a rebellion because, though it commenced with a military mutiny, it speedily extended itself and changed its character, and there is every reason to believe that circumstances will be discovered tending to prove the existence of an organized conspiracy against the British Government. The population of the country had no love for us. It would have been strange if they had. What did they owe to us? Nothing. The widely-circulated notion that the natives had never been happy and contented till they came under British rule will never be entertained by any one who has seen them in independent states under native rule. The corruption and venality of our law-courts and subordinate law officers has of late years begun to be exposed; had the natives anything to thank us for on that score? But we brought them the blessings of civilization—they were not far enough advanced to appreciate them. Our professions were a great deal too vast and high-sounding to be put faith in. We might as well attempt to persuade the illiterate and semi-barbarous inhabitants of Hindostan that we tried to govern the country for their good, and not for our own profit, as to induce them to believe that the Government had no design against their religion in giving them a liberal education in the State schools. It is the nature of men to judge others by their own standard, and the natives of India judge of us by theirs. By far the greater portion of the population never came in contact with an Englishman at all, and of those who did, a great part encountered the Anglo-Saxon in some unpleasant way, either as a magistrate deciding a case against him, or perhaps awarding some punishment, or as a hard tax-gatherer, only more hated than the race of tax-gatherers or revenue collectors who went before, inasmuch as his commands were more inexorable, and there was less chance of escaping from his clutches. Of the large, very large majority that never knew practically what an Englishman was, nearly the whole would have heard plenty about him; and what did they hear? What did the inhabitants of Oude think about us?—the very people, perhaps, of all others, that ought to have heard nothing but what was favourable, seeing that they were so intimately connected with our Sepoys, and had scarcely a village among them in which there were not some pensioners who had served their time, or some relatives of men killed in action under the British Government, who were dependent on its bounty for their support. Even these people believed we were slayers of men and women, and that the English soldier refreshed himself after a day's work by a meal of children's flesh. There was supposed to be some wonderful specific in common use among us, made out of the bones of children killed for the purpose. The gross injustice so often perpetrated under the name of law in our own provinces—to whom was that ascribed but to the English magistrate? The native subordinates of our civil and criminal courts, allowed on all hands to be most corrupt, never took a bribe, or gave a blow, or subjected a victim to torture, but he did it in the name of the 'Sahib.' What wonder that when the Sepoys took the lead, and proclaimed the British Government overthrown, thousands hailed the intelligence as good news of better times? The only marvel is that there was a single native in the country on our side. And that there were so many speaks volumes in favour not so much of British rule, as of the character of those who formed the executive.

That we have never much to fear from a general rising of the population is evident to any one who has studied the practical features of the late revolt. The Rajpoots are a warlike race—at least they always carry arms—and are strong, if not in present spirit, at any rate in tradition and heroic stories of the past, yet a small band of Sepoys, disorganized to a great extent by mutiny, and deprived of their English officers, marched through the whole territory of Marwar, and carried terror with them wherever they went, in spite of the exertions of the Maharaja to induce his subjects to stop them. In one day he might have assembled a force of armed men as many as ten to one against the mutinous Jodhpore Legion, but the people were afraid to go near them. They were a scourge to the country; they went where they pleased, and did exactly what they liked. The same thing may be said of a band of Sepoys with British officers, only their effect would be probably ten times as great as without; and a compact force of English soldiers might march through the length and breadth of the land carrying victory with them. The manner in which the late campaign against the rebels has been conducted has given the natives a very low idea of English statesmanship, but of the prowess of English soldiers they have acquired a most exalted notion. An anecdote I heard in Oude will show how far native soldiers are to be dreaded in the field. A civil officer was riding along the road in that district one day during Lord Clyde's last campaign. The British army had taken the field, but the country through which our solitary horseman was wending his way—like the heroes in James's novels—was in possession of rebels. His steed was, unlike the animals usually bestridden by the worthies of romance alluded to, lame, and the rider was unarmed. He was pursued, if pursuit it can be called, by three well-mounted and well-armed rebels, who emerged from the jungle on the side of the road. To fly was impossible, as the lame horse would soon be overtaken; to stand and make a fight for it was equally out of the question, as the Englishman had no arms; so as it was useless to walk away from the rebels, he turned and walked towards them. They stood, watched his steady advance for a few seconds, and then turned and fairly fled from the field.

Natives are no doubt liable to sudden impulses and fits of excitement, under which they are capable of doing deeds of valour. From temporary outbursts of this kind we shall always be in danger of suffering, and it is against these that we must chiefly guard. Religious fanaticism is undoubtedly the strongest incentive to impulsive action that can be put in operation, and every one knows what a large share of the origin of the late rebellion is to be attributed to this cause. There is, I believe, more excitement on the subject throughout the country now than many are disposed to admit. It is well known that in numerous parts of the country the Queen's proclamation was interpreted to signify that henceforward the natives might revert to old usages and customs which had been put down by the Government. Three cases of suttee have lately taken place in the North-west Provinces; formerly such a thing was never heard of. The people appear to think that, finding how distasteful to them were the laws and regulations of civilized society, we—at least Her Majesty's Government—had determined to cease their introduction into the country, and let them revert to the old order of things. Yet it is strange that while the natives hold this idea, a stronger attack than was ever yet made is being organized against the bulwarks of their superstition. The education question is a difficult subject to handle, yet I cannot close these desultory remarks without doing what little may be in my power to urge upon the English people the necessity of pausing and reflecting carefully before they act in this matter of State education. The movement that is now going on in England in 1859, unless guided by temperate and clear-headed men, is calculated, if anything can, to raise a general revolt in India. An education, such as an English Government need not be ashamed to give, must be conducted on Christian principles; at least, as Englishmen we have need to be ashamed of ever having given any other. In many parts of India, I believe, such an education might be offered to the people without producing any evil effects, or raising any suspicion. But the worst of our system of Government is, that difficult and important questions, affecting the whole empire, are too often settled in Calcutta, or at the seats of Government, by members of that Government who forget that all the numberless races and tribes of India—races and tribes, be it recollected, in every conceivable stage of civilization, from the barbarous and half-naked denizen of the mountains and forests, to the polished, subtle inhabitant of our military cantonments and large cities—are not fitted for one and the same legislation. That measures which in one part of the country would be safe and beneficial, in another are calculated to breed disaffection, suspicion, revolt. And so it is with education. In many places the Bible might be introduced into Government Schools, and Christianity openly taught without exciting so much as a murmur or a thought of suspicion; in others it would be held to verify the prophecies and warnings we have heard so much about of late, that the Kaffirs were bent on making every one Kaffirs like themselves. But no discretion is allowed; the measure, if passed at all, is to be universal in its operation. There must be one law for all.

What India wants has been told often before, and by many abler pens than mine. Yet I may be excused, perhaps, for raising one more voice in favour of the course which prudence and common sense in vain call for against prejudice and traditional policy. Much discretionary power must be entrusted to individual officers; no one system of Government, no set of regulations, however well drawn up, will ever suit the diverse cases and peculiar circumstances in which the magistrate is called upon to act. The administration must be made as personal as possible; every officer must learn to govern his district by his own personal influence, and let it be an established rule that a civil officer who is the most respected, the most feared, and the most liked in his district, shall be the first to be promoted, without reference to regulation, or examination, or red tape. The species of government required for India (I am speaking of the provinces and not of the Presidency towns) is as distinct from that required for a country like England as one thing can possibly be from another. Englishmen in England cannot learn the art; no course of instruction at college can teach it, no book can describe it, no lecturer delineate it. It must be acquired by experience, and the officer who mixes the most with the natives of all classes, and rides or drives about his district unattended by a host of chuprassees and hangers-on, and a retinue of officious servants, and who is guided in his duty by a conscientious desire to act justly and kindly towards those whose welfare and happiness Providence has placed in his hands, will be the first to acquire that practical knowledge of it which alone constitutes the efficiency of an Indian magistrate.

CHAPTER XVI.

ADDITIONAL REMARKS.

ALTHOUGH the real history of the mutiny has yet to be written, and the origin of it is so deeply seated as to have hitherto baffled all efforts at inquiry, sufficient time has elapsed to enable us to see pretty clearly how it has affected our position in India, and what our chances are, humanly speaking, for the future. But before offering the few remarks on this subject that have occurred to me as worthy of attention, I must say a word or two regarding the immediate 'fons et origo mali,' the greased cartridges. Since the former portion of this narrative was written, I have accidentally acquired additional information on the subject from the best authorities, and as an erroneous impression respecting the conduct of Government in the affair has been promulgated, and is entertained by a large majority, it may be as well to state what actually occurred.

For the purpose of teaching the use of the Enfield rifle, three depôts of instruction were established, as I have before remarked, to which small parties of selected native officers and men from native infantry regiments were sent. In the regiments themselves no Enfield rifles and no cartridges for them were issued. This is very important to remember, because whatever was done in regard to the cartridges was done at the three depôts of instruction only, and neither rifles nor cartridges were sent anywhere except to the depôts. That a large portion of the Enfield rifle cartridges were greased is undeniable; but I believe I am right in stating that not a single greased cartridge was issued, for the purpose of being used in practice, to any Sepoy. They must have got some into their possession, because our party brought some with them from the Umballa depôt to Nusseerabad, and it was by this means that I had an opportunity of examining them myself. It has also been asserted that the Sepoys of the Nusseeree battalion, nominally a Goorkha regiment, were supplied with them at their own request—a request preferred ostensibly to demonstrate their fidelity to Government.

The three depôts were respectively at Dumdum, Umballa, and Sealkote. At each there was a good deal of preliminary drill to be gone through, to teach the men how to handle, how to take to pieces and put together again, how to poise the rifle for the aim at different distances, how to make up the cartridge to load, &c.

The Dumdum depôt was under command of Captain Bontein, and being near Calcutta, this officer was in constant communication with the military secretary to Government, General Birch. While the instruction was being carried on, and before the men had arrived at the stage when it was necessary to load, Captain Bontein communicated the following information to General Birch. A Sepoy belonging to the 2nd Grenadiers, and attached to the party at the depôt, was passing along the road in the cantonment at Dumdum, when one of the magazine classies accosting him, asked him for a drink of water. The Sepoy replied that he had just bathed and filled his lota, and not knowing the caste of the classie, doubted whether he could give him a drink of water out of his lota. On this the classie rejoined, 'You talk of caste! why, where will your caste be a few days hence, when you are made to bite cartridges which are greased with bullocks' and cows' fat?' The Sepoy spread the story at once among his comrades at the depôt, and some of them having gone to the arsenal in Fort William, ascertained that there were greased cartridges there. I may observe here, in passing, that two separate and distinct objections were urged against the cartridges by the men; one was that the paper composing them had already been greased, and the second that the grease into which the end of each cartridge had to be dipped before loading was of impure material. There was no doubt about the latter. The objectionable materials were being used in the arsenal, where the grease was being made up, and no doubt the Sepoy of the 2nd Grenadiers, who was the first to communicate the intelligence to his comrades, and set the snowball rolling, made a good deal of his discovery that the grease was actually being prepared just as the classie had said. It was no less true that the grease was never issued, but the suspicions of the men had been aroused, and were subsequently confirmed by the fact that it was undeniably in course of preparation.

As soon as General Birch had received this information, he addressed a letter to the Inspector-General of Ordnance, calling for an immediate report on the grease made for the cartridges in the arsenal, and the reply was that there probably was beef fat used in it.

Without any delay, General Birch, by order of the Governor-General, telegraphed to the depôts of instruction at Umballa and Sealkote, prohibiting the issue of any cartridges except in a dry state, and directing that the officers commanding the depôts should send proper men from among those under their command into the bazaars to procure such materials for greasing the cartridges as were unobjectionable in the eyes of either Mahometans or Hindoos. A court of inquiry was also assembled at Dumdum to hear what the Sepoys had to allege against the cartridges, and the glazed appearance of the sized paper in which they were enclosed was objected to. It would appear that the men's objections on this occasion were overruled. While the investigation was being carried on, a native present produced a 'khareeta,' or royal letter, sent by Goolab Sing, the Maharaja of Cashmere, to an officer who was travelling in the valley. The paper used by the natives is glazed, and has just the same appearance as that of which the cartridges were made. The objector was called upon to examine the two, and point out the difference. He was obliged of course to confess there was none.

Now, seeing that the measures taken by Government were in time to stop the issue, and seeing that no Sepoy was ever called upon by authority to touch a greased cartridge at all, how is it possible to account for the tremendous effect produced, except on the theory of a premeditated plot, and a regularly organized conspiracy? Who then was the active agent?

I think it is much to be regretted that the opposite theory should be received as true, because it will necessarily have the effect of preventing further inquiry, and if it turns out to be true, after all, that there was a directing agent, it is a pity he should be allowed to remain any longer *incognito*.

The cartridge question, dry as it is, may, after all, be the means of affording a clue to the origin of the whole disturbance, just as it proved the engine in the hands of the disaffected to ruin the army.

Another unfortunate occurrence took place at the same time, which had the undoubted effect of strengthening the suspicions already engendered in the mind of the Sepoy, and that was the issue of cartridge paper of a different colour from that which the men were accustomed to, from the manufactory at Serampore. This was merely accidental.

I have before alluded to the introduction of a new system of platoon exercise. The history of it was as follows. When the objection of the Sepoys to the Enfield cartridge was first brought to the notice of Government, it was determined (suggested in the first instance, I believe, by Captain Bontein and General Birch) to introduce a system of platoon exercise which should obviate the necessity of the soldiers putting the cartridges to their mouths at all. The Indian Government having at once adopted the idea, sent to the Horse Guards suggesting or requesting that the new system, having been introduced into India, might be introduced throughout the whole British army, for the sake of uniformity. The Horse Guards signified their approval, and the alteration was made. The only man in authority who objected was Sir Patrick Grant, Commander-in-Chief of Madras; but the supreme military authority having confirmed it, his objections were of course overruled.

Now, all this was done on the best motive in the world; but it will be, I think, apparent to every one that it was very bad policy. Suspicions of the intention of Government with regard to the new cartridges were universally entertained by the native army. The men, however, were solemnly assured over and over again that their suspicions were groundless, that they would not be required to use the obnoxious articles; yet at the same time a new platoon exercise is introduced, with the very object of obviating the necessity for putting the cartridge to the mouth. If the Government stated what was not the truth, how could its asseveration be depended on, and what might not its policy be? if it stated the truth, why introduce a new system of platoon exercise at all? The inference was obvious and inevitable, and we may be sure did not escape the notice of the Sepoys, whose attention was now thoroughly aroused, who watched every proceeding of Government jealously and carefully, and who were in a frame of mind which rendered them almost incapable of judging fairly, while they fell an easy prey to the machinations of designing men.

While therefore future history will acquit the Government of wilfully ignoring the question, it cannot but attribute to it an error, or succession of errors in policy which were attended with the most disastrous results. Not that the mutiny would have been prevented had there been no such thing in the world as an Enfield rifle. Had the cartridge grievance never turned up at all, some other matter would have been made an instrument for kindling the flame which was already smouldering in the breasts of the Sepoys, and ready to burst forth at any moment it might find a vent.

Disastrous as were the immediate consequences of the outbreak, we cannot but entertain the hope that they will be overruled by Providence to our good; nay, we may even now see many instances in which good has already resulted from it. Our position in India is undoubtedly far stronger than before; not stronger than we imagined it, but stronger than we now know it to have been. In the expressive words made use of the other day by a native of rank while conversing with me on the subject, the 'spirit of disaffection has burnt itself out, and is reduced to ashes.' The chains of British dominion which before held the Indian people in subjection are now riveted, and without powerful external aid it seems impossible, humanly speaking, that they should ever be shaken off. While we cannot but condemn the policy of Government in raising so large a native army anew on the ruins of the old, we cannot be blind to the fact that the power of combination which the former army possessed—though they made so little use of it—is beyond the reach of the present. Less useful as a support to the State, because formed of inferior material, they are less dangerous as internal foes. I am alluding now to the troops raised in Hindostan; the Sikhs of course, of whom there are now about 90,000 in the service of Government, would, if they were to mutiny, form a most dangerous enemy, far more so than the old Sepoys. But it is to be hoped that the Government will be wise in time, and though it has not learnt as much as we could wish by the past, yet it must be blind indeed to the best interests of the empire if it neglects to adopt measures which will make a combined movement on the part of the Sikhs almost an impossibility.

It must, I think, be obvious to every one who has studied the history of the rebellion, that the cause which operated more than any other in hampering the Government and paralysing its action, was the enormous and unwieldy size of the Presidency over the greater part of which rebellion was one time raging. I have before alluded to the evil which resulted from officers in high and responsible situations being afraid to act for themselves, and being tied down by orders transmitted from the seat of Government, a thousand miles off perhaps from the scene of action. If the Presidency were broken up into three or more minor Governorships, the authority would be more concentrated, its influence more rapidly communicated to the executive, officers would feel more freedom of action, and be more capable of consulting their superiors, and would feel more confident of support; the actual intercourse between the head of a comparatively small province and his subordinates being much greater in a dependency the size of the Punjaub or Sind than in so widely-spread a domain as that of the whole Bengal Presidency. It has been frequently asserted that the Punjaub was saved owing to the accident of telegraphic communication between Lahore and Calcutta having been cut off; the able and energetic Governor of the Punjaub was thus thrown on his own resources, and in a position where he could act independently, and follow the guiding of his own almost unerring judgment. Had he been able, he would have been forced to refer every question to Calcutta, where it would have been discussed by a council, nearly every member of which was practically ignorant of the country beyond the suburbs of Calcutta; and whether his suggestions were confirmed or negatived, in either case time would have been lost, and with it that which told with immense force upon the excited minds of the inhabitants of the Punjaub and the country north of Delhi—the vigorous action of a dictator bent on carrying out his will, and turning every instrument within his reach into a means of re-establishing British power.

When the outbreak occurred we were taken at every disadvantage; everything was against us. The number of European soldiers in the country had been reduced to an unprecedentedly low limit. Never before, since our empire had begun to extend itself, had India been denuded to such an extent of English soldiers. The native army, on the other hand, was strong out of all proportion. Almost all our strongholds, and arsenals, and treasures were either in their hands, or at any rate within their reach. They had all the prestige which the adherence to their cause of the lineal descendant of the house of Timour could give. To all appearance there was scarce a single circumstance wanting that could contribute to render their success certain, yet they failed, and that signally. It is scarcely within the bounds of possibility that a similar combination of circumstances can occur again, nor is it at all probable that we shall ever again have such a number of incompetent men in situations of authority in almost every department of the State. If we have a second rebellion, the chances are at any rate a hundred to one that we shall not have a weak government at the time, and with a strong one attempts at revolution would be harmless, even as the mutiny of 1857 would have been, had it been dealt with by a strong hand, and strangled at its birth.

The disarming of the country, which, though not thoroughly carried out, has been completed to a certain extent, is another undoubted source of future security. There may be thousands of smaller weapons concealed in the rural districts that have escaped the vigilance of our magistrates, but Oude is no longer full of forts bristling with cannon; we have no native artillery to supply rebels with ready-made batteries, and troops of horse artillery efficiently equipped; our arsenals, well stocked with ordnance and ammunition, are no longer in the hands of native soldiers, so that were a rebellion to occur, it is really difficult to see where the disaffected could procure their guns, and without them natives are powerless.

One remarkable feature in the late rebellion was the want of support it met with from the higher orders, and men of influence and good family in the country. With very few exceptions, the principal men in India stood aloof. It is true many, even of those reputed loyal and treated as such, wavered in their allegiance, and, true to their national character as Asiatics, contrived to secure themselves on both sides, so that if their mainstay, the British Government, failed, they might fall upon their feet. And this was not difficult. They could write to the puppet King of Delhi and express their sympathy with his cause, but beyond that, they would allege, it was impossible for them to go. They were ready, they would urge, to join, directly the defeat of the British troops gave them room and freedom of action. Many, however, abstained from doing even this, but honestly and heartily aided the Government. The Maharaja of Pattiala deserves especially to be mentioned, because he was in a position where he could, had he been so disposed, have inflicted perhaps greater injuries upon us than any other native prince. Yet his alliance was hearty and entire. It was not so with some other chiefs who have nevertheless, out of motives of policy—whether good or bad I will not stop now to inquire—been treated and rewarded as if they really were what they pretended to be. Had all or any of the independent chiefs, men of family and great influence in the country, placed themselves at the head of the rebels, the result of the mutiny would have been very different from what it was.

In a future attempt to throw off our yoke, if such be made, it is scarcely possible that this important fact should be left out of the calculations of conspirators. Without men of influence to lead them, their cause would fail as it failed before; and with the experience of the past before their eyes, no independent chief, unless driven by ill-treatment or unwise policy into rebellion, is likely to come forward to head a movement against us. The British Government as the paramount power, supported on all sides by the hearty alliance of the neighbouring States, would be impregnable. That support the States are ready and willing to accord. They are now bound to us by closer ties than ever existed before, nor, as long as the British Government is true to its own interests, will these ties ever be broken. 'As long as we rest our empire on the sound basis of a firm government and British cannon (for be it recollected that physical force is, after all, the only real foundation on which every government depends) we shall never want the hearty and vigorous support of allied States; if, by foolish policy or mismanagement, or a desire to sacrifice everything to principles of government plausible in theory but faulty in practice, we weaken our position, we shall be abandoned to our fate by our allies, who, however willing to support the paramount power to serve their own ends, have, we may be sure, no desire to be buried under its ruins. To side with the strongest is the ruling principle of Asiatic (perhaps of all human) policy. In giving us their support, the independent States in nowise ran counter to the national characteristic. What is so much to the credit of these princes, is not that they acted contrary to their hereditary policy, but that they had the good sense, and tact, and wisdom to see clearly through the cloud of difficulties that beset us, and, without being dazzled by the temporary success of the rebellion, and the appearance of things upon the surface, beheld in the background the resources of the British Empire and the power of civilization, and acted accordingly.'*

A great deal too much stress has been laid by many writers who advocate the immediate formation of railways at any expense, upon their political results as affording a source of security to the empire. Some go so far as to assert that when the chief lines of railway are completed, we shall be able to dispense with a large

---

* *Delhi Gazette*, Dec. 13, 1859.

portion of our European force, and look forward to the time when the expenditure under the head of military requirements will be capable of reduction to the extent of half its present amount, by diminishing the European garrison of India. Those on whom rests the responsibility of maintaining the British Indian Empire in its integrity would do well to pause and reflect ere they sanction any practical application of this grievous error. The importance of railways in a commercial point of view, and their powerful effect in stimulating enterprise and in facilitating the transport of country produce from inland districts to seaport or market-towns, it is not my intention to underrate, nor can it be denied that as a means of moving troops long distances at short notice they will prove invaluable; but if we trust them to such an extent as to reduce materially our European force on the ground that the remaining portion of it can be so easily transported from one place to another, that fifty thousand men then will be as good as a hundred thousand now, we shall meet with disaster. The arrangements that in India devolve upon the commissariat department for the transport of troops and supplies are brought as near perfection as they can be. Carriage is difficult to procure and expensive to keep up; still the Government manage to procure it in almost any quantity, and have little or no difficulty in keeping it up, because it is almost always wanted and almost always kept up. Let us trust entirely or mainly to railways for means of transport, and in a very short time the wheels of the commissariat machine that are now in good working order will become rusted from disuse, and incapable of being set in motion. On the occasion of a revolt in any part of India ten rebels armed with axes and crowbars would be able in one night to break up a line of rail, and effectually stop all communication between a garrison or depôt of troops and a disturbed district. India is not like England, where such an injury to a line might be repaired in a few hours. I am not speaking of the danger of accident to a large body of troops moving by rail, which might be averted by common prudence, that would, under such circumstances, no doubt be exercised, but of the impossibility of maintaining communication. We must not forget that the natives of India are capable of combination. We used to imagine that nothing would ever serve to reconcile the Hindoos and Mahometans, and to induce them to act in concert against a third sect. It was the commonest thing in the world for men to say, and for almost every one in India to think, that happen what might, we should always have either the one or the other race allied in its integrity to us. Experience has proved the fallacy of this. The antagonism of religious animosity is not irreconcilable, and though the late revolt has shown how badly the co-operation of different bodies of rebels was managed, it has proved that different races and sects can suppress mutual enmity when they have a common object in view. Experience has taught them the importance of combination; they cannot fail to see that had they acted in concert all over India in 1857, success was certain. Long lines of railway running necessarily for immense distances through tracts often uninhabited, must be left to the guardianship of native police. A handful of men could in an hour stop all communication at any given spot, and before the mischief could be repaired whole embankments might be cut away, the line torn up and destroyed for miles, and the whole railway rendered useless. A native of rank, conversing on the late rebellion, remarked to an officer—'There was one thing we totally forgot, and that was the telegraph.' This omission would not occur again. With our telegraphic communication cut off entirely, and our railway rendered useless for a time, with no other means of transport ready at hand, and no carriage of ordinary kinds available (which would be the case if we had ceased for any length of time to require it), and a combined movement against us originated in many different parts of the country simultaneously, we should be worse off than we were in 1857, or before a mile of permanent way ever reached these shores.

It cannot be impressed too strongly upon the British public and the Home Government, that India is only to be retained by an overpowering British force. Seventy-five or eighty thousand men should be the minimum strength of our European army. The country may be held with less; a brigade of British soldiers, ably handled and well led, may reconquer a whole province. But it is not our object to be perpetually at war with our fellow-subjects, to be perpetually putting down *émeutes*. We can conquer Asiatics with ease, we can beat them at the greatest odds, we can take their strongest fortresses even when at every disadvantage. But our object is to maintain peace, to improve the condition of the people, to promote civilization, commerce, education; and the best way, nay, the only way to do it, is to discourage strife, and suppress as far and as speedily as possible that unhappy antagonism of race that has always existed, and that has been so much fostered by late events. It is not enough to be able to crush disaffection when it openly displays itself, to trample out the flame of rebellion when the conflagration has begun; we must take up such a position in the country as will effectually prevent all attempts at throwing off our yoke. As long as the natives see no hope, no chance of success in a struggle against us, we may be sure they will not try it. To reduce materially our British force, and to hold India as we held it before, is to induce rebellion. We throw a tempting bait—the bait of independence—before the natives, and when they attempt to take it we punish them, and the land is deluged with blood; with the blood of our own countrymen and countrywomen, and with that of the natives themselves. It may suit the purposes of certain parties in England to dwell upon the Utopian scheme of holding a great part of Asia by moral influence—the force of education, the willing subjection of many millions of aliens, are high sounding phrases—but history will teach us that no country and no people in the world, least of all in the Asiatic continent, were ever held in subjection by such means. Let us by an overwhelming superiority of physical force retain the country, keep it safe from external attacks and maintain peace within; and when a century has passed, our successors may be able to dispense with the greater part of their English troops. Till then, the attempt to do so will be premature, and will end in nothing but disaster.

APPENDIX.

Dr. Murray's Narrative of his Escape from Neemuch on the night of the Mutiny, June the 3rd, 1857.

The explosion at Neemuch took place on the night of the 3rd June. For many days before, I, in common with others, felt that we were upon a mine, and expected a 'smash' at any given signal; it was owing, I fully believe (under Providence), to the tact and management of Colonel Abbott, that it wasaverted for a time.

From the day we heard of the disastrous outbreak at Meerut and horrible massacre at Delhi, no end of reports were constantly flying about, set on foot by wretches anxious for our overthrow and the restoration of the Mahometan rule; indeed it soon became evident that unless Delhi was speedily retaken, Neemuch would *go.* Scarcely a night passed but incendiary fires blazed in different directions, and on two or three occasions panics were 'got up' in the bazaars, alarm bugles sounded in camp, drums beat, and the whole station was in commotion.

On the 1st of June, Colonel Abbott assembled the whole of the native officers of the different regiments composing the brigade, and talked to them so persuasively that they agreed to swear, in the most solemn manner, that they would remain loyal to the State, and stand by their European officers in any emergency. Oaths were accordingly taken; the Mahometans swore on the Koran, and the Hindoos on the waters of the Ganges, or whatever else was most sacred to them. After this solemn compact, confidence was restored, but only until the following day, for the Sepoys then heard that the troops at Nusseerabad had mutinied, and the most exaggerated reports were circulated; among others, that every European there had been killed, &c. It now became apparent that an outbreak was inevitable; it seemed no longer a question of days, but hours. Whether the native officers would keep their oaths or not, remained to be seen.

The night of the 3rd June was one of the loveliest I have ever seen: the moon shone bright and clear, and not a cloud was visible throughout the whole expanse of heaven. About eleven o'clock I had my bed brought outside as usual, where the sentry was pacing up and down, and lay down in my clothes, having merely changed my coat for a dressing-gown. I had not been half an hour on my bed when two guns were fired, at intervals of a few seconds, by the artillery. This was evidently a preconcerted signal, for immediately after several shots were fired in the direction of the cavalry lines, and bungalow after bungalow was set on fire. I assembled my night guard at once, and wanted them to accompany me to Captain Lawrie's house, where I expected to find some ladies, whom I intended to escort towards the fort. The naick said there was no use in going, that we should be killed by the cavalry, and strongly advised me to retire. I was going over myself, when I saw the naick of Captain M'Donald's guard running towards me; he was in a great state of excitement, and taking hold of me by the arm, begged me not to go that way; the 'mém log,' he said, had all fled, and the place was now filled with the mutineers. I saw some natives running about wildly, and presently several shots were fired not far from where I was standing. 'Chullo, sahib, gole chulte,' said the naick, who now entreated me to leave the place, or I should be killed. Seeing that matters had at last become serious, that in fact the long-expected crisis had arrived, I desired my syce to saddle my nag, and bring him over to the fort; the naick said, 'For God's sake, sahib, don't go to the fort; fly at once into the country.' I asked him what he meant; he answered, 'All the fighting will take place in the fort.' 'All right,' I said; 'we will fight, too.' Upon this he insisted on going with me, and called out to two Sepoys of the guard to follow; they came immediately, and on our way to the fort (which was only about three hundred yards from our house), he told me that as soon as the bungalows were plundered and burnt, the mutineers would attack the fort in order to carry off the treasure. I asked him how *he* knew that; he replied, 'Such is the report.'

I arrived at the fort just as the left wing of the regiment, under Lieutenant Rose, was entering; the right wing, under Captain M'Donald, had already lined the ramparts and bastions, and presented a somewhat formidable appearance; the whole regiment being now inside, the gate was shut, the drawbridge taken up, and a strong party under Lieutenants Gordon and Davenport was planted to guard the entrance. I went on the ramparts, where I found Captain M'Donald encouraging the men, and telling them that the artillery could do them no harm, as they had no shells. Lieutenant Rose was also on the ramparts, and doing his best to encourage them; I was sorry to hear from him that he had been fired at by a Sepoy of the regiment immediately after he had given the order for the left wing to march to the fort. I looked upon this as a bad sign, for I had all along felt confident that, come what would, the greater part of the regiment would stand by us; the fact of their not attempting to seize the man who fired at Lieutenant Rose, and who was known, shook my faith in them very much.

Shortly after, we were all in the fort, and whilst the work of destruction was being carried on outside by the mutineers of the other regiments composing the force—viz., wing 1st Light Cavalry, 72nd Regiment N.I., and Walker's troop Native Horse Artillery—Captain

M'Donald got out the colours of the regiment, carried them himself along the ramparts, and unfurling them on the right front bastion, called on the Sepoys to protect them. This they declared they would do.

From time to time I walked along the ramparts talking to the Sepoys, and encouraging them to hold out. I explained to many of them the high reward that Captain Lloyd, Superintendent of Neemuch, had guaranteed to every individual among them who assisted in protecting the treasure and fort, and that if they behaved well, and remained 'true to their salt,' the Government would reward them handsomely. Several of the men assured me they would die rather than surrender; others said they would hold out against infantry and cavalry, but if artillery attacked them they would be obliged to give in. I told them the artillery had nothing but grape, and that could not possibly injure the fort or them either, as they were behind walls. The reward that Captain Lloyd offered, was one hundred rupees to every Sepoy, three hundred to each naick, five hundred to each havildar, and five thousand to the senior native officer, or the one who should most distinguish himself in preserving order.

About a quarter to three o'clock, A.M., four men of the grenadier company came up to me, and said, 'Doctor Sahib, it is no use holding out any longer; we are not now under the orders of the Major Sahib, we are commanded by Pirthee Sing, subadar of the grenadier company. If you don't believe us,' they continued, 'come and see for yourself.' I went with them to the left rear bastion, where I found a large body of the regiment (at least one hundred and fifty), and Pirthee Sing at their head. One of the Sepoys said to him, 'The Doctor Sahib has come.' He had just then been addressing some of the men, and turning round to me, said, 'You had better all leave the fort before it be too late.' Another Sepoy standing close by, said aloud, 'We are now under Pirthee Sing's orders.' I went back to report the circumstance to Captain

M'Donald, but meeting Lieutenant Rose (second in command), I mentioned it to him; he said it was a bad business, and he would go at once and tell M'Donald. A few minutes after, the artillery commenced firing again, and hearing a 'row' at the gate, and some of the Sepoys shouting, 'Deen, deen,' I hastened down, and found that the party under Lieutenants Gordon and Davenport had mutinied, and were forcing their way through the gate. Hevia Sing, subadar, had just before countermanded an order of Lieutenant Gordon, by saying, 'Oouka hookum mut mâno, humara hookum chulte.'* Captain M'Donald, Lieutenants Rose, Gordon, Davenport, and myself, with Sergeants Nesbitt and Lane, tried all we could to prevent their leaving the fort, but to no purpose. Many of the men had their bayonets fixed, all were loaded; and the whole regiment, nearly seven hundred strong, left the ramparts and bastions, and slowly but steadily forced their way through the gate. We (some half-dozen Europeans) were taken on by the tide, and got separated in the crowd. Two Sepoys of the grenadier company who were with me all this time insisted on my going away before the cavalry came down upon us. They said, 'Your lives are safe with us, but we cannot answer for the artillery and cavalry.' Seeing it would be madness to remain any longer, I and Doctor Gane left them. I should have mentioned that Doctor Gane of the Bombay service was with us all the evening; he had only that day returned from Nusseerabad, where he had seen the station in a blaze, and had now, unfortunately, a second edition, attended with more serious consequences as far as he was personally concerned.

On leaving the regiment, we made our way to the garden in rear of the fort, where we hoped to stumble upon the rest of our party; the moon, however, had now gone down, and it being dark we missed them, so after

* 'Don't attend to his orders; I am in command.'

staying in the garden a few minutes, and feeling certain that all the other officers of the regiment must have gone on, which was the case, we decided on leaving the place at once (luckily for us as it afterwards turned out). We accordingly shaped a south-west course into the country, avoiding public roads, along which we thought it not unlikely cavalry videttes might be thrown out, and for the rest trusting to the same Providence that had hitherto protected us in all our difficulties.

Just as the day began to dawn, we arrived at a village which we afterwards found to be Kussounda. Although we had not walked above six miles, yet the ground being heavy, we were quite tired, and half dead with thirst. We knocked up one of the villagers, an old man, and asked him for some water; he immediately brought us to a well where there was a cistern quite full, and we both sat down and had a regular libation. I verily believe our guide thought we would never leave off drinking. I gave him a rupee, which pleased him mightily, and asked him to show us the 'head man' of the village; this he did at once. We found him in a small fort, about forty or fifty yards square, surrounded by some half-dozen men. I told him we wished to rest there for an hour or so, and asked him if we could do so; he said most certainly, and received us with great civility, had a place cleared for us immediately in his own house, and begged we would make ourselves comfortable. He sent for milk, chuppatees, dâll, rice, and mangoes, and entreated us to eat. After partaking of some refreshment, and congratulating ourselves upon falling into such good hands, we lay down and had a nap. We were not destined, however, to remain long at rest; about nine A.M. a party of cavalry who were scouring the country, probably foraging for carriage, arrived at Kussounda, and insisted on having the sahibs out, in order that they might 'sâf kuro' them. Doctor Gane and I would have stood no chance against these scoundrels, and we were indebted for our lives to the noble conduct of the Rajpoots of the village, viz., Jâdoo Ram, Oonkar Sing, Késree Sing, Mothee, and several others, who swore they would stand by us to the last. They said, 'You have eaten with us, and are our guests, and now, if you were our enemy, we would defend you.' They put us into a small dilapidated shed on one of the bastions, and when the troopers demanded us, declared we were not there. After much altercation, the troopers threatened to attack the village if we were not given up. The Rajpoots warned them to be careful. They said, 'Kussounda belongs to the Rana (the Rana of Oodeypore), we are *her* subjects, and if you molest us, she will send ten thousand soldiers after you.' After a short time they went away, threatening to return with the guns in the evening, and blow us to pieces.

About one o'clock we were agreeably surprised by seeing an artillery sergeant (sergeant Supple, of the Bengal Horse Artillery, an active and gallant soldier,) walk into our little fort. We thought at first he was pursued by the cavalry, but he informed us that he was in search of the Brigade Major; he told us also that Captains Lloyd and M'Donald, with several officers of the 7th Gwalior Contingent, were at the village of Darroo, only three miles off. This was good news. He said he would gallop off and bring us assistance, and soon we were glad to see him put his horse out at full speed, and scour across the country in the direction of Darroo. Had I been alone, I would have galloped off with him, but I felt I could not leave Doctor Gane by himself at so critical a time, particularly as he could not speak the language.

Hour after hour passed away, and no assistance arriving from Darroo, we began to think that our friends there were in as great a 'fix' as ourselves, and such we afterwards discovered was really the case.

In consultation with our Rajpoot friends, it was decided that we should go on to Chota Sâdree, a distance of about

x 2

sixteen miles, that same night. Accordingly we left Kussounda shortly after sunset, escorted by several Rajpoots, and arrived at Chota Sâdree about ten o'clock. Our route lay through dense jungle, and being on foot (for my nag had been stolen), we were a good deal knocked up by the time we arrived there, and, to our great disappointment, were told that all the sahibs had left an hour before for Burra Sâdree, sixteen miles further on. Our reception was cold in the extreme; they did not want us to remain there a moment, and would scarcely give us even a drink of water. I sent two men to inform the kumashdar that we wanted to see him, but they came back saying it was too late, he would not see us; and advised us to hasten on after the other sahibs. There were lots of horses and camels picketed about, a couple of which we wanted to hire, but they refused to let us have them, saying they would sell them to us if we liked; this was of course out of the question, as we had only a few rupees left between us. One man asked two hundred rupees for a tattoo that was worth about ten. Nothing remained therefore but to push on for Burra Sâdree. Our escort from Kussounda left us, and in their place we got two Bheel guides; so, after remaining about twenty minutes in Chota Sâpree, we pushed on for the next stage. In about an hour and a half we reached a small village in the heart of the jungle, called Bheeliga-ke-gaon. Here we received very great kindness: the Bheels seemed to vie with each other in their hospitality. They spoke to us of the benefits they received under British rule, and abused the mutineers in no measured terms; the women appeared to be very indignant at the treatment they heard we had received, and expressed a hope that vengeance would speedily overtake the traitors. We remained with the worthy Bheels about an hour, and having procured a couple of ponies, started for Burra Sâdree, which place we reached about nine o'clock next day, and were delighted to meet all our friends of the 7th Gwalior Contingent,

1st Cavalry, and Artillery. The fate of the officers and families of the 72nd N.I., and staff, was still a mystery. At Burra Sâdree we parted with our Bheel guides, to whom we gave a present of a few rupees, nearly all we had, and in place of the pony, I was fortunate in getting the loan of a spare cavalry charger, and Doctor Gane succeeded in getting a gharry. We were now a strong party, comparatively speaking, mustering about twenty 'fighting men,' most of us well armed and well mounted. and would have been ugly customers in a life and death struggle. About half-past one P.M., our whole party, numbering in all about six-and-thirty—men, women, and children—started from Burra Sâdree, *en route* towards Oodeypore. We arrived at Doongla about seven o'clock that same evening, and put up in a small mud fort, where we remained two days, when we were joined by Captain Showers, political agent of Meywar, who hastened from Oodeypore, with a strong force of the rana's troops, and determined on giving chase to the mutineers at once. Leaving, therefore, a guard to escort the women and children and sick to Oodeypore, Captain Showers, accompanied by Captain Sir John Hill, Bart., Captain M'Donald, Lieutenant Ellice, Lieutenant Barnes, and myself as volunteers, started next morning in pursuit. From Chota Sâdree, Captain M'Donald proceeded to Neemuch, with a party of Bheels, and at Chittore we were joined by Lieutenant Stapleton, of the 1st Cavalry. Neemuch in the meantime had been re-occupied by Captain Lloyd, superintendent of the district, and Major Burton, with some of the Kotah troops.

We pushed on rapidly, in the best possible spirits, at the rate of thirty and forty miles a day, as far as Lehazghur, bordering on the territories of the Jeypore Rajah, where we hoped to have fallen in with two hundred of H.M.'s 83rd Regiment, and some Bombay Horse Artillery (Europeans). To our disappointment, however, we found that, for various reasons, they could not be spared from

Nusseerabad. This was to be regretted, as we were within an easy march of the mutineers, and if we had had a couple of hundred of the 83rd, and a few guns, under a dashing commander, we would have scattered them to the four winds. The fact is, the mutineers rushed from Neemuch in the greatest haste possible, a report having got among them that the much dreaded 'gora log' were close at hand, and the appearance at this juncture of a very small European force would in all probability have accomplished their destruction. This is no haphazard remark, for we all know what the gallant Major Vincent Eyre, of the Bengal Artillery, effected near Arrah, when, with a hundred and sixty of H.M.'s 5th Fusiliers, three guns, and twelve mounted Englishmen (volunteers), he defeated and utterly routed *twenty times his own number of native regular troops.*

At Jehaz-ghur we rescued three European women, six children, and one sergeant, who were flying for their lives from Deolee, the head-quarters of the Kotah Contingent, that station having been plundered and burnt by the Neemuch mutineers.

Numerous were the hair-breadth escapes at Neemuch, and, considering the character of the outbreak, it was providential that many lives were not lost. One European woman (the wife of the artillery sergeant above alluded to), and three children, were unfortunately butchered at the commencement of the mutiny. The sergeant was on duty over the guns at the time, and it appears had no opportunity of defending his family. Happily there were no other lives lost.

The Mahometans throughout were most cruel, ferocious, and bloodthirsty; those of the artillery and cavalry were the worst; excited with *bhang*, they galloped about like fiends, intent only on bloodshed and murder.

A subadar of the 72nd N.I. persuaded Colonel Abbott, and the officers of the regiment, with their families, to take shelter in his house. They were no sooner in, than he fastened the door upon them outside, and sent for the guns. Fortunately a Hindoo Sepoy, who remained true to his salt, broke open the door, and warned the officers of their danger in time to enable them to escape.

The quartermaster-sergeant's wife of the 7th Gwalior Contingent was attacked by some Mahometans, and would have been killed but for some Hindoo Sepoys who came to the rescue, and escorted her in safety to a village some miles out of the station. She afterwards joined her husband, and proceeded with the rest of the party to Oodeypore.

The conduct of the Oodeypore durbar at this crisis was beyond all praise. The rana appears to have entered heart and soul into our cause; indeed, had it not been for her loyalty to the British Government, and co-operation with the authorities, there is no saying what might have been the aspect of affairs in Rajpootana at the present moment.

THE END.

www.ingramcontent.com/pod-product-compliance
Ingram Content Group UK Ltd.
Pitfield, Milton Keynes, MK11 3LW, UK
UKHW041952190726
13854UKWH00005B/1926

9 781845 742256